BLACK HERETICS, BLACK PROPHETS

BLACK HERETICS, BLACK PROPHETS

RADICAL POLITICAL INTELLECTUALS

ANTHONY BOGUES

Routledge
New York and London

Published in 2003 by
Routledge
29 West 35th Street
New York, NY 10001
www.routledge-ny.com

Published in Great Britain by
Routledge
11 New Fetter Lane
London EC4P 4EE
www.routledge.co.uk

Routledge is an imprint of the Taylor & Francis Group.
Copyright © 2003 by Taylor & Francis Books, Inc.

Printed in the United States of America on acid-free paper.

10 9 8 7 6 5 4 3 2 1

Cataloging-in-Publication Data is available from the Library of Congress.
ISBN–0-415-94324-8 (hbk.)—0-415-94325-6 (pbk.)

To all the youthman and youthdawtas of Craig Town and for my sons Samori, Machel, Nzinga, and Kilamba.

Contents

Acknowledgments

The writing of a book has many legs, and we should recognize that these legs make it a collective enterprise. Writing is a dialogue not only with the self but also with the social world. So one needs at the end of a writing project to explore these legs, to reflect upon the making of the book. This book originated in a series of night classes held in the inner-city community of Craig Town, Kingston, Jamaica, in 1999. In this community I was asked to conduct a series of classes in black history. What was amazing was that for about six months a group of young men, most of them unemployed and all living under oppressive conditions, came twice a week, learning the rudiments of reading and writing, staying late into the night speaking, listening, and questioning the ideas of some of the figures in this book. What began as a class in black history quickly became a discussion group about black radical ideas. The decision was made to write a book about the black radical intellectual tradition when one of these young men, in Jamaican vernacular, recounted some of the key political ideas of Walter Rodney, eloquently stating what those ideas had meant to him and the rest of the group as young black men living in a society that oppressed them along class and color lines. To these young men I owe a great deal, and I hope that the book will reflect some of the ideas we intensely discussed many nights, trying to keep alive a hope that their lives could be changed.

Since then a few of these young men have died at the hands of state forces, others have left the area, and still others are trying to make their lives better. A book is in no way a substitute for making social change, but writing can help to clarify some of the ideas about history and politics, ideas that are important for the execution of social change. It is because the unemployed youths of Craig Town for a brief moment demonstrated what was possible for all human beings, once we recognized ourselves in history and as active agents who can change both our condition and history, that the book was written.

In the fall of 1999, Lewis Gordon, with an intellectual generosity rare in the academy, suggested that I write the book for the *Africana Thought* series. He argued that another book I was working on could be done later. I want to thank him for his insistence. Paget Henry, the other editor of the series, provided valuable support during the writing, reading some of the drafts and making extensive comments. I wish to acknowledge his support. Since coming to Brown University in the fall of 1999, I have taught a senior undergraduate seminar, "Africans and the West: A History of Ideas," in which the students have forced me to sharpen my analysis of the black radical intellectual tradition; their probing questions have reshaped many ideas in this text. I want to thank them for their contributions to this project.

Various chapters in different guises were given as talks at several forums. The ideas about Cugoano were first developed for a paper presented in 1999 at the American Philosophical Association conference in Boston, and I want to thank the audience who attended that panel for their questions. After that panel Robert Gooding-Williams invited me to present some of the ideas of the book at the Humanities Center at Northwestern University. Both the faculty and the student seminars stimulated me to think how the ideas about a black radical intellectual tradition could be reworked in the academy as integral to the study of political theory. I want to thank Robert for this invitation and for his continued support of my work. At Howard University the chapter on James and Du Bois was presented, and the rich discussion which ensued that Sunday morning shaped the historical ideas of that chapter; I want to thank Patrick Goodin for making that seminar possible. Patrick also hosted a conference on Afro-Caribbean philosophy at Howard in which I first outlined the nature of Dread history. I want to thank Linden Lewis for his encouraging comments at that forum. At the University of California, Irvine, I presented an overall conception of the book and ideas about the nature of the black radical intellectual tradition to the Afro-American Studies Program. I wish to thank all who participated in that seminar particularly those who saw the work as an attempt in the history of ideas.

Particular sections of this book would not have been written without the rich discussions that I have with members of the Small Axe Collective. In particular I want to thank David Scott for arguments about Dread history; Nadi Edwards, who knows more than most about the nature of the popular Caribbean aesthetic; and Val Carnegie, whose brief article on Robert Marley proved very valuable. Thanks are also due to the filmmaker Julian Henriques, for discussions about Dread history, and to one of my most talented graduate students, Greg Graham, who did the newspaper research on the Claudius Henry trial. Jana Lipman of Yale University allowed me to look at some original documents she found in the National Archives in Washington, D.C., that helped shaped the Rastafari chapter. Thanks are also due to my friend and colleague Rupert Lewis, who ever since he was my dissertation adviser has served as a sounding board for my ideas in gestation.

If the youths of Craig Town stimulated the ideas for this book, then the person who has seen it through is my partner, Geri. Her ideas and critical comments are all over the text, in particular the chapters on Ida B. Wells and Julius Nyerere. She insisted on Wells as a central figure in the black radical tradition and someone who had been overlooked by political theorists. Her insistence that the book be written in plain English, I do not know if I have satisfied, but I am sure that my attempts have made it a better book. When the manuscript was completed, Don Pease of Dartmouth College facilitated a series of invigorating lectures on sections of it. I want to thank Don for his immense intellectual generosity, acumen and support. My colleague at Brown University, James Campbell, made an important comment on the final section, which I greatly appreciated. Finally, I would like to thank Damon Zucca, Damian Treffs, and Julie Ho for making the post-writing phase a smooth one. Much appreciation also to Beth Wilson for great copy editing.

In the end, I take responsibility for what has been written.

Opening Chant
The Full Has Never Been Told: Heresy, Prophecy, Praxis, and the Black Radical Political Intellectual

> *I came into the world imbued with the will to find meanings in things*
> *My spirit filled with the desire to attain to the source of the world, and then*
> *Found that I was an object in the midst of other objects.*
> —Frantz Fanon

> *We refuse to be*
> *What you wanted us to be*
> *We are what we are*
> *That's the way it's going to be*
> —Bob Marley

Introduction

For the last five hundred years or so, the practices of the black radical political intellectual have been in large part a product of modernity. Her or his contributions to radical thought should not be ghettoized into closed discursive boxes which marginalize those contributions, making them specific and unique only to what has loosely been called "the black experience." This "black experience" had its origins within the interstices of modernity and is often a counterpoint to its progressive universalist claims.

The various narratives of modernity generally agree that modernity's emergence was accompanied by what Hans Blumenberg has called the "self-assertion of reason." Many accounts also argue that in the radical political domain, the 1789 French Revolution inaugurated conceptions of citizenship and sovereignty as forms of political modernity replacing previous religious and aristocratic ones; the 1776 American Revolution cleared new political horizons; and the remarkable works of the several European Enlightenments provided new grounds for our studies of both the human and the natural sciences. What is oftentimes elided is that the overarching framework for modernity's emergence was the rise of racial slavery, colonialism, and new forms of empires; that the conceptions of "rational self-interested subjects" were embedded in a philosophical anthropology of bourgeois Enlightenment and Eurocentrism. This has enormous consequences for the history of thought. Thus, even when it is now widely accepted that any history of modern thought which privileges the Western intellectual tradition is Eurocentric and flawed,[1] there still remains another layer of difficulty in the history of thought and the study of black thinkers.

Lewis Gordon has noted that it is a common habit to study the thought of black thinkers as primarily derivative.[2] The practice results from the confluence of five different sources. The first is the assumption that Africana thinkers should be studied primarily for their experiences. Here the notions, the political and historical conceptions that have animated Africana radical thinkers' historic engagement with the West (racial slavery, colonialism, and racial oppression), are reduced to a series of actions and musings bereft of any serious thought. Reason still remains the preserve of the West. What this means is that thinkers like C. L. R. James, Frantz Fanon, and W. E. B. Du Bois are never credited with intellectual independence or originality. Their ideas exist only *in relationship to* and *because* of the already accepted systems of thought. Consequently, there is a great chain of thought constructed around a hierarchical order wherein Africana thinkers are located on the margins. In this chain, radical Africana thinkers piggyback on Marx or Sartre, their intellectual validation passing through the ideas of the accepted "giants."

The second source is a more general one and concerns the way political ideas and political thought are studied. Quentin Skinner, in his call for a form of linguistic historicism, has made the point that the traditional methods for the study of political thought and the history of ideas are fraught with difficulties. He suggests a revisionist methodology that pays more attention to linguistic codes, authorial intentions, and historicism.[3] Such procedures obviously mean revisiting methodologies that privilege the autonomy of the text and broaden the perennial context-text debate. While Skinner's revisionist procedures push us in the direction of his injunction that "We must learn to think for ourselves,"[4] they are still problematic. Skinner is right to destabilize the way in which the traditional history of political thought is studied as a seamless system of ideas of great thinkers. But in narrowly focusing on linguistic historicism he misses the ways in which political questions that are not yet fully answered keep on reappearing in different periods. It is a point which Joseph Femia makes when he argues that "social practice determines what is thought; it does not follow, however, that what is thought cannot, in some cases and in varying degrees, transcend its context."[5]

What is accurate is that when we deploy the traditional method of studying ideas which searches for links, coherence and integration, regularity and linearity, it excludes from our horizon that which is different, and forces us into a false canonization process. As Michel Foucault notes, "A discursive formation is not . . . a smooth text."[6] And since a smooth text brooks neither ruptures nor contradictions, the fever and fret of the thinker, of his or her life and its complexities are reduced to patterns of thought already organized and consolidated. Such smooth, settled patterns yield negligible results in the study of Africana thinkers, particularly those who have a complex engagement with the Western intellectual tradition.

The third source of the difficulty resides in the relationship of power, 3. knowledge, and the creation of discursive systems. Both Michel Foucault and Antonio Gramsci were preoccupied in different ways with this conundrum of an ideational system. Foucault's discussion of the problematic of power—knowledge relations and the way in which power structures an epistemic field—and Gramsci's notion of hegemony and its various modes of structuring thought suggest possible directions of how to study black radical thought and black political intellectuals. Radical Africana thought is obviously engaged in the creation of counterhegemonic texts. However, the critical question is: At what moment does rupture begin? The contestation typically begins as dialogical; there is intertextuality, and then rupture. The study of black radical intellectual production requires us to be historically concrete not so much in very carefully tracing its original sources as in finding the critical points of rupture and understanding the new categories when they are thrown up. In this regard, as I will attempt to show later on, while Foucault and Gramsci are valuable touchstones for plotting the genealogy of the black radical intellectual tradition, they are not the complete guides.

The fourth problem resides in the fact that many of the theories and 4. frameworks which currently reject the privileged position of the Western episteme are themselves rooted in the conceptual protocols of this tradition. In particular they ignore the black or anticolonial intellectual tradition, and as such their critique of the Western intellectual tradition is oftentimes an internalist one that, while useful and important, displays similar assumptions about the "native" or black.[7] So when the Western tradition is unmasked, deconstructed, and decentered by these writers, the intellectual resources called upon are the thinkers who critiqued the modern project but who themselves are an integral part of the canon. This is not to reject the extraordinary importance of many of the theorists who have critiqued modernity (e.g., Nietzsche; Heidegger, rescued from his explicit

Nazi associations; and Wittgenstein). These thinkers' writings have spawned a wide range of criticisms that are of current significance in the field of postcolonial studies. Instead, I wish to draw attention to a problem that still remains (and it is both an intellectual and political one)—what do those who were "outside," who have been "objects amongst objects," have to say? What are their discursive practices, and how should we study them? Do they form an independent intellectual tradition that we need to recognize and then critically engage? Finally, can we lump the discursive practices of these thinkers only in the category of the postcolonial?

S.   The fifth difficulty is the ways in which Africa is still represented, and its politics and human experiences are portrayed and studied in the so-called serious press, the prestigious organs of the Western intellectual tradition, and the popular mind. Conradian "heart of darkness" leitmotifs in contemporary writings and political discourses concerning Africa still abound. The internationally famous *Economist,* in a bold headline superimposed on an African male placed in the middle of a map of the African continent with a modern instrument of death, proclaimed on one of its cover pages in May 2000 that Africa was "The hopeless continent." Not to be outdone, *The New York Review of Books,* on June 29, 2000, against a black-bordered backdrop, announced that Sierra Leone was "the worst place on earth." We are not reviewing here nineteenth-century travel writings of European explorers or missionaries, but the productions of some of the West's most prestigious contemporary publications.

What is intriguing is that none of the above representations of Africa attempts in any substantive way to tell the full story. For example, we still do not get in any discussions of the conflict in the Congo an account of the years of complicity between the "civilized" nations of Belgium and the United States that led to Western intervention in the Congo and the murder of Patrice Lumumba, his body dismembered by a "hacksaw and dissolved in sulfuric acid."[8] Nor do we get any insight into how the gruesome practice of the chopping of hands was a common habit encouraged by colonial powers in central Africa in their rush to extract rubber.[9] At the core of the present-day Western "invention of Africa" is a knowledge regime that fails to grapple both with African realities and with its own internal mythological representations constructed over centuries.

This is not an apology for the African elite who have constructed a set of politics that continues to oppress Africans. It is simply to point out that a number of these practices of the African elite are in many instances continuations of various models of "colonial governmentality."[10] Africa has fifty-two nation-states. In 2000 there were five war zones: Sierra Leone, Angola, Sudan, Ethiopia and Eritrea, and the Democratic Republic of Congo (DRC). The northern border of the DRC is a porous one in which groups from Rwanda and Uganda move back and forth engaging in military conflict. Therefore to stretch things a bit, we might say eight African nations at that time were involved in some sort of military conflict. That certainly does not constitute a hopeless continent. But this continued "Conradian" representation of Africa is only the latest expression of the persistent location of African human experiences in a global racial hierarchical order.[11] Historically embedded inside the major categories of Western political thought are conceptions of "civilization" and the unpreparedness of the colonized for self-rule. Such ideas still profoundly shape the ways in which mainstream history of thought negotiates the nature of Africana ideas.

Intellectuals and Politics

The legacies of being a racial-slave-colonial object haunt twentieth-century black radical thinkers. As descendants of slaves they master the protocols, the conventions, and the traditions of the modern Western intellectual tradition. The Western tradition was initially constructed on natural history classificatory schemes of racial order which located those of African descent as nonhuman. One consequence is that a stream of the black radical intellectual tradition deals with thought through the mastering of both the language and the culture of the dominant power—white supremacy or colonialism. Such a process establishes epistemic boundaries. Thus many black radical intellectuals consistently wrestle with language, consciousness, the nature of the ordinary, and the meaning of Africa to their life and work. This cauldron opens different spaces for the twentieth-century radical black intellectual—spaces that cannot be captured in studies of thought which trace in smooth fashion the emergence, attribution, and trajectory of ideas.

In grappling with these issues, I began to work through the precise meaning of the black radical political intellectual, using many of the standard paradigms. My first stop was an engagement with Gramsci's conceptions of the nature and functions of intellectuals. Gramsci's primary concern was the location and function of intellectuals as a social group, and the relationship of knowledge production to both questions of domination and the proletarian revolution. In examining these questions he states, "One is referring in reality only to the immediate social function of the professional category of the intellectuals, that is, one has in mind the direction in which their specific professional activity is weighed, whether towards intellectual elaboration or towards muscular-nervous effort."[12] From this perspective Gramsci moves to develop two categories of intellectuals—"traditional" and "organic."

In radical political thought the "organic" intellectual has become a central preoccupation. For example, Cornel West deploys a broad notion of the "organic" which affirms that there are two "organic traditions in African-American life: the Christian tradition of preaching and the black musical tradition of performance."[13] West's conception points to two central dimensions of black intellectual production, but it does not explore what each means nor, most important, their interiority. Indeed, West's main preoccupations are the various applications of Western categories to black intellectual production rather than excavating the tradition itself. In "The Dilemma of the Black Intellectual," West's categories of the black intellectual simply follow the different schools of Western thought, and in the end he delineates a separation between the "life of the mind," political activists, and cultural artists which seems to deny that politics is also an expression of profound cognitive capacities.

Second, West bemoans the fact that there are no really great black literary intellectuals except Toni Morrison, nor great black Marxists other than, perhaps, C. L. R. James. Historical accuracy aside, what is ignored here is how the dialogical engagement of black thinkers with the Western intellectual tradition produces thought that needs to be both documented and analyzed. To see the black radical intellectual tradition as operating wholly inside the Western canon, and then to judge its many contributors solely from that angle, is both to miss the tradition's complexity and to negate the tremendous knowledge that this tradition has postulated about the nature of the West.[14]

How Cornel West misses the fact that Du Bois was one of the major radical political thinkers of the twentieth century, contributing new knowledge not only to politics but also to historical theory, is partly a result of the ways in which he allows the category "organic" to flavor his view of the black radical intellectual. The Gramscian conception of "organic" intellectual is an unsatisfactory one to explain the black radical intellectual tradition primarily because it deals with functions and sociological relationships of intellectuals. This analytical notion does not spell out the nature and the engagement of the black radical political intellectual in the struggles for political and human freedom. Indeed, its purpose was not to do so.[15] Without doubt the black radical political intellectual often functions as an "organic" intellectual. But this is only part of the story. The key question is the nature of his or her political engagements and the character of his or her contributions to radical thought. To call the black radical intellectual an "organic" intellectual describes only function and relationships, not what that functioning means both for radical thought and for the topography of the black intellectual tradition. Thus, to rely solely on Gramsci in this instance limits our exploration.

Edward Said, in grappling with the nature of twentieth-century intellectual life, suggests that the radical intellectual is an outsider and asserts,
"The interest, the challenge of intellectual life is to be found in dissent
against the status quo."[16] Said pays some attention to Gramscian conceptions, but is more concerned to make the distinction between the professional intellectual and the amateur. He argues that the latter is committed
to "engagement with ideas and values in the public sphere."[17] The character of the amateur's engagement, Said says, is to "represent . . . the collective suffering of your own people . . . reinforcing memory."[18] This stance,
he argues, "universalizes the crisis, to give further human scope to what a
particular race or nation suffered, to associate that experience with the suffering of others."[19] I want to suggest that Said's radical intellectual is a *public* intellectual, who functions as a social critic.

Over the last decade there has been substantial concern about the nature of intellectuals and their relationship to politics and social criticism.[20]
The debates have focused on the issues of autonomy, "self-marginality,"
and the conception of the intellectual as an interpreter. The core assumption of the debate is that of Karl Mannheim, who argued that in the modern world, "in the place of a closed and thoroughly organized stratum, a
free intelligentsia has risen."[21] However when elements of this group become radical, then the issue is how they should function. The response of
Said and others is to detail the radical intellectual as a *public* intellectual.
Perhaps part of this response was generated by the controversy surrounding Russell Jacoby's stance in *The Last Intellectuals*.[22] However, what Jacoby
was lamenting was the supposed eclipse of the public intellectual who
spoke to a "public world and [in] a public language."[23]

This is different species of intellectual practice from that of a *political*
intellectual, although the latter includes some elements of the *public* intellectual. Because even though "speaking truth to power" as a form of social
criticism is to some degree a political act, any observation of black radical
intellectual production would illustrate that the central figures of this tradition were explicitly *political,* seeking to organize, having the courage to
stand by or break with organizations and programs while developing an
intellectual praxis that made politics not a god but a practice for human
good. Theirs was not just a practice of social criticism but oftentimes of organized efforts to intervene in social and political life.

Michael Walzer notes that the languages of radical intellectuals consisted of "political censure, moral indictment, skeptical question, satiric
comment, angry prophecy, utopian speculation."[24] However, as we will see
in the various chapters, there was more within the black radical tradition.
In the end, many of the contemporary arguments about the radical intellectual do not adequately describe black radical intellectual production,

and are woefully inadequate in supporting any hermeneutical practice on the writings and political activities of C. L. R. James, Franz Fanon, Malcolm X, and James Baldwin, to cite a few important members of the black radical intellectual tradition.

But what, you may ask, about the classic arguments of Julien Benda? In *Treason of Intellectuals* Benda argues that the real intellectuals are "those whose activity is essentially *not* the pursuit of practical aims . . . and hence in a certain manner say: their kingdom is not of this world."[25] Benda designates these individuals as "clerks" who live in "opposition" to the multitude and adopt "abstract principles . . . superior to and directly opposed to these passions."[26] Writing in 1928, Benda is preoccupied with what he calls the "rise in political passions" and the way it seems to him that many intellectuals "betrayed" their vocation of "abstract principles." His portrayal of intellectuals as persons with abstract principles in direct opposition to political passions is not particularly relevant to any serious discussion of black radical intellectual production, except to remind us that his work is an important marker in the Western conceptual history of the intellectual. Benda draws his inspiration from both Platonic conceptions of knowledge and the early European clergy's historic practices of knowledge keeping and dissemination. His other importance for our present discussion is that his views are still frequently echoed to suggest that intellectuals and the enterprise of thought should not be contaminated by existence.

There is, however, another set of conceptions about intellectuals to which we should pay some attention. Isaiah Berlin has written extensively about the history of ideas. It is generally acknowledged that his work on Russian thinkers and on Giambattista Vico were much-needed additions to the history of Western thought. However what is of interest to us here is Berlin's sense about the role of the Russian intelligentsia. Berlin begins his arguments about the Russian intelligentsia with a rehearsal of the nature of Russian society in the late nineteenth century. He makes the point that the Russian intelligentsia was "a minority of persons who had access to the civilization of the West and freely read languages. They were almost foreigners in their own land . . . those among them with sensitive consciences were acutely aware of a natural obligation to help their fellows."[27]

It is generally acknowledged that by the turn of the twentieth century, the Russian intelligentsia as a group was one of the most radical. It produced writers such as Tolstoy and Turgenev and political intellectuals such as Plekhanov, Lenin, and Trotsky. Berlin argues that this intelligentsia was remarkable for its commitment to the salvation of Russia. He suggests that its achievements resided in their application of Western ideas to "backward Russia."[28] On the surface this argument seems to fit the radical black intellectual particularly in the colonial context. But closer scrutiny reveals flaws. Colonialism attempts to be a totalizing knowledge regime. The radical colonized intellectual finds herself, as Fanon says, sometimes a foreigner in her own land once she begins the process of reconnecting with the native population.[29] Reconnection leads to new knowledge and the rejection of the Western episteme rooted in the negation of the colonized.

Thus the problem of black radical intellectual production is a different one. Black radical intellectual production is not simply reducible to an application of Western modernity in the ways that Berlin suggested the radical Russian intelligentsia did; instead it is a critique of, and oftentimes a counterdiscourse about, the nature of Western modernity. So while Berlin's analysis of the Russian intelligentsia is useful in our efforts to grapple with the complex history of radical intellectuals, it does not offer a real model for our study of black radical intellectual production.

Much of the contemporary debates on the nature of the intellectual within mainstream history of thought still revolves around two issues— the intellectual as expert and the intellectual as critic. Jürgen Habermas, in discussing this, explains that the

> intellectual commits himself on behalf of public interests as a sideline so to speak (something that distinguishes him from both journalists and dilettantes) without giving up his professional involvement in contexts of meaning that have an autonomous logic of their own, but also being swallowed up by the organizational forms of political activity.[30]

Such a conception of intellectuals continues the binary opposition in Western thought identified by Hannah Arendt in her 1958 text, *The Human Condition*. Arendt argues that this binary opposition between a life of the mind and that of the body and action is a false distinction between *vita activa* and *vita comtemplativa*. Of course, Arendt is primarily concerned with a phenomenological analysis of political philosophy, but her insights into the ways in which the history of Western political thought is organized is largely accurate. Habermas, by operating within this dichotomous frame, does not supply adequate conceptual tools for us to critically engage the ideas of the black radical intellectual tradition.

The Study of Black Radicals

The study of radical black intellectuals requires us to excavate the ideas of black radicals, to probe and discover the questions they raise in their political discourses and practices. This route may allow us to theorize about the discursive practices of black radicalism while deploying the conceptual resources that emerge from our examination. In this regard I want to suggest that there are two major streams of black radical intellectual production—the heretic and the prophetic. Let us first turn to the heretic stream. This stream is represented by the highly educated figures of C. L. R. James, Anna Julia Cooper, Richard Wright, W. E. B Du Bois, Walter Rodney, Ida B. Wells, and Julius Nyerere, among many others.

We are aware that all discursive practices are historical. Thought abstracted from history and context, from human agency, can become a textual plaything in insignificant language games, "all sound and fury, signifying nothing." So in our study of black radicals it behooves us to rehearse briefly some of the intellectual and contextual legacies and ideas that shape the black radical intellectual. Cedric Robinson in his seminal text *Black Marxism* observes that by the twentieth century, the black intelligentsia was rooted in the growth of a black "middle-class" which had developed in the world system. He describes the life of this group thus:

> In the Anglophone, Francophone, and Latin territories of both hemispheres, the Black "middle-class" had become broadly identified by culture and language, that is their abilities to absorb the cultures of their ruling classes and the reading and speaking of European tongues. Deracination, social and cultural alienation had become the measures of their "civility," loyalty and usefulness.[31]

There are three things of import here. First is the perception of this "middle-class" by the colonial powers as a native class formed ideationally in its own mirror image and designated as the all-important buffer group between the colonial powers and the native lower orders. This "class" had an ambiguous political relationship to the colonial power because even when it trained itself in the protocols of the West and imbibed Western language and civilization, it was still oftentimes excluded. Thus, the black or native middle class found itself alienated from the lower orders on class terms, cultural norms, and horizons, as well as excluded from the upper echelons of the ruling elite. The "in-betweenness" of this group is acute. Listen to W. E. B. Du Bois in *Souls of Black Folk* describing rural blacks at the turn of the twentieth century:

> The Sea Islands of the Carolinas where they met were filled with a black folk of primitive type, touched and moulded less by the world about them than any others outside the Black Belt. Their appearance was uncouth, their language funny, but their hearts were human and their singing stirred men with a mighty power.[32]

Or to C. L. R. James describing Matthew Bondman in *Beyond a Boundary:* "For ne'er-do-well in fact vicious character, as he was, Matthew had one saving grace—Matthew could bat. More than that, Matthew so crude and vulgar in every aspect of his life with a bat in his hand was all grace and style."[33] What saves the ordinary people who are located within the lower-class orders, in the eyes of these black radicals, is their ability to perform remarkable artistic endeavors. The alienation of the black middle class runs deep and, like all other forms of class hubris, involves conceptions of "decency and propriety." What is critical to note is that this social distance, which is normal in classbound societies, becomes exaggerated within colonial and racialized societies, and the educated black or native "middle class" becomes a most tortured creature. Why?

The normative definitions of the colonial and racial order made all blacks and natives inferior. The educated black "middle-class," clothed in the intellectual protocols of the West, must pay special attention to this distance from the black lower orders by engaging in a set of social practices that includes language, dress, speech, eating habits, religious and cultural practices. But they do this in a context of anti-black racism. This leads to our second point. The black intellectual through formal education becomes a European intellectual by training, learning to live within the framework of the Western episteme. James puts it well when he announces in *Beyond a Boundary,* "When I left school I was an educated person, but I had educated myself into a member of the British middle class with literary gifts."[34] This leads to the third point. When black radical intellectuals immerse themselves in the Western intellectual tradition, they often find their mimetic efforts futile. They become the native intellectuals who speak well, the black artists who have mastered *the* form very well, and if they begin to speak in the critical language and idiom of radical theory, they become specimens to behold, living examples that indeed the black native can be civilized. The native colonial intellectual or the black intellectual in an anti-black society is always proving himself or herself. All this, given the nature of the Western intellectual tradition, should be expected. But there is a more insidious problem that has faced the black radical intellectual since the inauguration of Western modernity.

Fanon points out in *Black Skin, White Masks* that to "speak means to be in a certain position to use a certain syntax, to grasp the morphology of this or that language, but it means above all to assume a culture, to support the weight of a civilization."[35] The implications of this are profound for radical black intellectuals. The question is, if words and language are the mechanisms by which intellectuals organize their practices, then in an anti-black society and colonial context, what is the political language they should speak? The problem is particularly acute for Africa, since colonialism attempted to impose linguistic control on the mosaic of African nations carved up at the late nineteenth-century Berlin conference.

Ngugi wa Thiong'o asserts that European languages became the discourse for literature and intellectual achievement, but it was the African peasantry who kept alive "their own mother tongues."[36] Within the African context this problem can be partly resolved by developing a political grammar and vocabulary rooted in the mother tongue.[37] One of the individuals whom we examine, Julius Nyerere, was able to achieve this with some degree of success in Tanzania by making KiSwahili the national political language. This action created the grounds for Tanzanian intellectuals to think in concrete Tanzanian and African terms.

For both continental and diasporic Africana thinkers, political language is central to political discourse. What do the terms and language of radical politics mean when invoked in the colonial context or in a situation of racial oppression? As black intellectuals become radicalized, they grapple with the categories of thought by which they have learned to live. However, they quickly find themselves in an intellectual cul-de-sac, for these categories are opaque; they shed little light on the nature of the colonial or racial condition. So the black radical intellectual begins the torturous passage of making her way back to the horizons of the native/lower-order population left behind. In doing so, she begins with history, with reclamation announcing the agency of the black colonized people. On deeper examination, the reclamation of *this* history becomes a practice and narrative that displaces what had been taught about the progressive universality of the Western intellectual categories. It also questions the accepted historical narratives and representations of who the colonized people are. At this point the black radical political intellectual becomes bereft of an anchor. Yet it is in the return passages to the native lower orders that the black radical intellectual begins to carve out the discursive space of the black radical intellectual tradition. It is then that he or she becomes a *heretic* intellectual . . . one significant stream of black intellectual production.

Heresy and Black Radical Intellectual Production

In modern usage the term "heresy" is defined as a form of deviation from orthodoxy. In the Spanish Inquisition, heresy was regarded as Muslim infidelity. The infidels were described as "the heretics and apostates of our time" who engaged in "betrayal and evasion of the truth." The *Repertorium Inquisitorium* defined how the meaning of heresy shifted from its original Greeks roots of the exercise of free will to the questioning of religious authority and the renunciation of faith.[38] Pierre Bourdieu in *Outline of a Theory of Practice* discusses heresy in relation to *doxa*. Bourdieu argues that the ideational domain of any social formation has limits. Within these limits, systems of classifications reproduce their own logic, and the nature of the social and natural world appears as both logical and natural.[39] Nothing is possible outside this constructed natural order. Therefore, underpinning social orders are theories of knowledge that in their symbolic power "impose the principles of the construction of reality—in particular social reality."[40] For Bourdieu, heresy occurs when the questioning of the *doxa* creates a new critical discourse.

When we use the word "heresy" to describe the actors of the black radical intellectual tradition, in what sense do we mean it? First, there is the sense of challenging orthodoxy. Black radical intellectual production oftentimes began with an engagement and dialogue with Western radical political ideas, and then moved on to a critique of these ideas as their incompleteness was revealed. Fanon's famous remark that one always had to stretch Marx when dealing with the colonial situation is apropos here. In other words, black radical intellectual production engages in a double operation—an engagement with Western radical theory and then a critique of this theory. In this sense black radical intellectual production is, to use Bourdieu's word, "unthinkable," breaking the epistemic limits established by the Western intellectual tradition. We are now well aware of the disciplinary dimension of orthodoxy, which fashions subjects into a specific set of social practices and customs—in the Spanish Inquisition, making the Muslim a Christian. For the black radical intellectual, "heresy" means becoming human, not white nor imitative of the colonial, but overturning white/European normativity—in the words of Robert Marley, refusing "what you wanted us to be." Third, for the black radical intellectual, heresy is a constructive project, sometimes developing a different set of political and social categories. But let us double back a bit to see how heresy operates inside black intellectual production, because for many radical black intellectuals, heresy is not the first recourse. It comes only when "double consciousness" is subordinated.

Reviewing the black intellectual tradition, one finds a conceptual frame that equips us for probing the heretic ideas of black thinkers—W. E. B. Du Bois's conception of "double consciousness." Much ink has been expended on the meaning of "double consciousness." In the manner typical of mainstream conceptual history, its antecedents have been traced to the writings of German romanticism, currents of American transcendentalism, and nineteenth-century psychology. Sometimes the notion has been used as a metaphor rather than a mode of analysis. In a remarkable text of intellectual excavation, Shamoon Zamir in *Dark Voices* posits an argument about the relationship of the notion of "double consciousness" to Du Bois's reading of Hegel's *Phenomenology of Mind*. He suggests that Du Bois's thinking at the time was not a simple adaptation or echo of Hegel's unhappy consciousness, but rather an attempt to creatively read the situation of African Americans at the start of the twentieth century. He further argues that it "represents the black middle class elite facing the failure of its own progressive ideals in the late nineteenth century . . . under the gaze of white America."[41]

While this insight is perhaps historically accurate, I think Du Bois as a radical black political intellectual was also getting at something else. A review of the passage, in *Souls of Black Folk* (1903), would reveal the following.[42] First, although "double consciousness" is called "strife," Du Bois makes the point that the African American is also gifted with what he calls a "second sight into this American world."[43] Second, "double consciousness" is how one sees oneself "through the eyes of others,"[44] and also hides what DuBois calls "true self-consciousness."[45] At the level of discursive practices, this means that there is a strange gray area of being master of a set of discursive practices, of thinking in the major categories of these practices while recognizing that the categories themselves negate one's self. This torturous conundrum is not a static one, and can generate creative deployment of ideas, particularly because those in this position inhabit a space and social location that facilitates radicalism—"the second sight." From this perspective I wish to deploy "double consciousness" as a conceptual frame to explain the tensions inherent in many of the heretic Africana thinkers of the twentieth century.

Coping with modernity that negated one's humanity created not only counternarratives of modernity's history, practices, and meanings but also a dilemma for the Africana intellectual in the West—to *be in* and *of* the West, and yet to create inside the West an identity, a personhood which required that the West, in the words of Fanon, be left behind. In deploying the notion of "double consciousness" as a conceptual framework, I am suggesting that the kernel of the problematic for the heretic Africana intellectual is one of disjointed reflective consciousness. For the highly educated black radical intellectual there is a profound disjuncture between the lived experiences of being a racial/colonial subject and the account of this lived experience by his or her learned discursive system. This disjuncture (it is deeper than a contradiction) is the source of acute tension in the political discourses of many radical black thinkers.

The tension led Du Bois in 1940 to plaintively write, "In the folds of this European civilization I was born and shall die, imprisoned, conditioned, depressed, exalted and inspired. Integrally a part and yet, of much more significance, one of its rejected parts."[46] It led James to retort sharply in the Caribbean in the 1960s, "I did not learn western civilization under a mango tree." There is a clear historic tension in this stream of radical black intellectual production. To remain consistently radical, to rupture the boundaries that confine, the Africana radical thinker transforms "double consciousness" into heresy. Although the context is somewhat different for the continental African radical intellectual, heresy is also related to what Amilcar Cabral calls "class-suicide," which translates, in discursive terms, into what I wish to call *epistemic displacement*. In black radical intellectual production, heresy becomes the resolution to the tensions and disjuncture created by "double consciousness" and the enchantment of the Western intellectual tradition.

Another possible way of thinking about this dimension of black radical and anticolonial intellectual production in general is through the metaphor of Caliban. This character in Shakespeare's 1623 play *The Tempest* has become representative of the thought of the "native" radical intellectual. C. L. R. James himself, in the epigraphs in *Beyond a Boundary,* invokes Caliban as the representative figure who, having learned the master's language, pioneers "into regions Caesar never knew."[47] The Caribbean political novelist George Lamming, in *Pleasures of Exile,* presents two essays in which he uses Caliban as representative of an anticolonial figure who contains "the seeds of revolt."[48] Lamming, though, is acutely aware of the problematic of the Caliban trope, and writes, "We shall never explode Prospero's old myth until we christen language afresh; until we show language as the product of human endeavors."[49] This tension about Caliban is partly located in what the Cuban cultural critic Roberto Retamar tells us: that "Caliban is Shakespeare's anagram for cannibal."[50] The word developed from the word Carib, the European name for the humans who inhabited the Caribbean at the time of the first European conquest. Although Retamar further claims that by the late 1960s, in the works of the Caribbean poet and historian Kamau Brathwaite and others, Caliban took on a new meaning and became a symbol of resistance, I wish to suggest that this symbolic representation is highly problematic.

Learning Prospero's language, Caliban uses it to curse him, but Caliban is already named. In other words, this deformed slave is already an *object,* a status given to him by Prospero. So the language he speaks is not only *foreign* to him, it also *describes* him. In the play, as Caliban curses Prospero, he wishes for freedom and notes that he is Prospero's *subject* primarily because he was cheated out of his land. From a radical perspective, it would seem that Caliban has to reclaim his land as well as his identity. Obviously, at this point there is no return to an original identity, yet we are forced to ask the question: What happens when Caliban curses Prospero, proclaims freedom, and reclaims his land? Is he still Caliban, a slave created and named by Prospero, or does he become something else? Does not Caliban's freedom require a second move on his part, one that creates a new language and political categories? Perhaps at this juncture we may move to Aimé Césaire's version of this play.[51] When Caliban first announces his entrance on the stage in Césaire's version, it is with "Uhuru."[52] Prospero responds, "Mumbling your native language again. . . ."[53]

In the dialogue which follows, Caliban announces to Prospero that he will never again answer to the name Caliban. When Prospero inquires why, Caliban responds in the following manner:

It's the name given me by your hatred, and every time it's spoken it's
an insult . . . [he continues] Call me X. That would be best. Like a
man without a name or, to be more precise, a man whose name has
been stolen. You talk about history . . . well that's history, and every-
one knows it! Every time you summon me it reminds me of a basic
fact, the fact that you've stolen everything from me, even my identity! Uhuru![54]

I wish to suggest that this second move being proposed by Césaire's Caliban is one where he casts away the trappings of colonial domination. So
while James and others may begin by using the language of the master, the
logic of emancipation carries them into uncharted waters. In other words,
by pioneering into unknown regions, Caliban casts off the name and cloak
of Caliban and ceases to exist. In the study of black radical and anticolonial
intellectual production, we now need to move into a post-Caliban period.
It is this sense of the need to break out of the discursive boxes in which
Western political thought has confined us that now turns our discussion to
the second stream of the Black radical intellectual tradition.

Another Stream

The second stream of the black radical intellectual tradition is that of the
"religious" men and women—those who constructed a set of practices and
rationalities that sustained Africans in the diaspora and in continental
Africa. This stream I wish to call *redemptive prophetic*. The figures in this
stream were involved in localized resistance movements in the eighteenth,
nineteenth, and twentieth centuries, in shaping the phenomenon that has
been called "Ethiopianism." In many instances these figures were the an-
tithesis of the Western-educated intellectuals. Rooted in the subsoil of the
African diaspora in the West in the period of early modernity, these persons (e.g., Boukman in Haiti and Gullah Jack in South Carolina) developed paradigmatic models of reasoning that were in sharp epistemological
conflict with the heretic stream.

Studies of these persons, or the groups they formed and sustained, have
yet to be formally recognized as a part of the accepted trajectory of the
black radical intellectual tradition. Here, the core of the problem partly resides with definitions of *who* and *what* are intellectuals. To facilitate a
breakout of these strictures, we might once more return to Gramsci, who
convincingly argues that "There is no human activity from which any form
of intellectual participation can be excluded: *Homo faber* cannot be sepa-
rated from *Homo sapiens*."[55] Although Gramsci then becomes entrapped
in a schema where revolutionary class consciousness is reposed in the "organic" proletarian intellectual, his conception of thought is useful because

it allows us to think in some different ways about radical political thought and practice. The political struggle of the colonized and racial subject is conducted in contexts of domination and oppression where traditional labor exploitation is overlaid with the negation of personhood. Thus labor exploitation is conjoined with racial and gender oppression. The native or the black, then, always exists in a zone of nonbeing. Resistance to this form of domination opens spaces for new political knowledge. In such contexts the formal public spaces of political action are sometimes the unlikely sites for the examination of forms of resistance and struggle. So if we fix our gaze there, we might end up in a state of disillusionment because when we look in the formal public spaces, we tend to look for the spectacular, the extraordinary explosive events, rather than the ordinary, deeply embedded in the cultural practices of the "lower orders" of the population.

If we accept—and history demonstrates this—that from the "subaltern" group there are the possibilities of elaboration of ideologies and conceptions which are oppositional to racism and colonial oppression, then new doors will be opened for us to understand different dimensions both of politics and of radical political thought. One of the intriguing features of the black radical political tradition is the number of individuals from the redemptive prophetic stream who conducted struggles for political freedom and against racial domination, and who were declared *insane* by the colonial authorities. Because their numbers litter black political history, we might pause here to reflect for a moment on the matter of insanity, confinement, and subject formation in the colonial context.

In *Madness and Civilization,* Foucault notes that "Madness and non madness, reason and non reason are inextricably involved . . . and existing for each other, in relation to each other, in the exchange which separates them."[56] He argues that the growth of asylums in eighteenth-century Europe was integral to the disciplinary procedures of subject formation and the "world of confinement." Foucault's remarkable work tracks how the emergence of a liberal market economy created a discourse around the treatment and conceptions of the poor population. He charts how economic thought developed a new foundation of the social category called "the poor." In Foucault's genealogy, the growth of the asylum was deeply connected to all these issues.

However, Megan Vaughan has pointed out that there was no great confinement in colonial Africa to "match that of 19th century Europe."[57] Madness in colonial Africa was related to the problems of colonial rule and the question of the nature of the African . . . was she or he civilized? Vaughan writes, "The madman and madwoman emerge in the colonial historical record not as standing for the 'other' but more often as being insufficiently 'other.' "[58] So although there was no "great confinement," colonial ideas of reason, civilization, progress, the role of religion in relation to secularism, and the privileging of scientism as the highest form of knowledge meant that African figures who disturbed these orders had to be confined because they broke the mold of discipline, and thus of subject formation. Within the colonial regimes the disciplinary function of subject formation, of creating regulative behavior, was of extraordinary importance.

Because colonial domination broke up earlier societies, the colonial order had to construct new ways of seeing politics, society, social life, love, the human, and all facets of human life. The confinement and classification of figures who broke these molds, of those who thought and organized in rationalities other than those created by Western modernity, had to be controlled. This does not mean that the colonial order did not arrest and control those who organized anticolonial politics through modern political forms—trade unions, political parties, and so on. Instead, it is to point us to other forms of politics that cannot be subsumed under protonationalist political forms. It is also to point to how this prophetic redemptive stream attempted to break the epistemological hold of the colonial knowledge regime. In such instances the first recourse of the colonial power, whether in Africa or in the Caribbean, was to confine and classify such persons or individuals as insane.

These prophetic redemptive figures, as was stated before, litter black political and social history, but their presence has been marginal in the study of black intellectual production. This is because, in large measure, black intellectual history continues to operate within the knowledge framework of an overweening Enlightenment historical reason. Many of these "mad" figures (Alexander Bedward, a nineteenth-century Jamaican healer; Leonard Howell, the acknowledged founder of the Rastafari movement; and Nontetha Nkwenke, a Xhosa prophetess and healer) attempted to reorder the epistemological rationalities of colonial conquest.[59] They were, in the colonial eyes, *unreason* as compared to European *reason* and disciplinary rationalities. Given the knowledge regime of colonialism, the practices of healing (of both body and polity) were confrontations with colonial power that struck at the very core of the modern colonial and racial project. The figures who were engaged in projects could neither be redeemed nor be fashioned. They were "mad" and seditious in the eyes of the colonial and racist order.

Certainly in Jamaica it must have seemed like a "madness" to the colonial order when in the 1930s Leonard Howell began to preach about a black king, denouncing the British monarchy, or when Alexander Bedward, resplendent in white robes, declared in August Town in the late nineteenth century that there was a black wall and a white wall, and that the former would soon crush the latter. The colonial white supremacist order of South Africa was deeply perturbed when Nontetha preached that the

Day of Judgment was nigh, and that African people should unite against the established racial order. If racial and colonial oppression rests upon attempts to dehumanize human subjects, and human beings are self-reflective, then it should not be surprising that from the "subaltern," those who have to reconstitute their humanness daily in ordinary ways, there would emerge ideas which over time became central to the black radical political tradition.[60]

So what are the elements of this prophetic redemptive stream? Historical scholarship on the nature of prophets in Africa suggests demarcations between three processes: divination, healing, and prophecy.[61] However, what is clear in any examination of the political role of prophetic figures is that to some degree they exercise all three functions. The political prophet in the Africana tradition gains knowledge by revelation, is able to prophesy, and heals and redeems. Let us use Leonard Howell and Alexander Bedward again as brief examples. Not only would they prophesy from dreams or revealed knowledge, but both were involved in healing practices. What makes the prophet redemptive in this tradition is that prophecy functions as a form of social criticism, a redemptive discourse that argues for the ending of colonial and racial oppression. This is a politics of the world upside down, which eschews the standard political forms and language of political modernity. As such, it is outside the pale of political modernity and is mistakenly viewed as "prelogical" or "prepolitical."

In his discussion on Jewish religious practice, Michael Walzer makes the point that the biblical prophets were social critics. He states as well that prophets speak to a large audience and do a kind of talking which is "not so much an educated as an inspired and poetic version of what must have been sometimes."[62] As a rule prophets call people to action; they remind them of their condition; they do not speak for themselves, but on behalf of other authorities that they claim hold the nation in judgment. The language of prophecy is poetic and visionary, and is rooted in conceptions of history. For the black radical political tradition, this language is embedded in two sources, biblical exegesis and the indigenous knowledge systems of the colonized native. This political form of struggle has created the religious/political category "millenarian."[63]

The Africana redemptive prophets narrate a different story and history of colonialism and redemption. In elaborating this narrative they sometimes break from monochronic time frames and develop conceptions and historical narratives that collapse past and present, making no linear chronological distinctions. This is particularly true in some historical conceptions of the Rastafari movement, where redemption is a destructive/constructive moment, an event rather than a process. In such frames history is a *now* between the past and the future, without transitions. Oftentimes when one is tackling the redemptive tradition of black radical thought, the figure of Walter Benjamin comes to mind. Benjamin's thesis on the philosophy of history affirms that "History is the subject of a structure whose site is not homogeneous, empty time, but time filled by the presence of the now."[64] The insight is remarkably similar to the prophetic vision of history in the black radical tradition and perhaps the similarities can be explained by the ways in which totalizing regimes locate "states of emergency" as they structure power and control.

The third feature to note of this redemptive stream is its creative usage of language to describe social conditions and affirm their humanity. In these instances the word —*la parole*—becomes a weapon, a chant, and an invocation beating against the walls of oppression as well as an "illocutionary force."[65] Language is a central feature for this stream as it reorders meanings. Used extensively, the different meanings of words contribute to an alternative political discourse. This discourse refigures political and religious languages, integrating them to create a new political grammar. Thus one of the most exciting things about mining this stream of the black radical intellectual tradition is the investigation of these new forms. In the study of political thought and philosophy, we now know that old political languages become transformed when they are exposed to new discursive practices. Within all streams of the black radical intellectual production this occurs. If we do not see it, perhaps it is because we are looking with the aid of categories that already shape our answers. We have to approach these issues humbly.

The final element of the redemptive stream is that it creates a "counter symbolic world and order."[66] The creation of a symbolic order that then overturns the hegemonic racist or colonial order is not only a semiotic challenge but also, importantly, a battle for human validation.

A Common Link

There is a common link between these two streams within the black radical intellectual tradition that returns us to some familiar arguments about the nature of Western political thought. Hannah Arendt remarked that Western political philosophy never fully recovered from its Platonic origins of opposition to "polis and citizenship." She further observed in *The Human Condition* that political philosophy can easily be interpreted "as various attempts to find theoretical formulations and practical ways to escape from politics altogether." Arendt also reminds us that "The central political activity is action," and as such, it would appear that the experiences of citizenship or the lack thereof, as well as the practices of the construction of a political community, should be issues for political theory and thought.

There exists a deep political practice in Africana political thought that connects the lived social and political experiences of Africans and the African diaspora to the categories of political thought. Any observation of the political activity and writings of many members of the black radical intellectual tradition illustrates this. Between the late nineteenth century and the mid-twentieth century, many figures represent this current of action and thought, "of praxis ascending to the level of thought"[67] (e.g., Ida B. Wells, Marcus Garvey, and Malcolm X). Wells's anti-lynching campaign and political writings mark new directions in Africana political thought about the nature of citizenship, rights, gender, race, and the political community in the context of the high noon of the white American republic. Marcus Garvey's political praxis of black internationalism and voluminous writings heralded a new stage for the international black movement against colonialism and racial oppression at the beginning of the twentieth century. Malcolm X's political praxis in the 1960s gave new meanings to notions of human rights and challenged the American liberal theory of rights.

By their political practices, all three figures collapsed the boundaries between political thought and political action. They were radical intellectuals who developed new political knowledge from a dialectical dialogue of lived experience and critical interpretation. This is a feature of the black radical intellectual tradition, where there is a radical hermeneutic of everyday experiences. Of such importance is this practice that it suggests to us a rethinking of the formulations about the relationships between political thought and political practice. Clearly, Malcolm X's thought on the relationship between human rights and civil rights, and Garvey's UNIA Manifesto for the black world, were not political *opinions* but political *knowledge* that raised foundational questions. Such a perspective debunks the idea expressed by the prominent political theorist John Dunn, that "The history of western political theory still for the present offers the richest resources available to human beings."[68]

Conclusion

This book of essays is an attempt to probe the ideas and the meanings of the two streams of the black radical intellectual tradition: the heretic and the prophetic/redemptive. Although essentially a hermeneutical exercise, it will offer meditations on the implications for radical thought that emerge from this tradition. The study is an exercise in the history of ideas and political thought, but in its very performance asks the reader to do what Fanon's private prayer always was—"O my body, make of me always a man who questions."[69] The book's chapters will be organized around figures and a movement that represent each of the streams. My choice has been guided by the questions that the particular figure or movement raised, and their contributions to radical thought in general. I will examine the thought of Quobna Cugoano, Ida B. Wells, W. E. B. Du Bois, C. L. R. James, Julius Nyerere, Walter Rodney, and Robert Marley. I will also examine the political philosophy of Rastafari.

Accounts of the present state of radical political thought are still embedded in a Western episteme that revolves around two historical events, the 1789 French Revolution and the 1917 Russian Revolution. Even those who proclaim the death of Eurocentrism still survey radical thought within these two historical exemplars. For example, Immanuel Wallerstein, in elaborating a left intellectual agenda for the twenty-first century, concedes that these two major historical moments and their conceptual histories have been the framing ones for radical thought, and *continue* to be so.[70] Michael Hardt and Antonio Negri's *Empire*, while attempting to draw "a new global order, a new logic and structure of rule—in short, a new form of sovereignty,"[71] still remains within the confines of the epistemic silences of radical political thought.[72] All of these works indicate the deep hold that the established Western categories, as the *sole ones of any import*, have on political thought. Such a perspective is clearly a blinkered one. If this book opens a small space for the reader to grapple with another source of radical theories and practices about human emancipation, then it will have been worthwhile. The African-American poet Langston Hughes asked us "to sit and dream, to sit and read, to sit and learn about the world," and to help "make our world anew."[73] This has been the trajectory of the black radical intellectual tradition. It is about time we explored it. So now we begin. . . .

THE HERETICS

CHAPTER 1

The Political Thought of Quobna Cugoano
Radicalized Natural Liberty

I write what I like.
—Steve Biko

The slaves shall be free . . . [through a] . . . combination of ideas.
—Robert Wedderburn, former slave

Introduction

The 1969 publication of African-American poet Arna Bontemps's *Great Slave Narratives* consolidated the study of slave narratives as a genre of literature.[1] Bontemps made the case for the slave narrative as an "American genre" of popular autobiography. This classification has meant that subsequent studies on slave narratives have been primarily framed as memoirs, autobiography, and a genre of literature. To consider these frames as the *only* ones for the study of slave narratives is today problematic. First, it is well known that a common problem within the domain of knowledge production is the misconception that blacks produce experience and whites produce theory.[2] Therefore, when we study the written productions of black slaves *only* within the autobiographical or literary frame, we can miss their political ideas and purposes. The second difficulty is that the narrow autobiographical frame which focuses on life experiences often ignores the broad context of textual production. When this occurs, the complex relationships between the written testimony of the slave and the political language and context in which the testimony is embedded are elided or reduced to a secondary position. The autobiographical/literary frame of slave narratives confines the politics of many narratives to a form of "literary black vindicationism" similar in some respects to the "vindicationism" of black history.[3] The autobiographical frame also ignores the fact that the late eighteenth century and a good deal of the nineteenth century were periods in which black abolitionism was a significant radical plank on the world's political stage.[4] This essay challenges the dominant interpretive mode of the slave narratives as primarily literary and autobiographical. In doing so, it argues that Quobna Cugoano's *Thoughts and Sentiments on the Evil of Slavery* is a major late eighteenth-century text of political discourse on natural liberty and natural rights.

Henry Louis Gates, Jr.'s book *The Signifying Monkey* (1988) opened wider spaces for thinking about the location of slave narratives. However, it did so within the boundaries of the established literary canonization of the narratives. In this seminal work Gates argues that the slave narratives were an integral part of the African-American literary tradition. He further suggests that this tradition was a "double-voiced" one, and characterizes the slave narrative as "a talking book." Positing a theory of origins, Gates asserts that the "literature of the slave" at the level of meaning was an oxymoron, and that for the slave, the capacity to read and write was his or her ability to "transgress [a] nebulous realm of liminality."[5] He further observes that, "The slave wrote not primarily to demonstrate humane letters, but to demonstrate his or her membership in the human community."[6]

For Gates, blacks became subjects in the eyes of the world through the crafting of a written text. Probing this point, he demonstrates how the privileging of reason by the various European Enlightenments created writing as a badge and expression of Reason, and therefore of humanity. It is common knowledge that after Descartes proclaimed, "I think; therefore I am," thinking was transformed into Reason, and that "I am" became an epistemological question rather than one of being.[7] Over time, the written word became the signifier for Reason as rationality. As such, African slaves living in the "Age of the Enlightenment" did use writing as *one* means of human agency. Gates and others have suggested that slave narratives were also the early beginnings of a "Black Atlantic literary and cultural tradition . . . [which shared] a common creolized cultural heritage that crossed national and ethnic boundaries . . . defined political categories, social norms, and even literary genres."[8]

In one sense this is accurate, and acknowledges the fact that modern Atlantic slavery was a large system and that the trade yoked different societies into a set of relationships. However, in spite of the above, we are still left with working through the specific forms of political writings and criticism that the narratives were embedded within. One way to grapple with the issue of the precise nature of slave narratives is to suggest that they were not only literature, political criticism, or narrative history, but integrated all these modes of writing into a form of critical exposition. This form of writing had an ethical dimension, and its primary modes were both communicative and calls to action, thereby making the narratives moments of slave critique. This shift in interpretation means that the narratives were something else; they were *documents of freedom* that can be interpreted within the context of the language and political ideas of their times. Today the act of reading these texts confronts one with a peculiar task of interpretation—the relationship between the meaning of these texts, the structural world of slavery, and the general ideas of natural liberty in what the critic Roland Barthes calls a "narrative communication."

This essay will attempt to address some of these issues. Using Cugoano's narrative, I want to suggest that perhaps another way to read *some* of the slave narratives of the late eighteenth century is to grapple with them as discursive practices of slave criticism and critique that probed alternative meanings of racial slavery, natural liberty, and natural rights, and countered the dominant eighteenth-century ideas of racial plantation slavery. As documents of slave political criticism and critique, the narratives have a great deal to tell us about eighteenth-century social and political ideas, and form a central part of an Africana radical intellectual political tradition.

Writing as Political Criticism

Dena Goodman tells us that there were many modes of critical writing during the eighteenth century: epistolary, historical narrative, letters, memoirs, treatises, and dialogical.[9] The major objective of these forms of writing was to shape a society's thinking. According to Goodman, these modes of writing constituted "conscious acts carried out by leading figures as part of the Enlightenment's civic project."[10] Critical writing during this period involved a kind of dialectic. The production of a text was an engaged moment whereby the writer hoped that he or she would affect society's thinking. As a mode of critical action, writing had three aspects— there was an audience who would be persuaded, who would be changed, and who would, eventually, act. From this standpoint we can better appreciate the emphasis that the English abolitionist movement placed upon written textual productions during the late eighteenth century as an integral part of its campaign to abolish the slave trade.

Another dimension of the discursive practices of the period was the language and vocabulary of political discourse. In general, four main themes provided the grammar for political discourse: state of nature, natural law, natural rights, and natural liberty. In England these themes were complicated by an older political tradition that had emerged in Stuart England— the Bible as the divine word of God and the application of the principles of the New Testament as a catalyst for conceptions of a harmonious political order. This tradition of appropriating biblical texts for radical purposes and reworking the language of revolution through the prism of religious beliefs was consolidated in the revolution of the 1640s when the major radical groups, the Levellers and the Diggers, conducted much of their revolutionary propaganda and journalism in the language of religious discourse.[11] For many African ex-slaves and slaves, the Bible was also a central source for reading and gaining literacy skills. Slaves' biblical exegesis readapted the narrative and prophetic forms of biblical discourse to explain and understand their condition. What is interesting in many slave narratives is how these forms functioned alongside secular Enlightenment discourse as part of the complex intellectual labor of the eighteenth-century black writer. Thus one could get in the slave narratives of the period the language of natural rights mixed with prophecy.[12] At the heart of the themes (natural law, natural liberty, state of nature, natural rights, theories of human origins) was what Michel Foucault has described as the political rationality of governing men.[13]

The third feature of the eighteenth-century intellectual context that should draw our attention is the conception of the "Great Chain of Being." This hierarchical conception formulated an originary theory of the universe in which human beings and the social order replicated "the divine hierarchy of heaven." Basing itself on the natural history classification of Carolus Linnaeus, this system of classification led to a vigorous debate on polygenesis versus monogenesis as the theory of human origin. At the center of this debate was the location of Africans in a natural inferior position.[14] This debate about the origins of the human became critical in late eighteenth- and early nineteenth-century mainstream arguments about the humanity of the black slave, and a major point of contention between abolitionists of all races and advocates of slavery.

The late eighteenth-century was a period when the questions that animated Western thinkers were framed around what Edmund Burke called the "great . . . unfolding map of mankind."[15] Part of this unfolding map was a preoccupation with the human and the development of a philosophical anthropology that postulated "natural" characteristics of the human. The evidence of this preoccupation can be discerned when we note the number of publications between George Berkeley's *Principles of Human Knowledge* (1710) and Mary Wollstonecraft's *Vindication of the Rights of Women* (1792), that had the human as a central focus. The following were some of the keys texts: Alexander Pope's *An Essay on Man* (1734), David Hume's *Enquiry Concerning Human Understanding* (1748), Gotthold Ephraim Lessing's *Education of the Human Race* (1780), and Johann von Herder's *Ideas for the Philosophy of the History of Mankind* (1784). The tragedy, of course, was that this *human subject* was narrowly defined, and excluded women, Africans, and other non-Europeans.[16] From within this exclusive paradigm the political grammar of natural liberty and natural rights was framed. However, because it was grounded in exclusions and silences, natural rights and natural liberty would morph over time to have narrow meanings.

Burke's "unfolding map" rested upon the notion of African inferiority, and was very dependent as well upon texts that reaffirmed Europe's "superiority" because many Western thinkers in this period drew heavily from the travel writings and literature of "explorers." Paul Kaufman's study of English reading habits of the period confirms the tremendous attraction of intellectuals and the literate public to travel literature and books.[17] Thus it is fair to say that there was during this period a general intellectual preoccupation in Europe with the nature of the New World and of colonialism. This preoccupation found its way into the writings and understandings of many early modern political thinkers, but via the musings and literate offerings of those who were conquering the New World. How these offerings infected political philosophy is detailed in Anthony Pagden's wonderful volume, *Lords of All the World* (1995).

Against the background of colonial conquest, and ideas of racial servitude and of African inferiority, Western political thinkers began their strivings for new forms of society that would replace crumbling European absolutism. In such a context, very few thinkers included the slave trade and racial slavery in their discussion of these questions, and when they did so, they were discussed within two main frameworks.

The first owed its foundational assumptions to Greek and Roman conceptions of slavery.[18] These conceptions stated that slavery was the result of war or of debt owed. John Locke's comments on slavery and natural liberty exemplify this current when he writes in *The Second Treatise of Government:*

> The *Natural Liberty* of Man is to be free from any Superior Power on Earth, and not to be under the Will or legislative Authority, but to have only the law of Nature for his Rule. . . . This *Freedom* from Absolute, Arbitrary Power, is so necessary to and closely joined with a Man's Preservation. . . . For a Man, not having the Power of his own life *cannot,* by Compact, or his own Consent, *enslave himself* to anyone . . . the prefect condition of *Slavery,* which *is* nothing else, but *the State of War continued between a lawful conqueror, and the captive.* For, if once *Compact* enter between them, and make an agreement for limited Power on the one side, and Obedience on the other, the State of War and *Slavery* ceases, as long as the Compact endures.[19]

An analysis of the above passage reveals not only that natural liberty was posed in terms of the relationship between government and citizens, what Isaiah Berlin has called "the central question in politics—the question of obedience and coercion"[20]—but also that Locke defined slavery as the result of conquest. For Locke, conquest meant that the conquered were outside the social contract, and since the compact was critical to the creation of conditions in which slavery as he defined it would cease, then wherever and among whomever slavery existed, such persons existed outside of the compact and had no rights.[21]

The second definition of slavery during this period was located within the ideas of what has been called "civic republicanism."[22] This "civic republicanism" some political theorists have argued meant that the conception of freedom and slavery was tied to ideas of citizenship that primarily focused on issues of how laws and the state shaped freedom as a form of political self-determination. Later on when this form of freedom is conceptualized as non-domination it is done so within the frame elaborated by Mill and Berlin, that of non-coercion and interference. I want to suggest that the elision of racial slavery and its meanings by the majority of the political thinkers of the period meant that over time, conceptions of natural liberty and natural rights narrowly folded into a set of political discourses about the state, government, and citizens' rights. This created a flawed space for a new discussion of rights, obligations, and notions of resistance for the male European citizen struggling against absolutism. At one level these new conceptions were perhaps best embodied in the 1789 French Declaration of Rights of Man and Citizen, and the American Constitution.

At another level there was a radical plebeian impulse that attempted to radicalize both the conception of rights and the notion of private property. This impulse drew its sources from Thomas Paine's defense of the French Revolution, *The Rights of Man*. In London it solidified around the formation of the London Correspondence Clubs, the writings and political activities of Thomas Spencer, and, by the 1820s, the preaching and chapels of persons like the former Jamaican slave Robert Wedderburn.[23]

Surveying the United States in this period, we can discern a preoccupation with natural liberty as a conception of republican civic freedom in the writings of Thomas Jefferson, John Adams, and James Madison. Mainstream American political thought in the late eighteenth century drew from two sources: republican political values of self-government and Lockean understandings of limited government and political liberty. Rogers Smith accurately sums up the early political goals of the American republic thus: "The goal remained a great but state-centric union of small agrarian republics, populated by self-supporting, educated white yeomen, joined and governed by the mutual consent of all those capable of being dedicated to free republican citizenship."[24] Within this political conception of republicanism, "slavery" was primarily identified as lack of self-government. Listen to Adams addressing the citizens of Massachusetts: "The people of Massachusetts uniformly think that the destruction of their Charter, making the council and judges wholly dependent upon the crown and the people subjected to the unlimited power of parliament as their supreme legislative is *slavery*."[25]

Thus we can safely say that by the late eighteenth century, the language of natural liberty in America was the discourse of self-government as political liberty. This language was oblivious to the overshadowing presence of the system of human domination (racial slavery).[26] However, some political thinkers did pay some attention to racial slavery, and in doing so developed a radicalized version of natural liberty. One of the most outstanding cases in this regard was Thomas Paine. Paine's 1775 essay "African Slavery in America" refuted the arguments that slavery in America was the result of a state of war. He forcefully asserted that the slaves were "not prisoners of war, and redeemed from savage conquerors, as some plead."[27] Paine called slavery a "savage practice" and appealed for its abolition.

For the French philosophers the situation was only slightly different. Montesquieu's satirical arguments against African slavery in *The Spirit of Laws* are well known. Nevertheless, he continued to hold the view that Africans were uncivilized and not energetic, compared to Europeans of cooler climes.[28] Diderot's joint work with Abbé Raynal, *The History of the Indies,* was a "philosophical and political history of European trade and settlements in the Indies." It was also an antislavery text with profound consequences. However, the text was deeply ambiguous, and while being anticolonial as well as antislavery, it maintained the view that Africans were "primitive" beings. In describing the African and Africa, the *History* states "that they are more indolent, more weak, and unhappily more fit for slavery."[29] Diderot and Raynal further note, "Arts are unknown amongst them. All their labors are confined to certain rustic employments, scarce one hundredth part of their country is cultivated and that in a very wretched manner."[30]

There is one other important political thinker of the period to whom we should pay some attention: Mary Wollstonecraft. Wollstonecraft belongs to the group of political thinkers who advocated a radicalized version of natural rights in the late eighteenth century. However, she could not escape the enmeshment of the "Great Chain of Being." So even while she pressed the claims for the equality of women in her pathbreaking text, *Vindication of the Rights of Women,* she continued to hold the view of Africans as an "unmeditative people."[31] In her 1789 review of Olaudah Equiano's narrative, Wollstonecraft writes that although they are interesting, these "volumes do not exhibit extraordinary intellectual powers . . . yet the activity and ingenuity, which conspicuously appear in the character of Gustavus, place him on par with the general mass of men who fill the subordinate stations in a more civilized society than that which he was thrown into at his birth."[32]

Diderot and Paine are comparable writers and thinkers, and their conceptions of natural liberty are closest to Cugoano's understanding of the relationship between natural liberty, natural rights, and the evil of racial slavery. However, there was a Rubicon that neither Paine nor Diderot seemed to be able to cross—the granting of *full human status* to Africans. In the end, many radical Enlightenment thinkers foundered on this point. The critical issue was that underneath the surface of modern political thought of this period lay a definition of the human that excluded African slaves.

Outside of these currents was another stream—the black abolitionist one. Cugoano belonged to this stream, and in many ways was for a short time one of its most radical exponents. From this frame we can now shift the focus to the study of Cugoano's narrative. Cugoano's work may be treated as a treatise or an essay on racial slavery that speaks in the language of natural rights and natural liberty. Second, Cugoano's notion of justice and human equality, his adaptation of Christianity, his condemnation of colonialism and support for the rights of rebellion of the colonized; his call for a universal community based on common humanity, and his advocacy for the abolition of the African slave trade and racial slavery make him a radical political thinker of early modernity. His writing therefore not only should be compared with that of the major white abolitionists of the period—Thomas Clarkson, Granville Sharp, and James Ramsey—but also placed alongside the other radical natural rights thinkers of the period.

The Political Discourse of Cugoano

Quobna Ottobah Cugoano's *Thoughts and Sentiments on the Evil of Slavery* was published in two versions, the first in 1787,[33] the year that the British Anti-Slavery Association was formally constituted, and the second in 1791. In 1788 a French version of the text appeared in Paris. The 1787 and 1791 texts were published for two different audiences. The first was "humbly submitted to the inhabitants of Great Britain," and the second, to the "Sons of Africa." Commentators on Cugoano—Paul Edwards (1969), Vincent Carretta (1999), Henry Louis Gates, Jr. (1998)—all locate his writings as major pieces of black Atlantic writing. Gates writes that "Cugoano leans heavily towards the side of polemic" and that the text is "constructed as a response to the eighteenth century's major treatises on African enslavement."[34] Carretta notes that Cugoano "raised the most overt and extended challenge to slavery ever made by a person of African descent."[35] In an interesting essay, "The Master's Tools: Abolitionist Arguments of Equiano and Cugoano," June Ward argues that Cugoano's work should also be studied as an abolitionist text and that the categories of his political discourse were ones which developed "wholly new formulations of the anti-slavery argument."[36]

I want to take a different track—Cugoano's *Thoughts and Sentiments* was not only an important abolitionist text but also a carefully crafted piece of political discourse written by a political thinker who was preoccupied with the nature of natural liberty and natural rights as "common rights."[37] This preoccupation forms the political ground for his arguments against slavery. As an explicit political essay, Cugoano's text does not follow the typical structural conventions of the slave narrative with detailed recapitulations of the cruelties of slavery and the slave trade. Instead, it goes in the opposite direction: Cugoano is explicit about what he is *not* writing.

Early in the text Cugoano makes the point that he is refuting the system of slavery at the level of *logic, reason,* and *religion.* He writes:

> What I intend to advance against that evil and criminal and wicked traffic of enslaving men, are only some Thoughts and Sentiments which occur to me, as being obvious from the Scriptures of Divine Truth, or such arguments as are chiefly deduced from thence, with other such observations as I have been able to collect. Some of these observations may lead into a larger field of consideration, than that of the African slave trade.[38]

Three things are immediately clear. First, that one conceptual resource of his discourse will be Christian notions; second, that he will use empirical observations about society to make his arguments; and third, that his field of criticism will be all forms of what he considers evil, as long as it connected in some way to the slave trade. By making the third move, Cugoano centers the Atlantic slave trade as a focal point of eighteenth century European civilization. Both this fact and his condemnation of colonialism immediately take him outside the boundaries of the political ideas and practices of the English abolitionist movement and place him on a track different from that of the radical natural rights thinkers. The title and some ideas of Cugoano's text draw from two earlier abolitionists' texts: Thomas Clarkson's *An Essay on the Slavery and Commerce of the Human Species, Particularly the African* (1786) and James Ramsey's *An Essay on the Treatment and Conversion of the Slaves in the British Sugar Colonies* (1784). What is of interest is that while other slave writings called themselves narratives, memoirs, or the life and confession of, Cugoano's essay does not do this. It therefore announces early on that it is a different text. Sidestepping the typical slave narrative structures, Cugoano pays very little attention to his own condition. He does, however, make an obligatory gesture toward the slave narrative biographical structure and writes brief passages on how he became a slave. But, these passages are quickly dispensed with when he states:

> But it would be needless to give a description of all the horrible scenes which we saw, and the base treatment which we met with in its dreadful captive situation, as the similar cases of thousands which suffer by this infernal traffic. Let it suffice to say, that I was thus lost to my dear indulgent parents and relations, and they to me. All my help was cries and tears, and those could not avail . . . brought from a state of innocence and freedom, and, in a barbarous and cruel manner, conveyed to state of horror and slavery. This abandoned situation may be easier conceived than described.[39]

Is it not clear that what Cugoano is concerned with is a *conception* of what slavery meant, not a simply description of its brutalities? This is important because, as David Brion Davis points out in his magisterial studies of mainly white antislavery opinions and movements, there existed a current of antislavery thought that was generated by what he calls the "man of feeling."[40] Davis argues that this current began to show itself in England when, contrary to Thomas Hobbes, ideas began to be asserted that "men were not discrete particles of self-interest, requiring for harmonious union, a coercive external will."[41]

I wish to suggest that this sentiment, combined with the notion that there were depravities attendant to the slave trade, played a huge role in the English abolitionist movement and was one of the reasons why the slave narratives often pressed home the brutalities of the slave trade and slavery. Cugoano departed from this view and sought to take the grounds of reason and religion. After describing how he gained his freedom and literacy, Cugoano decides that any improvement in his condition should be used in the struggle against slavery. He writes: "Since, I have endeavored to improve my mind in reading, and have sought to get all the intelligence I could, in my situation of life, towards the state of my brethren and countrymen in complexion, and of the miserable situation of those who are barbarously sold into captivity, and unlawfully held in slavery."[42]

What are the main elements of Cugoano's political ideas that emerge from this text, and how are they similar to and different from the ideas and political language of late eighteenth-century radical political discourses on natural rights and natural liberty?

Natural Liberty as Political Horizon

I will proceed at two levels here. First, I will list what I consider to be the major tenets of Cugoano's political thought, then choose three for elaboration. The major political ideas of Cugoano can be distilled into the following themes and propositions:

1. Opposition to African slavery
2. A theory of history that conflates Enlightenment concerns surrounding geography and climate empiricism with a Christian notion of monogenesis
3. An overarching framework of natural liberty that is located in the emergence of civil society and not in a state of nature
4. That natural liberty is enriched rather than diminished by the growth of civil society
5. That natural liberty and monogenesis mean that all "men" (heathens, pagans, Christians) have property, civil, and political rights.
6. That racial slavery is evil and contrary to divine law, natural human law, and "common humanity"
7. That a consequence of racial slavery is restitutions to Africans who had suffered because of the trade
8. That colonialism and colonial conquest are contrary to civilization (civil society), natural law, and divine law
9. That society should be constructed as a common harmonious community which looks after its poor
10. A definition of natural liberty as self-ownership, and a critical attitude to the British crown and its involvement in the slave trade.

This chapter will focus on Cugoano's antislavery ideas, his conceptions of evil, and his views on the relationship between natural liberty and natural rights.

Cugoano regards slavery as an activity that is rooted in stealing, kidnapping, and the selling of human beings, and as such is contrary to what he calls the "common rights of nature."[43] Declaring himself a liberal,[44] he announces that the enslavement of Africans is against the "common rights of nature," evil, and thus contrary to notions of justice, reason, and humanity. Here Cugoano is using the political language of radical eighteenth-century political thinkers. In his essay on slavery, Paine had declared:

> Our traders in MEN (*an unnatural commodity*) must know the wickedness of that SLAVE-TRADE. . . . Such men may as well join

with a band of robbers, buy their ill-got goods . . . but none can law-
fully buy without evidence that they are not concurring with men-
stealers . . . so the slave who is the proper owner of his freedom, has
a right to reclaim it, however often sold.[45]

The general conception of slavery posited by the radical natural rights
thinkers was that slavery was the robbery of natural liberty. Cugoano puts
the position plainly when he writes: "But the robbers of men, the kidnappers, ensnarers and slave-holders, who take away the common rights . . .
are . . . pitiful and detestable wretches; for the ensnaring of others and taking away their liberty by slavery and oppression, is the worst kind of robbery."[45]

Cugoano's foundational assumption was that there existed a state of
natural freedom which each person had. Slavery therefore was not just
about brutality or inhumane conditions, but at root was the taking away of
the freedom made possible by natural liberty. That robbery of natural liberty was therefore slavery's worst element. This was a view of natural liberty very different from that promulgated by the mainstream natural
rights thinkers of the period. Cugoano sees natural rights as "common
rights," and applies these rights to African slaves. In doing this he universalizes natural rights in ways others did not. The notion of "common
rights" was a popular one in radical natural rights theory at the time. For
example, in Paine's hands the notion was meant to convey "*the unity of
man*; by which I mean, that men are all of *one degree,* and consequently
that all men are born equal and with equal natural right."[47] Cugoano deploys the notion in a similar manner, but he uses slavery as his benchmark
to characterize whether or not a country is really free and Christian.

Slavery as Evil

We now turn to Cugoano's characterization of slavery as evil. Cugoano argues that slavery is evil because it is contradictory to three elements: justice, humanity in a collective sense, and reason—that most celebrated dimension of the European Enlightenment. This is different from the
descriptions of slavery as evil by both the radical natural right thinkers of
the period and the white abolitionists. Thomas Paine calls slavery evil and
a crime because it goes against natural rights. Many abolitionists felt that it
was against divine law, and therefore a sin and evil. However, Cugoano
links all these, and adds reason:

> By taking away the natural liberties of men, and compelling them to
> any involuntary slavery or compulsory service, is an injury and rob-
> bery contrary to all law, civilization, reason, justice, equity, and hu-

manity: therefore when men break through the laws of God, and the rules of civilization among men, and go forth and steal, to rob, to plunder, to oppress and to enslave and to destroy their fellow creatures. . . .[48]

For Cugoano the heart of this form of evil is that human beings are reduced from their human status. He writes that the "slaves, like animals, are bought and sold, and dealt with as their capricious owners may think fit."[49] Thinking about the meaning of evil has had a long history ranging from metaphysical and theological interpretations, to Manichaeanism (where good and evil are seen as binary opposites), to the psychology of evil, to Hannah Arendt's efforts to understand evil as banality.[50] In Arendt's thought there is a distinction between the "radical evil" of mid-twentieth-century totalitarianism and the "banality of evil" of Adolf Eichmann. In the latter, Arendt attempts to understand the quotidian nature of Eichmann's actions—what she calls its "normality." In describing "radical evil," Arendt wants to point to one way in which we might understand evil. She makes the point in a letter to Karl Jaspers:

> Evil has proved to be more radical than expected. In objective terms, modern crimes are not provided for in the Ten Commandments. Or: the Western Tradition is suffering from the preconception that the most evil things human beings can do arise from the vice of selfishness. . . . What radical evil really is I don't know but it seems to me it somehow has to do with the following phenomenon: making human beings as human beings superfluous.[51]

"Making human beings as human beings superfluous"—is this not what racial slavery did? Arendt also makes the point that one of the steps of domination which opens the pathways to evil is the process that kills "the juridical person in man."[52] In another letter to Jaspers, she argues that one dimension of evil "is the organized attempt . . . to eradicate the concept of the human being."[53] In this regard evil is not simply about excessive selfishness or human wickedness, although both these traits can be involved. If, as Orlando Patterson has successfully argued, slavery was a system of "social death" in which human beings are a "subcategory of human proprietary objects," then this system that continued for hundred of years and marked early modernity was not only an inhumane system but an evil one as well.[54] It was particularly so because one context of the emergence of racial slavery was the great flowering of debates and revolutionary action that placed the "rights of man" on the political and social agendas, what Cugoano referred to as "civil society." This perspective suggests that Cugoano was very prescient when he argued that one evil of slavery was its turning of Africans into a subhuman category species. His deployment of the conception of evil therefore opens up vistas for moral philosophy to examine racial slavery and the slave trade as crimes against humanity.

A point that may startle the contemporary reader is how Cugoano argues about the nature of reason. For Cugoano, reason was the developed consciousness of the human being, and as such was contrary to racial slavery. Other writers, such as Paine, Diderot, and Montesquieu, would suggest that slavery was against natural liberty, but *reason*—none would venture there. For Cugoano, reason demanded a "common humanity" that could not tolerate slavery. The final point to make here is that by positing that the core of African slavery was the kidnapping and stealing of human flesh, Cugoano develops a conception of slavery different from that of other writers of the period except Thomas Paine and the founder of Methodism, John Wesley.

In developing his analysis of the nature of slavery, Cugoano distinguishes racial slavery from other forms of slavery and servitude in world history, and notes that African slavery and slave trade required robbery of natural rights in a context where society had evolved to a stage he calls "civilization." Cugoano posits a history of servitude with a narration that argues about the necessity of historical forms of servitude. Using biblical sources, he points out that although servitude existed under Mosaic law, it was in a state of equity and justice because such servitude was entered into by "a covenant with another man as a bond-servant."[55] His conceptions of the history of slavery and forms of servitude rely on the then accepted history that ancient slavery was the result of debt or war.

However, Cugoano makes three distinctions in drawing comparisons between ancient and racial slavery. First, he notes the conditions of racial slavery with specific reference to the West Indian colonies. Second, he remarks on its racial element. Third, Cugoano argues that there is no evidence to suggest that the foundation of African slavery resided in the fact the African slaves were already prisoners of war. This was an important distinction at the time, because one of the major pro-slavery arguments was that Africans were already slaves or prisoners of war. The argument attempted to absolve Europeans' conduct of the Atlantic slave trade and plantation slavery from any culpability. The heart of the argument was that Africans were an inferior species already in slavery and were heathens; thus it was legitimate for Europeans to bring them to civilization and Christianity, even if it was done through the Atlantic slave trade. Cugoano rejects this and calls these arguments specious: "If the argument were true, it could afford no just and warrantable matter for any society of men to hold slaves. But the argument is false; there can be no ignorance, dispersion, or unsociableness so found among them, which can be made better by bringing them away to a state of degree equal to that of a cow or a horse."[56]

As for African slavery, Cugoano asserts that "The continent of Africa is of a vast extent, and the numerous inhabitants are divided into several kingdoms and principalities, which are governed by their kings and princes, and those are absolutely maintained by their free subjects. Very few nations make slaves of any of those under government; but such as are taken prisoners of war . . . until they can be exchanged and dispose of them otherwise."[57] This process, Cugoano claims, creates a group of "slave-procurers" who are, he says, "a species of African villains, which are greatly corrupted, and even vitiated by their intercourse with the Europeans."[58] As an African who had been kidnapped by an African slave procurer, Cugoano does not shy away from condemning Africans who were European allies in the Atlantic slave trade. He wants to make the point, however, that there was no widespread slavery in Africa, and that where slavery existed, it was not based upon race. The majority of the slaves brought to the New World, Cugoano argues, were "born as free, and are brought up with as great a predilection for their own country, freedom and liberty, as the sons and daughters of fair Britain."[59] All these arguments laid the foundation for Cugoano to stake the profound claim that racial slavery was the robbery of human beings and resulted in the reduction of the status of the African human.

With regard to the racial element of slavery, Cugoano sets out in the text a series of arguments which demonstrates that Africans were not inferior to Europeans, and refutes the arguments about supposed African inferiority as a basis for slavery. He notes that ". . . we find that the difference of color among men is only incidental, and equally natural to all, and agreeable to the place of their habitation; and if nothing else be different or contrary among them, but that of features and complexion, in that they are all equally alike."[60] Engaging the common argument that the color black was a result of sin, Cugoano makes the following point:

> The external blackness of the Ethiopians, is as innocent and natural, as the spots in the leopards; and that the differences of colour and complexion, which it hath pleased God to appoint among men, are no more unbecoming unto either of them, than the different shades of the rainbow. . . . It does not alter the nature and quality of a man, whether he wears a black or a white coat, whether he puts it on or strips it off, he is still the same man.[61]

Cugoano therefore was firmly within the camp which believed that the origin of the human was a monogenetic creation by God and that variety did not mean hierarchical differences which could then be transformed into justifications for racial slavery.

Thoughts and Sentiments moves seamlessly from the themes of racial slavery to natural liberty and colonialism. Cugoano notes that both colonialism and slavery were against divine law, and therefore those who participated in such ventures were not only un-Christian but also unhuman. *Thoughts and Sentiments* details a complex set of religious and historical refutations of the claims of those who favored slavery or the supposed inferiority of the African at the time. These included David Hume, Gordon Turnbull, James Tobin, and the infamous Edward Long. As could be expected, Cugoano is preoccupied with the notion of supposed African inferiority, and returns to it in different ways. In the text he flays the proponents of the then popular religious/historical arguments that the reason for African slavery could be found in the curse of Ham or the climatic conditions under which blacks lived.

The need for both secular and sacred refutations of racial arguments led Cugoano to a conception of history. He developed this conception by drawing from a providential cast of history, popular then in the plebeian radicalism of the times, as well as from eighteenth-century thinkers who framed the study of history and historical analysis in secular terms. Cugoano's conception of history mixed his radical Methodism and elements of secularism to form an interesting hybrid. The God of Cugoano was an interventionist one who watched over the evolution of civil society and civilization. However, his interventions were through humans (the prophets). Cugoano's historical analysis attempted to synthesize three things: biblical exegesis, an interpretation of divine law, and the affirmation of the secular in the growth of civilization. His assertion about the lawlike requirements for human equality amply demonstrates this point:

> . . . there is but *one law and one manner* prescribed universally for all mankind, *for you and for the stranger that sojourneth with you*, and wherever they may be scattered throughout the face of the whole earth, the differences of superiority and inferiority which are found to be subsisting amongst them is in no way incompatible with the universal law of love, honor, righteousness, and equity.[62]

Here Cugoano is obviously referring to inequities in social status, not in what one might call foundational equality, and it is interesting that alongside what one would consider biblical injunctions, he places equity.

Historical analysis was an important element in Cugoano's writings, because the construction of racial oppression required a theory of human history and origins that justified the so-called inferiority of the African. Overturning racial conceptions of human history required an alternative historical discourse that could support alternative ideas of "natural liberty" and "common humanity."

Radicalized Liberty

I now wish to focus on Cugoano's conception of "natural liberty" and demonstrate how it was both different from and similar to conceptions of other political thinkers of the period. Cugoano establishes in *Thoughts and Sentiments* that in human history there were different forms of human servitude, all of which violated natural liberty. However, he concedes that these different forms may have been necessary, given the different stages of the evolution of human society. Employing an evolutionary notion of history, very typical of Enlightenment historical discourse, Cugoano makes the point that the emergence of "civil society" negated all forms of servitude. This was a distinctive position. Cugoano's articulation of natural liberty is one in which natural liberty is enriched by the growth of a civil society (civilization). This conception of natural liberty is different from the way many political thinkers of the period perceived the relationship between civil society, the state of nature, and natural rights. The clearest example is of course that of Rousseau, who proclaimed, "Man is born free; and everywhere he is in chains." In *The Rights of Man,* Paine considered this problem in natural rights theory and argued that there was a distinction between natural rights and civil rights. Natural rights, Paine argued, are "those which appertain to man in the right of his existence . . . [while] civil rights are those which appertain to man in the right of his being a member of society."[63] Paine further argued that in civil society, humans give up some of those natural rights: "The natural rights which are not retained, are all those in which, though the right is perfect in the individual, the power to execute them is defective."[64]

The problem that then faced many natural rights thinkers of the late eighteenth century was how to construct a civil and political society which returned elements of natural liberty and natural rights that had been lost when civil society emerged. For Cugoano, on the other hand, *civil society developed natural rights and liberty* in two ways. In the first, Cugoano, unlike other radical natural rights thinkers of the period, claims that the laws of civilization are derived from divine laws, and therefore they enhance rather than diminish man's natural rights. In the second, he makes the point that civilization, and therefore civil society, had now removed any necessity for forms of slavery and servitude. This perspective, he argues, was confirmed by the emergence of Christianity: "In the establishment of Christianity there is nothing remaining in the law for a rule of practice to men, but the ever abiding obligations, and ever binding injunctions of moral rectitude, justice, equity and righteousness."[65] However, as regards civilization there is a contradiction in Cugoano's thought, because a few pages later he argues that "When [men] break . . . the laws of God, and the rules of civilization among men, and go forth to steal and rob, to plunder, to oppress and to enslave, and to destroy their fellow-creatures, the laws of God and man require that they should be suppressed, and deprived of their liberty, and perhaps their lives."[66]

Perhaps one answer to this apparent contradiction is that Cugoano was very aware of his audience, and felt that appeals to biblical injunctions did not necessarily carry enough weight to convince some of the slaveholders and their allies. In this regard he observes, "I am aware that some of these arguments will weigh nothing against such men as do not believe the scriptures themselves nor care to understand."[67] Another way to think about this apparent contradiction is to suggest that Cugoano, drawing on the two intellectual sources, secular and religious, was not able to satisfactorily resolve them. This is not unusual in the history of political thought, and certainly Paine in this period deployed notions of sacred history in some of his writings. However, the weight of Paine's gaze was on issues of political rule, whereas for Cugoano it was on racial slavery and colonialism.

Natural liberty, for Cugoano, was the foundation of human society. In such a condition human beings were distinct from property, and should be treated accordingly. They could neither be bought nor be sold, and any system based upon robbing human beings of this natural liberty was evil. Cugoano, while speaking the language of natural rights, extends those rights to the African slave. As a consequence, the basis of his political thought shifts from the traditional elements that then made up natural rights as political discourse. Natural liberty became the basis of all natural rights, including property rights. In Cugoano's political thought, nations, land, or properties could not be conquered with any justification. He observes: "The Spaniards began their settlements in the West Indies and America, by depredations of rapine, injustice, treachery and murder; and they have continued in the barbarous practice of devastation . . . ever since . . . and the maxims in planting colonies have been adopted in some measure in every other nation in Europe."[68] The remarkableness of this position should be obvious when we think of Locke's theory of property, which facilitated colonial conquest of lands in North America, and the general sentiment even of radical thinkers that although colonialism involved violence and domination, it brought "civilization."[69]

Cugoano's position is even more remarkable because he proudly embraced the Christian faith. However, for him Christianity was neither a marker of civilization nor an exclusive doctrine of humanness. For Cugoano the lands of the "pagans" and "heathens" could not be conquered even for missionary purposes. This was in direct opposition to the then official Catholic Church position instituted after the 1550 debate between Juan Ginas de Sepúlveda and Bartolomé de Las Casas. Colonialism for Cugoano was a "dreadfully perfidious method of forming settlements, and acquiring riches and territory."[70]

Cugoano's doctrines of natural rights and liberty were the foundations for his radical anticolonialism. He was also concerned about the poor, and argues that although they are free in a natural sense, poverty means the existence of problems of equity and justice.[71] He asked whether a London poor person would give up his condition of poverty to be a well-fed slave,[72] refuting the argument of James Tobin that the African slaves in the Caribbean were materially better off than the English poor.

The defining feature of Cugoano's conception of natural liberty is *self-ownership*, a radicalized version of natural liberty. The conception of self-ownership and its relationship to natural liberty were central to Diderot's and Paine's political ideas. Diderot writes in *History of the Indies,* "Natural liberty is the right which nature has given every man to dispose of himself as he wishes."[73] However, in his elaboration, Diderot makes a distinction between natural, civil, and political liberty. Cugoano, on the other hand, collapses all forms of liberty into "natural and common liberty." There is no separation in Cugoano's thought between different forms of liberty. For him, without political liberty there is no natural liberty, and certainly civil liberty is a function of the scope of natural liberty as well as the application of divine law. He consistently reinforces the point that slavery and servitude in any form are not compatible with civilized human society. While both Diderot and Cugoano concur that natural liberty was man's most marked feature second only to reason, Cugoano, while deploying the language of natural liberty, gave it a new set of meanings that focused on the nature of racial slavery during the late eighteenth century as a system of human domination. This meaning of natural liberty later found resonance in the black plebeian radicalism of Robert Wedderburn.

As was stated before, in Western political thought, natural liberty emerges alongside the issues of popular sovereignty and the questions of political obligation. When John Locke inveighed against Robert Filmer, he asserted a counterposition to the conservative view that natural liberty was license.[74] However, Locke's description of natural liberty slid into civil liberty and instituted a historic practice of natural liberty as civil liberty. This practice became a formidable part of the political horizon in Enlightenment political thinking. It then worked to foreclose all other possible political languages about the meaning of natural liberty. Cugoano opens this closure by shifting the focus of natural liberty from issues of civil liberty, and sovereignty to racial slavery: "But the robbers of men, the kidnappers, ensnarers and slave-holders, who take away the common rights and privileges of others to support and enrich themselves . . . for the ensnaring of others, and taking away their liberty by slavery and oppression, is the worst kind of robbery."[75] Natural liberty in this sense is for Cugoano not sovereignty over political self-determination but the absence of forms of human domination. He describes West Indian slave laws thus: "They do not take away a man's property like other robbers; but they take a *man himself* and subject him to their service and bondage, which is a greater robbery and a greater crime, than taking away property from men."[76]

This shift created by Cugoano's gaze places his perspective of natural liberty outside of the state of nature. The radical thinker with whom we have compared Cugoano, Thomas Paine, had a notion of a compact that was created and that distinguished the different stages of humanity's political evolution. Cugoano seems to operate with no such historical fiction, and his notion of civil society is one that emerged when sacred history and man's evolution began a unified development with the widespread emergence of Christianity. However Cugoano grants civil society to non-Christians and in Africa sees civil society as a form of government. He is not concerned with the practices of ruling, but rather with seeking to answer the question of the nature of racial slavery.

If for many of the political thinkers racial slavery was a side issue, subordinated to the issues of ruling and political obedience, for the slave it was the major issue. The European political thinkers who turned their attention to the role of colonialism and slavery in the building of empire, particularly after the American Revolution, did so, in the words of Edmund Burke, with a concern for "how to govern a Large Empire upon a plan of Liberty."[77] This liberty was a clear reference to the question of self-government and by the mid-nineteenth century it would become another marker for civilization.[78] Slavery and colonialism were not marginal to European and American life, and in the words of Daniel Defoe, "No African Trade, no Negroes, no Negroes, no Sugar; no Sugar, no Islands, no Islands no Continent, no Continent no Trade; that is to say farewell to your American Trade, your West Indian Trade."[79] Because slavery and colonialism were not marginal to the European experience of empire at the time, any questions of natural rights and natural liberty that did not take these two things into consideration would be unable to offer universal answers to the central problems of the human polity.

With his focus on modern racial slavery and colonialism, Cugoano developed a radical program for the period. It called for the total abolition of slavery and the slave trade, the ending of colonialism and colonial empires, and the dismantling of the Dutch Cape Colony (South Africa). It also advocated that the trade in human beings be replaced with agricultural trade, using some of the economic statements employed by Adam Smith in the *Wealth of Nations* (1776) to argue that free labor was cheaper than slave labor.

Conclusion

What are we to make of this extraordinary African ex-slave? First, the text on which I have based this essay clearly needs to be studied as part of modern political thought. It should be placed alongside Paine's *Rights of Man* and Wollstonecraft's *A Vindication of the Rights of Women* as representative of a different current of radical natural rights thinking in the late eighteenth century. In the history of political theory, natural rights discourse has been both connected to natural law (Locke) and disconnected from it (Thomas Hobbes). However, until Jeremy Bentham in the nineteenth century launched his attack upon natural rights as "nonsense upon stilts," the frame of natural rights and natural liberty was *the* frame of Western political thought. Cugoano's political discourse suggests the existence of a different stream that articulates notions about natural liberty and natural rights that do not fold into other conceptions of rights. For Cugoano, the fundamental natural right was the right of the individual to be free and equal, not in relationship to government but in relationship to other human beings.

This, I want to suggest was not only a radicalized version of natural rights but also, at the time, a heretic one. Keith A. Sandiford's comment in a fine critical essay on Cugoano states, "From the axiom that slavery was against sensibility, Cugoano moved . . . to enunciate the axiom that slavery was against humanity."[80] This is an accurate interpretation, as any reading of some of the major abolitionist writings of the period will reveal. Then there is Cugoano's positive self-affirmation of blackness in an anti-black racist world.[81] Cugoano's dethronement of blackness as curse and badge of inferiority was astonishing for its time, given the normative weight of hegemonic whiteness naturalized as the universal self. Again this would separate him from many of the white abolitionists who argued against slavery but felt that Africans were uncivilized and could benefit from freedom only if they were subjected to a process of tutelage by civilized persons. When we add these things together, we cannot escape the conclusion that there existed in Cugoano's slave narrative a political counternarrative that moved in a different direction than the political horizons of the Enlightenment.

So we come to the final point, the subtext of this essay. What, precisely, was the discursive practice of Cugoano? An early critic of Cugoano, Henri Gregoire, opines that Cugoano's work is not "very methodical. There are repetitions, because grief is verbose. An individual deeply affected, is always afraid of not having said enough. . . . We see talents without cultivation, and to which a good education would have given great progress."[82] One consequence of this is that *Thoughts and Sentiments* has been reviewed as a form of jeremiad. There is no doubt that the text does have elements of this form of denunciation and prophecy. However, I wish to suggest that *Thoughts and Sentiments* should not be confined to the limits of prophetic denunciation, but that in this instance the jeremiad typical of eighteenth-century English polemics was crafted onto a form of political writing, the treatise/essay, which emphasizes historical explanations and appeals to reason. Quobna Cugoano worked through many traditions, plucking from available intellectual resources, but his labor transformed his choices into a political language and discourse that had a meaning different from those which constituted the major traditions of political thought. The discursive practice in which he engaged forms a central part of a radical black intellectual tradition that circles around freedom. In the genealogy of this discursive practice he stands as a figure who raised the fundamental question that engaged all Enlightenment thinkers: What does it mean to be truly human? His heretical answers opened up spaces where none dared to go.

CHAPTER **2**

The Radical Praxis of Ida B. Wells-Barnett
Telling the Truth Freely

> *Southern trees bear a strange fruit*
> *Blood on the leaves and blood at the root*
> *Black body swinging in the Southern breeze*
> *Strange fruit hanging from the poplar trees.*
> —Billie Holiday

> *The Afro-American is not a bestial race.*
> —Ida B. Wells-Barnett

Introduction

Late nineteenth-century America was a site of trauma and regular murder of ex-slaves. The defeat of the Radical Reconstruction signaled extraordinary times for African Americans. Reconstruction had granted all blacks freedom from slavery, and voting rights to black men. These victories attempted to reorder the political system of the South, eroding some of the basis for white supremacy rule. But they were ephemeral, for the Southern elites successfully launched a fierce counterreform movement with the objective of defeating black male political equality and reestablishing white supremacy, thereby making sure that the American state continued to be a racial one.[1] The battles to accomplish this were major and brutal. At stake were not only political and economic fortunes but also a human order that had constructed itself upon white privilege for over two hundred years. This order was not restricted to the South. The South was the epicenter for racial slavery after the American Revolution, but the human order based upon white privilege as a way in which human nature was ordained and structured was also evident in the North. Thus the defeat of Radical Reconstruction shaped the entire American society and the meanings of the human social order. It was in this context of defeat, the brutal pushes against black male equality and citizenship, and the desire to preserve the order of white supremacy that America became a place where there were "bulging eyes and twisted mouth, scent of magnolia sweet and fresh, and the sudden smell of burning flesh."[2] How to stem this tide of defeat, to assert black male and female equality, to end the mass ritual of flesh burning, to establish a new set of practices for black women that redefined womanhood—how to do these things while thinking and writing about them—was the profound challenge that Ida B. Wells-Barnett undertook.

Ida B. Wells-Barnett was not only the single most important campaigner against lynching in the late nineteenth and early twentieth centuries; she was also a black woman radical who grappled with one core idea of American thought of the period: the nature of the black body and the subhumanness of the African American. Hazel Carby notes that Wells was a "woman with an analysis of the relationship among political terrorism, economic oppression, and conventional codes of sexuality and morality that has still to be surpassed in its incisive condemnation of the patriarchal manipulation of race and gender."[3] In grappling with these issues, Wells practiced a form of black feminism.

The activities of Wells-Barnett are representative of a stream of the black radical intellectual tradition in which activity and theoretical reflection merge into praxis. In this frame, practical activity is *critical practical activity*, which confronts the ideas and practices of the old order. Wells-Barnett's writings mark a different stage in the African-American tradition. Her essays on lynching are interventionist texts in which the issues about the referential functions of language are replaced with notions about language and writing as truth claims. If the slave narratives in their literary form were badges of reason, then Wells-Barnett's writings were polemical sociological excursions. At the level of representation, they were constructed to demonstrate truth, to deconstruct some of the deepest racist arguments of the period, and in the end, to mobilize a reform movement against the ritual burning of the black body—known as lynching.

This style of writing utilized conventional investigative journalistic techniques that were embedded in a profound, considered analysis of why things happened. The preoccupation with the why is, as we know, a large part of the basis for theoretical reflection. It also might be useful to remember that although the etymological root of theory—*theoria*—is oftentimes translated as contemplation, Richard Bernstein points out that contemplation is not a passive posture.[4] What we have in the writings of

Wells-Barnett is an integrated relationship between writing, reflection, and action. We now turn to the story of how she did all these things and their significance for the study of the black intellectual tradition.

Slavery, Equality, and Racial Uplift

Entering the world in 1862, Wells-Barnett was born in slavery. Some of her important memories of slavery were the conversations she heard between her parents. In her incomplete autobiography she recollects one such conversation, in which her father responds to an invitation to see his former mistress. "Mother," said her father, "I never want to see that old woman as long as I live. I'll never forget how she had you stripped and whipped the day after the old man died."[5] There are two things about this specific memory. In the first place, it is clear that the whipping which Wells's grandmother received was the result of the fact that she had borne a child for the slave master. Second, if we think about some of the central elements of Wells's campaign against lynched black bodies and the dominant accusations of black male rape, this memory functioned to make the point about the regular practice of white male rape of black female slaves.

Wells's life took the normal turn of many black women growing up in the period after slavery. Her parents placed a great deal of emphasis on education, and she attended the freedmen's school in Holly Springs, Mississippi, and Rust University. She did not complete her degree, and economic circumstances forced her to begin teaching at age sixteen. By the time Wells was a young adult, Reconstruction had been defeated, the systematic institution of Black Codes had begun, and the effects of the repeal of civil rights laws in 1877 were in full swing as segregation began to consolidate. In 1884, after being forcibly removed from the first-class compartment of a train, Wells sued the railroad.

Under segregation, the everyday world of the black person was a dangerous one. It was a time when traveling, shopping, eating, or just being in the right place at the wrong time could cause one great harm, for the public spaces of freedom for ex-slaves were sharply constricted. In this constriction the drive to reduce the black human being to the status of an object became paramount.

The construction of Jim Crow involved many things: the passing of laws, court decisions, the political defeat of the Radical Republicans, and the crushing of what were generally called, at the time, "uppity blacks." The black male population's political demands for equality focused on inclusion under the rubric of American male citizenship. This is how one meeting of the South Carolina convention put it:

> We simply ask that we be recognized as *men,* that there be no ob-
> structions placed in our way; that the same laws which govern white
> men shall govern black men . . . that in short we are dealt with as
> others are—in equity and justice.[6]

But this was not to be, and the black population (both male and female)
had to turn to other avenues to carve out human lives for themselves.

The conditions of constricted freedom for the African-American community during this period created two currents that are central to our discussion of Ida B. Wells. One current was a group of black males who
worked hard, saved, and attempted through small-scale economic development to shield themselves from the effects of Jim Crow. This group became important members of the black community, eventually representing a small black male middle class. Belonging to this group were
individuals who went to college and formed the core of a black male intelligentsia. The second current was the black women who studied at various
freedmen's schools, and those who received further education at colleges
such as Oberlin. Many of these women came to believe in a version of
womanhood that challenged the dominant conceptions of the time. There
were some common features of the two currents. Both believed in hard
work, education, duty, and what has been described as the ideology of
"racial uplift."[7]

Commentators on this period have pointed out the emergence of the
male current and the figures of Alexander Crummell, W. E. B. Du Bois,
Thomas Fortune, and Booker T. Washington, to list the most obvious ones.
They also point to the debates about politics, racism, and the struggles
against racial oppression as often surrounding the writings and activities
of these men. However, as Hazel Carby and others have pointed out, there
existed as well during this period a group of black females whose work is
just as significant.[8] Carby makes the point that one should consider the
decade of the 1890s as "the woman's era not merely in order to insert
women into the gaps in our cultural history . . . but to shift the object of interpretation from examples of individual genius to the collective production and interrelation of forms of knowledge among black women intellectuals."[9]

Carby further states that the period was marked by many writings by
black females, including Anna Julia Cooper, Frances Harper, Pauline Hopkins, and of course Ida B. Wells.[10] Cooper enunciated the clearest statement about black womanhood during this period. Of the ten chapters that
constitute her *A Voice from the South,* Cooper devotes five to discussing the
condition of women in America, paying great attention to the roles and
possibilities for black women. In her essay "Womanhood: A Vital Element

in the Regeneration and Progress of Race" (1886), Cooper, referring to Martin Delany, asserts:

> No man can represent the race . . . we must point to homes, average homes. Homes of rank and file of horny handed toiling men and women of the South . . . only the BLACK WOMAN can say "when and where I enter, in the quiet, undisputed dignity of my woman-hood, without violence and without suing or special patronage, then and there the whole *Negro race enters with me.*"[11]

Cooper's view of the role of the black woman was not unusual among progressive black women of the period, and rested upon an understanding that women were a source of strength and that "the retraining of the race, as well as the ground work and starting point of its progress upwards, must be the *black woman.*"[12] This understanding of the "training of the race" was a very prevalent one. The argument rested on the ground that slavery had led to the degeneracy of the black population and that freedom now required retraining. Cooper herself noted that:

> The race is just twenty-one years removed from the conception and experience of a chattel, just at the age of ruddy manhood. It is well enough to pause a moment for retrospection, introspection and prospection . . . we look within that we may gather together once more our forces, and, by improved and more practical methods, ad-dress ourselves to the tasks before us.[13]

One major element of this task was the role of education in the training and creation of a certain kind of subject. The political language of freedom in the American South was in many ways similar to that of the hegemonic language of emancipation of an earlier period in the Caribbean when is-sues of subject formation were critical.[14] In these political languages there was a model of citizenship in which women played pivotal domestic roles. These elements of citizenship were taken up by some elements of the black community and solidified into the "uplift program," alluded to earlier. In his study of the nature of "racial uplift," Kevin K. Gaines makes the point that it espoused "a vision of racial solidarity uniting black elites with the masses. For many black elites, uplift came to mean an emphasis on self-help, racial solidarity, temperance, thrift, chastity, social purity, patriarchal authority, and the accumulation of wealth."[15]

Certainly this meant that a woman's place was in the domestic sphere. What is intriguing about women like Cooper is that they often stepped outside the bounds of that sphere and constructed a public role for them-selves in which the cause of Black "uplift" was paramount. One reason for this was that the context of Jim Crow and the repeal of black male citizenship placed many obstacles before the drive for "racial uplift." In working through these obstacles and attempting at the same time to develop strategies for female suffrage, female thinkers and activists like Ida B. Wells challenged both the overarching notion of uplift and the concept of womanhood. Wells turned the notion of domestic responsibility on its head. For her, responsibility was not a personal matter centered on home confinement, but was linked to the entire black community. She made this point eloquently in her first anti-lynching pamphlet: "Somebody must show that the Afro-American race is more sinned against than sinning, and it seems to have fallen upon me to do so."[16] Wells was engaged in two things. First, she struggled mightily against the consequences of Jim Crow and the loss of black male equality. Second, she overturned some of the dominant conceptions inside the black community about women. In the end, she radicalized the ideology of "racial uplift."

The defeat of Reconstruction was a profound event in world history and, as stated before, it marked the reorganization of America as a racial state of white supremacy. The character of this reorganization was bolstered by the development and popularity of a set of ideas about human evolution, biology, and the manifest destiny of the Anglo-Saxons. Embedded within these ideas was a continuing discourse about the black body and blackness in general. We cannot fully grasp the importance of Wells's writings and campaigns, and how they confronted a main plank of social Darwinism in American thought, if we do not pay some attention to the then popular racist discourses about the nature and character of the African American.

The Negro as Savage—Take Two

The impact of Charles Darwin's *On the Origin of Species* on American thought was mediated by a growing preoccupation with the writings of Herbert Spencer.[17] Spencer had argued that there was biological evolutionary primacy in the emergence of human society. In explicating this theory, he developed notions of human selection and coined the phrase "the survival of the fittest" while drawing from Jean Baptiste Lamarck the idea of inherited mental features. In America the coalescing of Spencerian and Darwinian theories laid the foundation for what became known as social Darwinism. Mike Hawkins argues that social Darwinism was a configuration.[18] Basic to this configuration was the application of biological laws to human social existence. This application constructed humans as primarily a bioeconomic species who over time had created an economic system and civilization. What is important for our purposes is that the working out of this application within the context of American white supremacy created the grounds for a "new" theory of "Negro inferiority." This "new" theory shifted the basis of black inferiority from primarily religious grounds to more naturalistic and cultural ones. It did not mean that the religious arguments were overthrown; instead, as is typical in ideological systems, new ideas were appropriated and grafted onto old ones. They were then reworked into a dominant ideological system. The ideas and theories of "Negro inferiority," combined with the brutal drive to defeat black male equality, provided the conditions for the ritual lynching of African Americans by the "hands of persons unknown."

The new ideas about black inferiority operated at two levels: in so-called scholarship and at the popular level. At the level of "scholarship," the advocates of these ideas included some of the leading scholars of the late nineteenth century. Among them was Louis Agassiz, the famous Swiss paleontologist who became central to Harvard University's anthropology, biology, and museum development. Agassiz decided that blacks were a different and inferior species, and concluded that they were a "degraded and degenerate race."[19] His work deeply shaped the early development of American anthropologists and natural historians. Another scholar, Nathaniel Southgate Shaler, introduced the idea that the real problem with the black population was that their skulls closed at too early an age, leaving "them unable to control their lower passions."[20] Then there was Edward Drinker Cope from the University of Pennsylvania, whose work on anatomy and zoology led him to anxieties about interracial sexual unions and caused him to call for the deportation "of all the black people as soon as possible, no matter what it cost."[21] Not to be left behind was Lester Ward from Brown University's sociology department, who believed that the lower passions of blacks made them sexually crazed and that a black male's rape of a white female was "the imperious voice of nature."[22]

Overarching these conceptions were the arguments of William Graham Sumner of Yale. In Sumner's social thought, "Millionaires are a product of natural selection, acting on the whole body of men to pick out those who can meet the requirement of certain work to be done."[23] Social existence was a Hobbesian exercise, and rights were part of a social game of "competition." What is important about Sumner's social thought is that he vigorously pursued the complete application of natural biological laws of evolution to social life and his mode of theorization represented the complete merger of biology with a theory of society, becoming popular among many scholars. Although Sumner was opposed to lynching, his theorization of the evolution of human society in general gave grist to those who claimed that the black population was subhuman.

Walter White's 1929 book on lynching demonstrates the perpetuation of theories of "Negro inferiority" at all levels of American social thought in the early twentieth century.[24] In the aftermath of the Civil War these theories provided the "rationale" for the ritual burning of flesh. Since the burning of a black body was a common occurrence that did not draw howls of condemnation from whites, it would be safe to say that the arguments about "Negro inferiority" did not operate only in the domain of scholars and universities. Although many scholars provided the core arguments that were popularized. Perhaps there was no more important popularizer than Rev. Josiah Strong, whose 1885 book, *Our Country: Its Possible Future and Its Present Crisis,* sold 175,000 copies.[25] With a clear sense of what the "survival of the fittest" meant, Strong pronounced that the "Anglo-Saxon people [were] the bearers of civil liberty."[26] With gusto he proclaimed that Anglo-Saxon civilization was the noblest and that the competition between the races would end in Anglo-Saxon victory.[27] For Strong this victory meant "extinction for the inferior races." The supremacy of Anglo-Saxon civilization was in Strong's mind, "God's final and complete solution of the dark problem of heathenism among many inferior peoples." Of course an integral part of Anglo-Saxonism was an attempt to purify white America, and it drew upon a version of comparative history which argued that American democracy was the direct descendant of a Teutonic theory of democracy. In this argument other white immigrant groups from other parts of Europe who were considered low-class and alien would over time become American white. Anglo-Saxonism then became not only a banner for American expansionism internally and externally, but also a popular white understanding of the providential destiny of the white race. Listen to the poem read in Grimes County, Texas, when the black populist figure Jack Haynes was murdered in 1899:

> Twas nature's laws that drew the lines
> Between the Anglo-Saxon and the African Races
> And we, the Anglo-Saxons of Grand Old Grimes
> Must force the African to keep his place.[29]

How to keep the African American in his place thus was an overriding preoccupation of white supremacy in the late nineteenth century, but it was not the whole story.

The Feast of Blood

Lynching is oftentimes viewed as a Southern aberration, its memory too grisly to be recounted as part of the American experience. In recent times it has been studied as systematic racial terror utilized to hold back black equality.[30] As this essay has been arguing, this frame is partly true. However, what is important for us is how the ritual practices of murdering black bodies and the discourses that surround such practices were deeply embedded in American thought of the period. Grappling with this will, I think, allow us to fully understand the achievements of Ida B. Wells.

As has been stated, American social thought of the period was shaped by social Darwinism. However, there was a deep contradiction in this ideological configuration. Although social Darwinism as a theory of human evolution was based on a biological understanding of human life, it often relegated the body and notions of corporeality to lower forms of life, to passion. By the time social Darwinism held sway, the body had been isolated as an anatomical structure to be inspected within the framework of illness or pathology. The modern emergence of biological science and the development of social Darwinism did not completely overthrow classificatory natural history, nor did it finally displace Cartesian anxieties of mind/body dualism. So even though the human was connected to nature and the natural, in social Darwinism human beings had mastered both and civilization was the product of that mastery. As a consequence, the divisions in the human species could be constructed around the relationship to nature. Evolution constructed along social Darwinism lines consisted of two stories; it gave a narrative of origins and also could tell humanity (or those who considered themselves human) why their particular variety of the human species had succeeded. These arguments, allied with the idea that the nature of the black body was close to nature, would, I suggest, become central in lynching debates. Tied to these arguments would be notions of gender, sexuality, and manliness about which more will be said later. However, what is critical for our discussion now is to see how these biological theories became integrated with the long held view of the black male as primarily a genital creature. The alchemy of these arguments would hold sway in America for many decades.

The figures are still staggering. Between 1880 and 1930, over three thousand African Americans were lynched. Although 90 percent of these lynchings occurred in the South, in the North during the same period 123 African Americans were lynched.[31] According to Ida B. Wells, in the 1890s however, the figure was much higher, in excess of the standard number given for the period 1880–1930.[32] On a large scale, lynching events were organized with all the trappings of special public events of central importance to social life. Wells describes one such feast of blood:

> The head was in plain view as, also were the limbs, and one arm which stood out high above the body, the elbow crooked, held in that position by a piece of wood. . . . Then came great blisters over all the exposed parts of the body; then in places the flesh was burned away and the bones begin to show through . . . two or three

white women, accompanied by their escorts, pushed to the front to obtain an unobstructed view.[33]

Before the burning, often the lynched black male had his penis cut off, and in the aftermath of the burning, people fought each other for bits of teeth, nails, and parts of burned flesh. There are many records that demonstrate how photographs of lynchings were turned into postcards and became widely used. The lynching of Sam Hose, which Du Bois recalled as an epiphany in his life, was reported in these terms by a newspaper of the day: "The excursionists returning tonight were loaded down with . . . pieces of flesh . . . persons were seen walking through the streets carrying bones in their hands."[34] What accounts for this grisly social spectacle and near cannibalism?

The primary argument used by the lynchers and sanctioned by officialdom was that the black male was a rapist, and that lynching was to protect virtuous white womanhood. This account could be found at many levels. Daniel G. Brinton of the University of Pennsylvania wrote in *Races and Peoples: Lectures on the Science of Ethnography* (1890): "It cannot be too often repeated, too emphatically urged, that it is to the women alone of the highest race that we must look to preserve the purity of the type . . . that religion is rotten, which would sanction a white woman enduring the embrace of a colored man."[35] In *The Mind of the South* (1941) W. J. Cash argues that in the Southern mind the abolition of slavery destroyed "the rigid fixity of the black at the bottom of the scale . . . and inevitably opened up in the mind of the Southerner a vista at the end of which stood the overthrow of this taboo."[36] This taboo, he suggests, was the place of the white woman in the Southern mind as the "perpetuator of that superiority in legitimate line."[37] Leading newspapers followed suit. The *New York Times,* for example, in 1892 opined that "The African Race is particularly prone" to rape.[38] Typically, ideas do not take hold in the popular mind unless they connect with ideas already formed or nascent. In this case the already formed or nascent idea was that of the nature of the black male.

Franz Fanon makes the point that "In relation to the Negro, everything takes place on the genital level."[39] He further argues that with the "Negro the cycle of the biological begins," and that "it is in his corporeality that the Negro is attacked. It is as a concrete personality that he is lynched. It is as an actual being that he is a threat."[40] Although Fanon here is speaking about black males, the black female also brings forth biology and untamed nature in Western thought. She is untamed sexuality who with her wiles seduces the white male, producing mulatto creatures. Thus it is important to note that in Western thought all black bodies bring forth nature and biology. If the black body has neither refined feeling nor any substantial intellect, then it can be treated with impunity, or so the argument runs. As a natural surface with no unifying logic other than wild lust, that body, when it cannot be tamed or disciplined under systems of slavery or colonial domination, must be crushed.

Thus it is no accident that there were similarities between the natures of punishment organized against the native African and that of lynching. While the contexts were vastly different and lynching developed as a ritual practice that drew from, and then transformed, an American practice, there were common points in the mental universes of both the colonial power and the lynchers.[41] In the Cape Colony in the late 1700s, the permutations of torture for the native African included breaking limbs, burning, decapitating, strangling, scorching, quartering and hanging up the pieces, and branding with red-hot iron.[42] Missing was the spectacle and the ways in which near cannibalism was organized. Also missing was the preoccupation with the sexual parts of the black body and how they were to be treated.

On one level, therefore, lynching was part of a pattern of Western oppression in which the crushing of the black body was a ritual enactment of domination and a public confirmation of white supremacy. At another level it was the negation of the very essence of personhood of the black population. Its practice would "keep the African in place" through fear and blunt the drive for black equality. Finally, it reinforced the idea that the black body had no interior life and was only surface, that it was rooted in primitive natural urges that could only be cleansed by fire when not chained. No wonder, then, that Ida B. Wells had to say, "The Afro-American is not a bestial race."

Lynching, Rape, and the Black Male Response

The argument about black male rape placed many advocates of black equality on the defensive, partly because many advocates of emancipation felt that slavery had so blighted the humanity of the male slave that he needed retraining. These persons argued that slavery had contaminated the slaves, and continued to keep them in a savage state. For many white Northerners this was *the* problem. Gail Bederman points out that the journalist Ray Baker, though opposed to lynching, felt that the crime was provoked by the "heinous crimes" of unmanly [w]orthless Negroes who refused to work, abandoned their wives and children."[43] In this argument the source of these feasts of blood was not the racial power of white supremacy and so-called civilization, but the pathology of the untamed black male. The successful invention of this pathology seeped into many mental crevices even when the empirical evidence demonstrated that this was not the case, and that a significant number of black males who were lynched were successful men attempting to "uplift" themselves and their families.

Perhaps nowhere is the ambiguity toward lynching and the notion of black male criminality more clearly expressed by black male leaders of the time than in the words of Bishop Henry Turner. A complex figure who straddled the nineteenth-century current of African identity, emigration and African colonization, and black equality, Turner in 1893 organized a black national convention to discuss the state of black America. The convention's call made reference to the "revolting, hideous, monstrous . . . shocking crimes charged upon us daily . . . and the reign of mobs, lynchers, and fire-fiends."[44] At the convention Turner proclaimed what the conditions of degradation led to: "In many instances we are guilty of doing a series of infamous things that we would not be guilty of, if our environments were different."[45]

Turner used an environmental argument to suggest that in a different context, black character could be changed. For him that context was Africa. The convention's resolutions on rape and lynching supported the arrest and conviction of "the foul fiend who sacrifices his manhood to the coercive lust of his passion" while condemning lynching.[46] Operating here were the ways in which the power of the dominant discourse, which surrounded the lynching ritual, limited the discourse that opposed it. Successfully tying lynching to rape and black criminality narrowed the grounds for opposition, particularly since in the minds of many black intellectuals at the time, the hegemonic general framework about the black male was rooted in conceptions of character uplift. To break the link between rape and lynching required more than thinking about lynching as a crime. It required confronting the major hegemonic ideas of the American racial state.

All observers agree that the major black political figure of the mid-nineteenth century was Frederick Douglass, and many periodizations of African-American history use the death of Douglass in 1895 as a watermark. Douglass's lecture "Why Is the Negro Lynched," published in 1894, attempted to provide a historical overview of the experiences of African Americans, offered a critique of lynching, and proposed a set of directions for black equality. For Douglass, lynching was part of what he called the "so-called Negro problem." He was clear that this "so-called problem" was really an American problem: "This so called but mis-called Negro problem is one of the most important and urgent subjects that can now engage public attention . . . it involves the honor or dishonor . . . of the whole American people."[47] In this text Douglass consistently calls the African-American population a class, making the point that "I am not a defender of any man guilty of this atrocious crime, but the defender of the coloured people as a class."[48]

For Douglass there was no denying that African Americans were "capable of committing the crime imputed to them, but [I] utterly deny that they are more addicted to the commission of that crime than is true of any other variety of the human family."[49] From this position Douglass proceeds to give a historical account of the African American which demonstrates that disfranchisement was the objective of what he called the "three stages of Negro persecution." In these three stages Douglas pointed out that the charge of rape was a new one, and was only a cover for the consistent violations of rights. He linked lynching to the Southern attempts to roll back black political equality. Although he did a comparative analysis of black life and denied the accusation of black criminality, however he did not decisively cut the links embedded within the rape/lynching argument. This was a very difficult thing to do, as Wells acknowledged in 1928:

> Like many another person who had read of lynching in the South, I had accepted the idea meant to be conveyed–that although lynching was irregular and contrary to law and order, unreasoning anger over the terrible crime of rape led to lynching, that perhaps the brute deserved death anyhow and the mob was justified in taking life.[50]

The personal encounter with lynching was both traumatic and galvanizing for many black intellectuals. Du Bois, when confronted with the ghoulish reminder of Sam Hose's lynching, stated, "One could not be [a] calm, cool, and detached scientist while Negroes were lynched, murdered, and starved."[51] Ida B. Wells, when confronted with the lynching of her associates in Memphis in 1892, wrote:

> The same program of hanging, then shooting bullets into the lifeless body was carried out to the letter. Nobody in this section believes the old threadbare lie that the Negro men assault white women. If Southern white men are not careful, then they will overreach themselves and public sentiment will have a reaction; a conclusion will then be reached which will be very damaging to the moral reputation of their women.[52]

Breaking the Link
From the inception of her campaign, Wells confronted the relationship between rape and lynching. She did this on several levels. First, she asked about the ways in which black women were raped by white slave masters,

thereby turning the argument on its head. In critical comments on an editorial she wrote: "Colored women have always had far more reason to complain of white men in this respect than ever white women have had of Negroes."[53] What is important to note about the editorial, she states, is that it asserted that black women had "no finer feelings nor virtue to be outraged."[54] Angela Davis commented that in American slave society, "The rights claimed by the slave owners and their agents over the bodies of female slaves were a direct expression of their presumed property rights over black people as a whole."[55] Wells, keenly aware of this fact, brought it into the debate about lynching. By doing this, she questioned the dominant conception of white male civilization. This point was forcibly in *A Red Record*, where Wells, in an ironic note on the frontispiece, wrote *Respectfully submitted to the Nineteenth Century civilization in the "Land of the Free and the Home of the Brave."*

The second point of Wells's interrogation centered around the conception of civilization. The term "civilization" was a central one in nineteenth-century Western thought. Raymond Williams observes that in this period its "modern meaning . . . [placed] emphasis . . . on social order, on ordered knowledge as [well as] on refinement and behavior."[56] The application of this definition was often contested by oppressed groups who asked through the "seas of oppression," who was civilized. Within the hegemonic framework of nineteenth-century Western thought, "civilization" denoted a specific stage of human evolution (at which whites had arrived) and was contrasted to barbarism. Following an evolutionary paradigm, it was a stage of human development. This stage folded into white normativity, with whites and the white societies in which they ruled being the norm. Blacks, as underdeveloped and savage, were not men, and black women were savage women who exhibited aggressive behavior patterns.

Wells was very aware of the civilization paradigm, and used it effectively as a counterdiscourse to lynching. In 1893, the World's Columbian Exposition was held in Chicago. Its objective was to showcase the achievements of white civilization.[57] Initially African Americans were not invited to participate in the fair, but after protest by Frederick Douglass, space was given. To protest their exclusion and to use the fair as a site for campaigning for black rights, four leading African Americans—Douglass, Wells, J. Garland Penn, and F. L. Barnett—produced an eighty-six-page pamphlet titled *The Reason Why the Colored American Is Not in the World's Columbian Exposition.* The text was divided into four sections. Douglass wrote the introduction, a chapter on the development of class inequality in America in regard to the black population, and a chapter on the convict lease system. Wells did the chapter on lynching. Penn wrote a chapter on the progress of the

African-American population since emancipation, focusing on the professions, literature, arts, journalism, the church, business, and education. He also paid some attention to the nature of black workers and tradesmen. Barnett ended the text with a summary of the efforts of the African-American population to be represented at the event and the nature of official racism. As a collaborative effort, the text was a remarkable document, and stands today as an important account of the ways in which the nineteenth-century African-American intelligentsia saw America and the critical issues that faced the black population.

Wells's contribution focuses on demonstrating that the argument about rape being the cause of lynching was a false one:

> The first fifteen years of his freedom he was murdered by masked mobs for trying to vote. Public opinion having made lynching for that reason unpopular, a new reason is given to justify the murders of the past 15 years. The Negro was first charged with attempting to rule white people, and hundreds were murdered on that pretended supposition. He is now charged with assaulting or attempting to assault white women. This charge is as false as it is foul.[58]

She goes on to call lynching "19th century barbarism."[59] Obviously Wells is contrasting the then accepted meaning of civilization with the ritual of lynching by calling attention to the question of who really practices civilized behavior. In the same chapter she writes, "As the number of lynchings have [*sic*] increased, so has the cruelty and barbarism of the lynchers."[60] Wells then asserts that lynching had two periods, one in which the overriding concern seems to have been pushing back black legal equality, and one in which the political purposes seem to have been replaced by a feast of blood. In the second, I wish to suggest that Wells was identifying the ways in which rituals as social drama become cognitive statements reinforcing dominant ideological frameworks. I think this is why her writings on lynching relied heavily on newspaper articles and why she always wrote with ironic flashes.

One central part of Wells's anti-lynching argument revolved around the place of white women in the patriarchal system of white America. The South had constructed a myth of honor and chivalry based both on the "virtuousness" of white women and on their role in the reproduction of the "superior race." This mythology, in the words of W. J. Cash, "was downright gyneolatry."[61] The depth of the mythology, Cash argued, identified the white woman with the very notion of the South itself. As such, he states, any assault on the South (and emancipation was one such assault) would "inevitably translate its whole battle into the terms of her defense."[62]

We know, of course, that this mythology was an integral part of the construction of a Southern manhood myth, and that the so-called virtuousness of the Southern white woman was in part an explanation for the white males' frequent forced sexual encounters upon black females.

Both black female sexual licentiousness and white female purity were mythological constructions of white male supremacy. Wells had to puncture this myth: "A few instances to substantiate the assertion that some white women love the company of the Afro-American will not be out of place. Most of these cases were reported by the daily papers of the South."[63] In her documentation of legitimate and emotional interracial sexual unions as well as other types of interracial relationships, Wells pointed out that in many cases white females initiated these relationships. Her point was that there were interracial unions with which white supremacy could not grapple because they eroded both the laws of miscengation and, more important, demonstrated the lies about black male sexuality: "The miscegenation laws of the South only operate against the legitimate union of the races; they leave the white man to seduce all the colored girls he can, but it is death to the colored man who yields to the force and advances of a similar attraction in white women."[64]

By demonstrating that there were many "legitimate" interracial unions, Wells attempted to destroy the myth that the protection of white female virtue was the objective of lynch mobs. At the same time, she was careful to point out that while lynching was an exercise in "white manhood," some white females and their children participated. She therefore says of her anti-lynching writings, "They will serve at the same time as a defense for the Afro-American Sampsons who suffer themselves to be betrayed by white Delilahs."[65]

Wells's militant anti-lynching stance and her debunking of the myth of savage black male sexuality ran counter to the views of many persons who condemned lynching as mob rule but were unwilling to tackle the underlying mythology.

One particular incident indicative of the different lines of the reform movements in America at the time, and of the ways in which some of these movements were still enmeshed in racial worldviews, was the controversy between Frances Willard and Ida B. Wells. In 1894 Willard, a key figure in the Woman's Christian Temperance Union (WCTU), flayed Wells's anti-lynching work. While condemning lynching as an abomination, Willard was critical of Wells's view about the role of some white women in legitimate interracial unions.[66] However, at the heart of the attack against Wells was the perspective of the temperance movement that perceived blacks as too tied to the saloon. For the temperance movement, blacks were deeply infected with alcohol, which they felt exacerbated blacks' "natural lasciviousness." As Philip Dray recounts it, many in this movement felt that once blacks became city dwellers, their "weakness for card games, brothels, and saloons [would ease] their quick relapse into animalism."[67]

This was the complex ideological configuration that faced Wells. That she was able to dent it, to question its veracity in the period, is a tribute not only to her campaigning and writings talents but also to her insight that if the South was successful in painting the Afro-American male as a bestial creature, it would sustain one of the most deeply felt ideological planks of white supremacy. In such a case, freedom and equality for all African Americans would be a chimera.

Feminism and Ida B. Wells

Wells's active life was preoccupied not only with lynching but also with female political and social equality. Her first pamphlet was published as a result of the resourcefulness of the black women's clubs of New York, and when Mary Church Terrell became the first president of the National Association of Colored Women (NACW) in 1896, Wells was a member attending the meeting with her four-year-old son.[68] According to reports of the meeting, Wells played an important role.[69] Linda McMurry explains that as the self-help ideology became stronger in the late nineteenth and early twentieth centuries, Wells's path diverged from that of the NACW. The NACW moved toward stressing the the "most vigorous efforts of the Negro woman should be done at the home."[70] Wells, her vision firmly fixed on full black equality, moved away from this group and began to work with the National Afro-American Council in an attempt to revive T. Thomas Fortune's National Afro-American League. Though her efforts were unsuccessful, they nevertheless allowed Wells to make new connections in the black community and to continue working for full black equality.

At this time many groups were influenced by Booker T. Washington's ideology of accommodation; Wells, along with others, opposed this. But for her this opposition meant that she also developed a form of community activism. She founded a kindergarten for black children, led community campaigns against police harassment of the black community, founded and led organizations conducting voter registration drives, ran for a state senate seat, and continued to speak out on all the major issues that impacted upon the African-American population. Her engagement in these activities broke the mold of the woman's place and constructed in action what some writers have called "community feminism." Ula Y. Taylor, in an article on Amy Jacques-Garvey, makes the point that "community feminism" attempts to integrate notions of self-determination with a "doctrine of equal rights for women that challenged women's oppression and subordination."[71] She argues, further, that in this form of feminism, "Activism discerns the configuration of oppressive power relations, shatters masculinist claims of women as intellectually inferior, and seeks to empower women by expanding their roles and options."[72]

The feminism of Ida. B. Wells cannot be judged by early twenty-first-century standards. Like all seminal ideas and practices, feminism has different sets of meanings at different times, and as Oyeronke Oyewumi shows, there is no one universal feminism, so one size does not fit all.[73] Making sense of Wells's feminism requires us to locate her within the main feminist discursive practices of the period and to see how she negotiated the tensions and conflicts of that period.

The birth of the movement for women's rights in America was contemporaneous with the rapid development of the general abolitionist movement. Two of the leading nationally recognized male abolitionists, Fredrick Douglass and William Lloyd Garrison, firmly supported women's equal rights and many of the leading advocates of women's rights supported the abolitionist cause, Elizabeth Cady Stanton and Susan B. Anthony being the most influential. In the minds of the radical abolitionists, these two causes were similar, and the end of slavery would mean black citizenship and political and social equality for women. Two black females who firmly supported both causes but paid special attention to black women were Sojourner Truth and Frances Ellen Watkins Harper.[74] These two women represented the complex tensions that emerged within the feminist movement during Reconstruction.

The ending of slavery and the period of Radical Reconstruction divided the womens rights and abolitionist movements since the passage of the Fourteenth and Fifteenth amendments gave black males voting rights. Immediately this posed a difficulty for the women's rights movement. Should one support black male suffrage as a consequence of the ending of racial slavery and continue to press for universal suffrage? In other words should one condemn it as a partial victory or as another form of institutional male supremacy? Many white feminists of the period took the latter stance, creating a rupture between abolitionism and the struggle for women's rights.

It is important to note that when one reviews the major documents and speeches of the white female abolitionists and feminists, one feature that stands out is the way in which racial slavery was used as a trope to describe the oppression of women. In her address to the New York State legislature, Elizabeth Cady Stanton made the point that "The prejudice against color, of which we hear so much, is no stronger than that against sex. It is produced by the same cause, and manifested very much in the same way."[75] In the same speech Stanton stated with regard to black male suffrage, "It is evident that the prejudice against sex is more deeply rooted and more unreasonably maintained than that against color."[76] Although Stanton was referring to limited black male equality in the North, it was clear that if racial slavery and women's political and social status were conceptualized within the same frame as *only* the consequences of the lack of *similar civil rights,* then any granting of black male suffrage, no matter how temporary, would be cause for consternation.

Once the movements began to differ over black male rights, what Frederick Douglass called the "Negro Hour," then the enactment of the Black Codes and the ritual murder of blacks would mean that the energies of many of the black abolitionists, both male and female, would shift to struggle against this new racial terror. In an 1868 letter to Josephine Sophie White Griffing, Douglass sums up the dilemma well:

> I am now devoting myself to a cause not more sacred, certainly more urgent, because it is life and death to the long-enslaved people of this country; and this is it: Negro suffrage. While the Negro is mobbed, beaten, shot, stabbed, hanged, burnt, and is the target of all that is malignant in the North and all that is murderous in the South his claim may be preferred by me.[77]

Many black female abolitionists/feminists also had to decide. In a response to the white feminists, Harper put the matter bluntly, making the case that race was at that moment the central defining feature of American society:

> You white women speak here of rights. I speak of wrongs I, as a colored woman, have had in this country which had made me feel as if I were in the situation of Ishmael, my hand against every man, and every man's hand against me. Let me go tomorrow morning and take my seat in one of your street cars . . . and the conductor will put up his hand and stop the car rather than let me ride.[78]

Between the conceptualization of *rights to be had* and *wrongs to be made right* there was a huge gap in political thought. As we have seen in chapter 1, the history of American political thought is primarily focused on rights, and the *meanings* of rights are constructed historically against the background of racial slavery. Even when slavery has been seen as a trope in American political thought, it has meant different things—from the lack of self-government, to dependency, to racial slavery. In general, the notion of rights is based upon the assumption of personhood, and thus eligibility for citizenship. Therefore, the struggle for rights was often a struggle against exclusion and an affirmation of the human quality of the agent. But the black slaves/ex-slaves, both female and male, were not considered human. Thus the struggle for rights was but one part of their struggle, for wrongs to be righted required a concept of rights larger than formal political or social equality. It required that the order be reversed. Freedom was the embodiment of rights, not rights morphed into freedom. Thus, for the black population what became important was the nature of the freedom that it could carve out in racist America.

In this there was no fundamental contradiction with the struggle for women's political equality. But in the counterposing of partial black suffrage with women's political equality, the grounds were being reinforced for the creation of a different kind of late nineteenth-century feminism in America. The most important document of the American nineteenth-century struggle for women's rights was the "Declaration of Sentiments and Resolutions, Seneca Falls." The resolutions contained in the document focused on social and political rights for women. They did not address the question of slavery. The document's presumption was that once women were granted social and political rights, female oppression would cease. It is interesting to note in the text the subtle distinctions between social class and native-born males contained in the document. It states in part: "He has withheld from her rights which are given to the most ignorant and degraded men—both native and foreigners."[79] The thrust of the document and its statement that "The history of mankind is a history of repeated injuries and usurpations on the part of man towards woman, having in direct object the establishment of an absolute tyranny over her."[80] is remarkable because it posits that rights in nineteenth-century America were embodied in patriarchal political power. However, what it misses is how racial slavery complicated this patriarchal power, making it not only patriarchal but also white supremacist in a racial state.

This is the situation that faced Ida B. Wells. Under slavery, white patriarchal power had expressed itself in the consistent rape of black women slaves. In the late nineteenth century the charge of rape was being hurled at the black male, in an attempt to create conditions that would be conducive to the reorganization of white supremacy in the new context of slave emancipation. Some black feminists made the choice to rally to the side of race alone, but Wells attempted to build a political praxis in which the issues of women's rights was not be subordinated to the race question, but formed part of a larger question about the reform of America. So at any one moment she was preoccupied with, say, lynching, or with police harassment in the black community, or with education and issues of general welfare, and at the next she would be campaigning for female political equality. All these things were part of a canvas of struggle that had been unrolled by the defeat of Reconstruction and the actions of the African-American population to make a form of freedom work.

Conclusion

So how should one locate Ida B. Wells within the black radical intellectual tradition? Joy James has suggested that Wells's politics "created a unique form of feminism shaped by race, sex, gender and class . . . [and] that it merged black feminism and black nationalism."[81] In a very perceptive introduction to Wells's lynching writings, Patricia Hill Collins argues that Wells collapses "contemporary distinctions . . . between intellectual production and activism . . . [which resulted in a] recursive and synergistic relationship between her ideas and activism."[82] I would like to suggest that Ida B. Wells represents that current within the black radical intellectual tradition in which the existential condition forces the black radical intellectual into new forms of praxis. In this form of praxis, political practice is an engaged critical social enterprise. It typically begins with community single-demand issues (e.g., end lynching or segregation) but then takes on wider issues of fundamental importance. In the case of Wells, one of those issues was the ideological configuration in which the "Afro-American was a bestial race." In this instance praxis is a form of concrete theoretical knowledge that rips the veil of normalcy, laying bare what is real. It is being able to tell the truth freely. It thereby follows one practice of heresy.

No one represented this current better in the late nineteenth-century black radical intellectual tradition than Ida B. Wells-Barnett. Rarely do political thought and theory examine historical actions; oftentimes they confine themselves mainly to textual exegesis of individual thinkers. What the praxis of Wells shows is that in the very practice of politics, ideas do contend. Of course here we are dealing with life and experiences as bearers of meaning and the relationship between these, reflection, and critical activity. The praxis of Wells should force us to think about this relationship in profoundly racialized societies. What we should also be aware of is that there exists another scale of human activities that have been ignored by mainstream scholarship. We ignore the heresy of Wells at our peril.

CHAPTER 3

C. L. R. James and W. E. B. Du Bois
Heresy, Double Consciousness, and Revisionist Histories

*The Negro is a sort of seventh son, born with a veil and gifted
with second sight in this American World.*
—W. E. B. Du Bois, *The Souls of Black Folk*

*To establish his own identity, Caliban, after three centuries,
must himself pioneer into regions Caesar never knew.*
—C. L. R. James, *Beyond a Boundary*

Introduction

The last two chapters have focused on individuals who are not normally
acknowledged as part of a black radical intellectual tradition. We now turn
to two figures whose writings and political practices are increasingly being
recognized as central to twentieth-century radical political thought. However, much of this recognition is still within the framework of the marginal
black and anticolonial experience. In this chapter, basing myself primarily
on two texts by James and Du Bois—*The Black Jacobins* and *Black Reconstruction*, respectively—we will explore what heresy meant for an understanding of the twentieth-century world.

We can now say that the Western intellectual tradition operates within
an exclusionary paradigm. Its systems of classification, naming, and categorization placed on the margins, made invisible, significant sections of
humankind. This invisibility and exclusion cannot be collapsed into sim-
plistic social constructions of savage/civilized, rational/irrational, Christ-
ian/heathen binaries, or into conceptions of the *other*. For the African
human, the exclusion was complete—it was both *ontological* and *epistemic*
erasure. Both these forms of erasure have profoundly shaped contemporary

discussions about thought—the meaning and construction of intellectual traditions. Erasure makes invisible, creates a veil that does not recognize a black intellectual tradition. At best this tradition continues to be viewed as particularistic, mired in fossilized, irrational conceptions and myths not worthy of serious study.

In the contemporary period we discuss the nature of racism and the barbarities of colonialism, but there is not much debate on the implication of these historic practices for political and historical knowledge. The issue here is what the Latin American philosopher Enrique Dussel calls the "underside of modernity," and how this "underside" has produced a radical intellectual tradition that engages in a critical dialogical relationship with various Western radical critiques (Marxism, existentialism, critical theory). In the field of postcolonial theory the engagement is oftentimes portrayed as mimetic and derivative, or as a "third space which eludes the politics of polarity."[1] What is generally missing is the understanding that oftentimes the products of the dialogical engagement have reopened the categories of radical political theory. Given the structures of racial oppression and, in the early twentieth century, of colonialism, the black radical intellectual finds himself or herself functioning in a mode of criticism that interrogates the essential elements of the Western intellectual tradition.

The reason for this is obvious. Regimes of domination do not rest solely upon economic, political, social, and cultural power. They also exist and conduct politics within a field of political and social knowledge, of ideas that form part of the self-consciousness of all members of a society. Given the nature of anti-black racism and the racialized object (who is human), the black radical intellectual as critic is first of all engaged with challenging the knowledge regime of the dominant power. Superficially this sounds similar to the Gramscian argument about the creation of counterhegemonic ideas. But there is a major difference. In their efforts at promulgating counterhegemonic conceptions, the subordinate classes and groups who are nonracialized subjects take seriously some principles that are normally enshrined in constitutional democracies, and expose the radical contradiction between enunciation, principles, and reality.[2] In these instances the creation of counterhegemonic ideas demands internal criticism and critique. There is no overturning of the philosophical anthropology of white normativity. On the other hand within the black radical intellectual, the process of overturning white normativity clears spaces, a terrain on which to accurately describe black or colonial life. This enterprise constructs a tradition.

What C. L. R. James and W. E. B. Du Bois did in their books *The Black Jacobins* (1938) and *Black Reconstruction* (1935) was to place squarely before us historical knowledge about two major events that reorder the narrative structures of Western radical history. Their projects created seismic shifts in twentieth-century radical historiography. One major development in twentieth-century historiography is the ways in which social theory became an integral part of historical understanding. In the early twentieth century, James and Du Bois wrote history with a "theoretical turn." They were concerned not so much with elaborating political or historical narratives as with "rewriting history." Reinhart Koselleck has suggested that no "rewriting of history takes place without recourse to the stock of experiences already captured."[3] Both James and Du Bois were rewriting history from a stance in which experiences were not captured—or, if they were, they had been captured from a standpoint that the black subject was a savage or, in the case of the Reconstruction, that black male political equality had led to the most corrupt and morally bankrupt state regimes in American history.

The matter becomes more complicated because both the Haitian Revolution and the Reconstruction have become contested sites of memory in the national imagery of Haiti and of America.[4] In writing *The Black Jacobins* and *Black Reconstruction,* the authors' gaze on the archival sources was shaped by the understanding that the African slave in the West was human. This simple but profound truth meant that while they deployed Marxian categories in their interpretation of events, both the categories and the events were invested with new meanings. In their historical writings James and Du Bois were guided by what St. Clair Drake has called "racial vindicationism." Finally, James and DuBois emplotted stories that challenged one of the major modes of historical narration in the 1930s, the nineteenth-century English novel. All of this was accomplished in a form of writing and intellectual practice far removed from the debates within the Western tradition about the nature of the political intellectual.

As we have already noted, the debates that traditionally animate the conceptual history of the intellectual do not neatly fit the black radical intellectual. Invisibility does not facilitate detached independence; exclusion does not mean isolation and loneliness. There are no priests who sustain cults of legitimacy, no black jesters who, in the words of Leszek Kolakowski, "stand outside . . . society from the sidelines in order to unveil the non-obvious behind the obvious, the non-final behind the final."[5] As well, we have already noted that the radical black intellectual is, to use Gramsci's term, an "organic" intellectual. But he or she is organic with a difference. While in the Gramscian mode radical organic intellectuals provide the missing inventory for the spontaneous philosophy of ordinary people, they do so within a framework and discursive practice that do not call into question their own ontological natures. The engagement of the black radical intellectual is different, then; critique and criticism become those of *heresy*, and categories deployed oftentimes are stretched to the limit. The examples of *Black Reconstruction* and *The Black Jacobins* will empirically demonstrate this process. But before we proceed, we should note some of the issues that confront any discussion of the black radical intellectual tradition and black intellectual production in general. Among them are whether or not this form of knowledge is a subjugated one; whether the tradition is a derivative or hybrid one. Finally, there is the large question of the meanings of the tradition and the relevance of the questions it poses to modernity. All these issues strike us forcibly when we examine the intellectual practices of C. L. R. James and W. E. B. Du Bois.

C. L. R. James: Political Practice and Intellectual Production

The interpretation of political texts requires a methodology that, among other things, distills the writer's political practice, the explicit political purpose of the text, and the political language and discursive practices of the tradition in which the author operates. Using such a methodology, let us first consider C. L. R. James.

James was born in 1901 in the British Caribbean colony of Trinidad. He was of a rebellious temperament and challenged the trajectory of the bright native intellectual then typical of the British colonial native intelligentsia.[6] Set on a literary career, James migrated to England in 1932 in order to pursue his ambitions. There he became absorbed with Marxist and anticolonial politics, and as a consequence, in his words, "Fiction writing drained out of me." Between 1934 and 1938, after joining the Trotskyite wing of the international Marxist movement, James became a leading Marxist theoretician in Europe. His reputation was consolidated by the publication in 1936 of *World Revolution (1917–1936)*, which in the opinion of many became the Trotskyite bible of the period.[7] He also became a leading cricket correspondent for the *Manchester Guardian*; wrote a popular pamphlet on the case for Caribbean self-government; published a novel, *Minty Alley;* and wrote a dramatic play, *The Black Jacobins*, in which Paul Robeson played the leading role.

By 1938, then, James was a leading figure in radical English political circles. His political practice, however, was a dual one. James moved easily between working with the small Trotskyite group and acting in concert with George Padmore, Jomo Kenyatta, Amy Ashwood-Garvey, and others in creating the organizational form and theoretical positions for the political independence of Africa, the International African Service Bureau (IASB). The intense political practice of this organization formed the immediate impetus for the writing of *The Black Jacobins*.

In Trinidad, James had shown interest in the Haitian Revolution when, in an article for the journal *Beacon,* he opined that Toussaint L'Ouverture was a seminal figure in Haitian history for uniting the country, a feat that had never been achieved before.[8] In a 1971 lecture in London, James noted that *The Black Jacobins* was published the same year as Aimé Césaire's *Return to Native Land.* He further commented, "I don't know why I was writing *The Black Jacobins* the way I did. I had long made up my mind to write a book about Toussaint L'Overture. Why I couldn't tell you. Something was in the atmosphere and I responded to it."[9] In the same year, in a series of lectures at the Institute of the Black World (IBW),[10] James again remarked on why he wrote the book. This time he was more specific:

> I also wanted to write a history of Toussaint L'Ouverture because I believe that of the books I had read none were satisfactory. I had a good knowledge of history, historical writing and biography, and I didn't see *a* good one. I had made up my mind, for no other reason than a *literary* reason, that when I reached England I would settle down to write a history of Toussaint L'Ouverture.[11]

Thus for James, in the first instance, it seems that purely literary reasons drove the writing of *The Black Jacobins.* This is an intriguing reflection and indicates the relationship between literary forms and historical narratives, particularly when the historical narrative is held together through the biographical form. It would seem that the protocols of the narrative form establish Western historical writing as partly one form of a literary genre that Aristotle referred to as "the emplotment of represented actions."[12] However, the problem of narrative form is also allied to a central problem of the philosophy of history: Is historical representation an accurate description of events? This is not the place to enter into a debate about this issue; instead, I wish to point out the following. Perhaps if one argues that there is no *direct* representation of the past, then it might be possible to operate with a conception of *historical truth.* Such a truth recognizes that its basis is interpretive and that while technical skills are applied to archives, the very act of historical writing is itself an imaginative one. The essential difference between *historical truth* and fiction is that archives act as an anchor and a trace of the past, informing and giving body to historical writings. This digression is an important one, since both James and Du Bois spent a great deal of time reflecting on their historical practices. James, for example, in the first preface of *The Black Jacobins* states, "The writer has sought not only to analyse, but to demonstrate their movement, the economic forces of the age; their moulding of society and politics, of men in the mass and individual men; the powerful reaction of these on their environment

... the analysis is the science and the demonstration the art which is history."[13]

Thus for James the writing of history was an art, while the analysis and marshaling of evidence called for scientific skills. In our attempt to examine the *historical truth* in *The Black Jacobins,* what becomes important in our investigation is to grapple with *all the conditions* that allowed the production of this form of truth. This does not mean some kind of cultural relativistism, but rather a focus on the influences, politics, and historical theories that shaped the writing of *The Black Jacobins.* In the end we will be able to see the ways in which James, while using certain radical historical categories, gave them new meanings.

In the 1971 IBW lecture James discerns that alongside his anticolonial political practice, Caribbean nationalism and his preoccupation with historical knowledge were the other ingredients which framed his writing. He ends a description of the influences on him in this way:

> So I hope that you understand now that this book was not an accident. It didn't just fall from a tree. It is the result of a whole series of circumstances by which I thoroughly master, as I did in those days, Marxism. I had come from the Caribbean with a certain understanding of Western Civilization. I had read the history of the Marxist movement, and I had written four hundred pages on the Marxist movement, from its beginning in 1864 to what was taking place in 1936. I was a highly trained Marxist, and that was the person who wrote *The Black Jacobins.*[14]

As a radical Marxist historian James had had his historical imagination stirred by reading Trotsky's *History of the Russian Revolution* and Oswald Spengler's *The Decline of the West.* Histories on an epic scale, the narrative of the large historical canvas, were to become for him essential elements of his historical practice. The audience for *The Black Jacobins* was the anticolonial revolutionaries in Africa and the Caribbean, and the European Marxists. Its political purposes were twofold. In the first instance the book was a vindication of the capacity of the colonized African to govern. James makes the point in his lectures: "I was trying to make clear that black people have a certain historical past . . . so by historical method, I tried to show that black people were able to make historical progress, they were able to produce men who could lead a revolution and write new pages in the book of history."[15] The second political purpose was that the text intervened in the intense political debates, swirling around the IASB, about the relevance of armed political struggle for the African anticolonial movement. In the end the text was organically linked to revolutionary political practice. The telling of the story of the only successful black slave revolt in modernity rewrote Marxist categories of labor, as well as the nature of the political economy of early capitalism and of radical historiography. As a consequence, James pushed Marxist theory in new directions.

Du Bois and *The Black Reconstruction*

If by 1938 C. L. R. James was a leading black Marxist in Europe, W. E. B. Du Bois at the time was the leading black radical intellectual in the western hemisphere. Born in New England in 1868, a few years after the Civil War, Du Bois exhibited intellectual and political practices that were chiefly shaped by his being a racial object in late nineteenth- and early twentieth-century America. He himself remarked in his first autobiography: "My life had its significance and its only significance because it was part of a problem; but that problem . . . the concept of race is today one of the most unyielding and threatening. . . . I have written then what is meant to be not so much my autobiography as the autobiography of a concept of race."[16] Determined at an early age to pursue an explicitly intellectual life, Du Bois dreamed of attending Harvard: ". . . my heart was set on Harvard. It was the greatest and oldest college and I therefore quite naturally thought it was the one I must attend."[17] However, the racial conditions did not allow the fulfillment of such a desire, and Du Bois attended a Southern black college, Fisk. The experience of Southern black life dismantled his Northern outlook. Reflecting on his period at Fisk, Du Bois stated: "The three years at Fisk were years of growth and development. I learnt new things about the world. . . . I came in contact for the first time with a sort of violence that I had never realized in New England."[18]

After Fisk, Du Bois gained admittance to Harvard, and continued there, with important sojourns in Germany, until he completed a Ph.D. in history in 1895. His dissertation, *The Suppression of the African Slave Trade to the United States of America, 1638–1870* was published by the Harvard Historical Studies program. Du Bois's education in the hallowed halls of an elite Western academy did not exclude him from racial oppression and the vicissitudes of being a racial object. He observes in his autobiography:

> . . . had it not been for the race problem early thrust upon me and enveloping me, I should have probably been an unquestioning worshipper at the shrine of the social order and economic development into which I was born. *But just that part of that order which seemed to most of my fellows nearest perfection, seemed to me most inequitable and wrong.*[19]

Du Bois's efforts to vanquish racial oppression in America made him a committed radical. In the late nineteenth century, clearly influenced by that century's developments in the social sciences and the discursive practices of the period, he announced: "The Negro Problem was in my mind a matter of systematic investigation and intelligent understanding." Upholding this position, DuBois produced *The Philadelphia Negro: A Social Study* (1899) and edited sixteen Atlanta University Studies covering all social aspects of African-American life at the time. All this was accomplished under onerous conditions. His sociological work exploded the American myth of "Negro pathology," the basis of the American so-called Negro Problem.[20] In 1903 he published what is perhaps today his most studied text, the seminal *Souls of Black Folks.* In 1909, he announced his return to historical writing when *John Brown,* was published. In that same year, the final meeting of the Niagra Movement was held and in the following year the National Association for the Advancement of Colored People (NAACP) was founded. It was racial terror that moved Du Bois from a man of science to a man of *political action and science.* He writes, after his encounter with the consequences of lynching," One could not be a calm, cool, and detached scientist while Negroes were lynched, murdered and starved."[21] In 1915, observing Europe's colonial hold over Africa, he turned his attention once more to history and produced his first major text on African history, *The Negro,* an attempt to begin "a complete history of the Negro people." By then Du Bois was obviously working well the historical practice of black historical writing —vindicationism. In this sense he and James were on similar tracks.

By the late 1930s Du Bois had come to the conclusion that the policy of liberalism which he advocated was politically exhausted. The NAACP had successfully led campaigns against lynching and had developed a wide-ranging set of legal strategies to fight racial discrimination. But the fight did not lead to political and formal procedural equality for the African-American population. Racial oppression was formidable. It had the capacity to reorganize itself and to be present in every aspect of American social life. In his early twentieth-century efforts there is no doubt that Du Bois was intellectually and politically engaged with American liberal pragmatism. Like other pragmatists of the time, he operated within the confines of what John Dewey has called a "renascent liberalism."[22] However, while pragmatism was the frame, the fact of race exploded its efficacy. The struggles against racial equality pushed the boundaries of liberal pragmatism. Du Bois observed: "The essential difficulty with the liberalism of the twentieth century was not to realize the fundamental change brought by the world-wide organization of work and trade and commerce."[23] All this once again opened the door for Du Bois to do what his common practice was throughout his entire life—grappling with political and intellectual practices that would vanquish American racial oppression and global anti-black racism.

The antecedents of *Black Reconstruction* are therefore to be found in Du Bois's search for theoretical answers to the extreme conditions of racial oppression that continued unabated in early twentieth-century America and his continual historical quest to dissect the meaning of America. In 1909 Du Bois made a presentation to the American Historical Association of a paper titled "Black Reconstruction and Its Benefits." The paper, though not very well received, appeared in the *American Historical Review*. For many years after, however, the Reconstruction period continued to intrigue him, and by 1931 he was ready to write about it. Du Bois was being driven to write about the Reconstruction because it had become clear to him that the construction of the memory of the period was a central one in the continued reworking of white racial ideology. In a perceptive essay on Du Bois, David W. Blight argues that "One of [Du Bois's] principal aims of all his future historical work [was] to forge a social memory . . . that might help solve or transcend the race problem, rather than simply getting rid of it."[24] In correspondence with friends, Du Bois explained that the "real hero and center of human interest in the period is the slave who is being emancipated."[25] But if the emancipated slave was the hero, what theory of history would facilitate Du Bois's telling of that story? Liberalism had been exhausted, so Du Bois turned to a study of Marxism.

He had first come into contact with Marxism as a student in Berlin. However, at the time he was not moved to engage in any serious theoretical study of it. In 1911 he had become a member of the Socialist Party, but left it a year later. In the 1920s he journeyed to the Soviet Union and wrote glowingly about what he saw. In spite of this he had initial problems with American Marxism. These were twofold. First, he felt that the American Communist movement was deeply racist and was unable to deal politically with racial oppression in the United States, second, he had discerned through study and political practice that race had complicated the character of the American class struggle.

In his article "Marxism and the Negro Problem," written for *The Crisis* in 1933, he states: "While Negro labor in America suffers because of the fundamental inequities of the whole capitalistic system, the lowest and most fatal degree of its suffering comes not from the capitalist but from fellow white workers." Continuing on this theme, he argues that the imperial expansion of industry had established a worldwide "proletariat of colored workers toiling under conditions of 19th century capitalism." Finally, he concludes that "Marxian philosophy is a true diagnosis of the situation in Europe in the middle of the 19th century despite some of its logical difficulties. But it must be modified in the United States of America and especially so far as the Negro group is concerned."

The article is an important one because it staked out a new political position that would inform the historical narrative of *Black Reconstruction*. It asserted: "In the hearts of black laborers alone, therefore, lie those ideals of democracy in politics and industry which may in time make the workers of the world effective dictators of civilization." The world had been turned upside down—black workers were to be the prime agents for a new order. This unorthodoxy—indeed heresy—became the central theme of *Black Reconstruction*.

The shape of the *Black Reconstruction* was also influenced by Du Bois's extensive political campaigns against racial oppression in the United States, his international political activity in three Pan-African congresses, and his consistent efforts to develop a mode of criticism and writing that debunked the notions of white supremacy and black "savagery." The final factor of influence was the nature of early twentieth-century American historiography, which argued that the Reconstruction period was "a hideous mistake." This position was the dominant one taught in schools, and formed the core of America's social memory at the time. It obviously served to reinforce the social location of the black population and white supremacy. It was compounded by the appearance of D. W. Griffith's film *Birth of a Nation*. In these contexts *Black Reconstruction*, like *The Black Jacobins*, became a text of political intervention.

I wish to suggest that radical political interventionist historical texts are works of *historical and political theory*, and that the requirements of political intervention mean that such texts elaborate a different narrative while they are theorizing. We now move to examine the historical theory that informed both texts, and to grapple with the ruptures implicit in the authors' historical and political analysis. In pursuing this path we will be exploring how black intellectual production occurs, how it engages radical theory, and what discursive practice ensues from this engagement.

The Heresy of *The Black Jacobins*

What theory of history informs *Black Reconstruction* and *The Black Jacobins*? Both writers deploy Marxist historical materialist categories. The major personalities of early twentieth-century Marxism haunt James's *The Black Jacobins*. His use of Lenin and Trotsky as the comparative political standard in his assessment of the political relationship between Toussaint L'Ouverture and Moïse; his paraphrasing of Marx's *Eighteenth Brumaire*, about how men make history; the organization of the text along the lines of social forces and their interplay in the vortex of class struggle and revolution; and the emphasis upon the dialectical relationship between external and internal factors in a political conjuncture all would seem to point to the fact that *The Black Jacobins* is a work of historical knowledge which reproduces, without additions or changes, the major categories of historical materialism. However, a more nuanced reading with an eye to the relationship of two elements—James's dual political praxis at the time and the requirements of vindicationism—opens the text in different ways. We also need to consider the event around which the text is organized, the Haitian Revolution. This revolution, called "unthinkable" by Michel-Rolph Trouillot, has been neglected in studies of revolution. Primarily, it has been studied as a slave revolt hardly worthy of the name "revolution." But the nature of the event encouraged James to tell a tale that shifted the main historical axis of the "Age of Revolution," narrating a different historical tale about the rise of modernity.[26] How did *The Black Jacobins* do this?

In the first place, the text has a remarkable opening. It argues that the wealth and economic strength of Europe were based on the slave trade and the products of slave plantation labor. Such claims were at that time neither common nor welcome within the discipline of history. Indeed, it was not until after the 1944 publication of Eric Williams's *Capitalism and Slavery* that major debates in Western historiography about the general relationship between racial slavery and capitalism occurred. Although Marx had made the point in *The Poverty of Philosophy* about the relationship between African slavery and the primitive accumulation of capital, *The Black Jacobins* reconfigures this relationship, placing colonialism and plantation slavery both at the rosy dawn of the accumulation process and central to nineteenth-century economic developments. This shift in periodization meant that James had to rethink the slave as a social type, thereby recasting the Marxist historical narrative of both revolution and the nature of the political economy of capitalism. In standard Marxist historical narrative, the birth of capitalist production originated during the late 1700s with the emergence of mills production and the production of textiles. Plantation slavery was subsidiary to this, and slave labor an anomaly. For James, such a historical narrative and interpretation would marginalize colonial plantation slavery, and thereby the political and social role of the slaves themselves. Confronted which this problem, he discusses Caribbean slaves in the following manner:

> The slaves worked on the land, and, like revolutionary peasants everywhere, they aimed at the extermination of their oppressors. But working and living together in gangs of hundreds on the huge sugar factories which covered the North Plain, they were closer to a modern proletariat than any group of workers in existence at the time.[27]

This categorization of the Caribbean slave was a rupture from formal Marxist categories of historical and social analysis, opening the door for a different set of interpretations of the social formation of Caribbean society and the characteristics of the black Caribbean colonial. For if racial slave plantation society was a modern society and the African slave a modern person, not only was racial slavery morally wrong, but the continued colonial domination of the Caribbean and Africa was untenable. Here James was also appropriating the notion of the modern and using it to make a case for political independence. The opening for a radical way of characterizing slavery created the conditions for *The Black Jacobins* to became a framing text in Caribbean radical social theory. *The Black Jacobins* seeks by its investigation of the Haitian Revolution to answer the question: What is the Caribbean? It is no accident that in the book's second edition (1963, one year after the colonies in the English Caribbean began to achieve their political independence), James affixed an appendix titled "From Toussaint L'Ouverture to Fidel Castro," in a postcolonial effort to interpret the history of the Caribbean on its own terms.

James was concerned to demonstrate the humanness of the African slave. Thus he avers," The slaves were subjected to the same historical laws as the advanced workers of colonial Paris."[28] Writing in 1939, James makes the point that "Negro revolutionary history is rich, inspiring and *unknown*."[29] However, it is worthwhile to note a problematic with the terms of James's vindication. His "enmeshment" with the Western intellectual tradition at the time meant that he granted slaves humanity on the grounds of their capacity to struggle.[30] It was their revolutionary actions that made them human. Part of the difficulty that James then faced was his failure to rework the premodern/modern divide in ways which would have been more reflective of African realities.[31] In the final analysis, James's achievement was to negate epistemic erasure, not to reclaim an African human self on its own terms. His operation therefore was a delicate one, so what were some of the conundrums that bedeviled him?

In the lecture to the Institute of the Black World, James states that if he were rewriting *The Black Jacobins,* there were two things he would do differently. In the first instance, he would not rely so heavily on the archives of French colonialism, and second, he would pay more attention to the activities of the slaves themselves. Both of these self-critical comments are important because they point to the central dilemma of *The Black Jacobins,* one that *Black Reconstruction* was not troubled by. The dilemma was this: In spite of rescuing the Haitian slave revolution from oblivion and granting the slaves agency, James had mixed feelings about these revolutionary slaves. Modern as they were, in James's mind they were sometimes the proletariat and at other times they were like "the peasants in the Jacquerie or the Luddite wreckers."[32] Even after defeating the best European armies, James noted, the ex-slave population was "backward" in relationship to Toussaint. He makes the point consistently: "Toussaint knew the backwardness of the labourers; he made them work, but he wanted to see them civilized and advanced in culture."[33] The real dilemma, in James's mind, was that the mode of production had yoked African slaves into modernity in the New World, but their worldview was still in rooted in the Old World. James did not grasp in 1938 (and it is very possible that he could not have) that there was a different African worldview which was central to their revolutionary upsurge.[34]

This meant that James, by not paying much attention to the archives of the slaves, writes an interventionist text on slave revolution and leadership but fails to grapple with the ideology of the revolution. In the end *The Black Jacobins* does not tell us why Dessalines, the slave general, became a *Lwa*[35] in the Haitian religious pantheon and L'Ouverture does not.[36] Another of the real tensions in *The Black Jacobins* is that while it wonderfully portrays the dialectic between the French Revolution and the Haitian Revolution, it does not answer the question of whether or not the latter was a black Jacobin revolution, a Caribbean revolution, or an African revolution in the Caribbean. Surely L'Ouverture was a black Jacobin, but was the rest of the revolutionary population?

One final point. James's text, written with its gaze firmly fixed on African independence, was extraordinarily prescient in understanding one of the central dilemmas of anticolonial leadership—the relationship in the postindependence period between former colony and colonial power. How that relationship could complicate political leadership is the story of many anticolonial movements in the later part of the twentieth century.

One of the principal purposes of making the unknown visible, of revoking *epistemic erasure,* is to fill the silences in history. James does this by drawing our attention to the relationship of the Haitian Revolution to the 1789 French Revolution. This narrative reconfigured the "Age of Revolution" and the nature of revolutions of the period. This "unthinkable" revolution raised the question that all the other European and the American revolutions of the period had dodged: what to do about racial slavery. This was not a minor question. The colonies of plantation slavery were the foundation of the colonial powers; racial slavery was embedded within American society alongside the conquest of the Native American population; and on those matters early twentieth-century radical thought was both blind and dumb. So with the sound of booming guns on the European battlefields and the marching of jackbooted fascists, James's *The Black Jacobins* was a valiant attempt to bring to the fore the position of colonial blacks. He deployed Marxism, but in his hands the categories used to describe historical processes were wrought into something else. The French Revolution became the permissive context for the Haitian Revolution, not *the* cause of the revolution; the Haitian Revolution was not the

French Revolution in Haiti. The radical actions of the slaves in the eighteenth and nineteenth centuries played a crucial role in the Western world's transition from feudalism to capitalism. The "magnitude of the contributions the Negroes" was an integral part of world revolutionary history, James said, and he chided the Marxists of the period for having "far less excuse for falling into the mistake" of historical neglect.[37]

The Black Jacobins as a historical text integrates the African slave population into modernity as human beings. The decade of the 1930s was alive with conceptions of the inferiority of the African. The development of social Darwinism, the emergence of the French eugenics movement, and the complex relationship between the civilizing mission of the colonizer and theories of human evolution combined to make historical narratives showing Africans in a positive light a difficult operation. I would suggest that to challenge these conceptions, even on flawed terms, committed James to heresy. But while C. L. R. James is nuanced, subtly reworking the Marxist categories and framework from which he is writing, Du Bois, on the other hand, makes a frontal challenge.

The Du Boisian Rupture

Black Reconstruction at once announces its rupture with Marxist orthodoxy, beginning with the bold enunciation that the black slaves in the United States were black workers. Early in the text Du Bois makes the point that there were two systems of labor in the United States linked to race and slavery. In one system there was the "exploitation of white labor," which existed both in Europe and the United States, and then there was slave labor in the Americas, based upon racial oppression. DuBois is not content to note the existence of these two systems, but thinks about their relationship. In doing so, he makes the following point:

> Black labor became the foundation stone not only of the Southern social structure, but of the northern manufacture and commerce, of the English factory system, of European commerce, of buying and selling on a world scale; new cities were built on the results of black labor, and a new labor problem, involving all white labor arose both in Europe and America.[38]

But there was more. Racial slavery created a unique set of complications for the Marxist notion of the revolutionary agency of the advanced proletariat in modern capitalism:

> Indeed, the plight of the white working class throughout the world today is directly traceable to Negro slavery in America, on which

modern commerce was founded ... the resulting color caste founded and retained by capitalism was adopted, forwarded and approved by white labor and resulted in subordination of colored labor to white profits the world over. Thus the majority of the world laborers by the insistence of white labor, became the basis of a system of Industry which ruined democracy and showed its perfect fruit in world war and depression.[39]

This statement obviously overturns the historical narrative of the nature of the American and European working class and its role as the revolutionary agency for a new social order. It suggests that capitalism was also a racial system and that race could not be reduced to an epiphenomenon in the American social formation. Second, it suggests that one had to reconsider issues related to Marx's notion of labor and the meaning of this category. In Marxist terms, wage labor is perceived as alienation, and the labor theory of value surrounds the issue of surplus value and notions of exploitation. The question that Du Bois raised was what would happen when labor was embodied in both body and person—in other words, when labor was combined with the property of a person. Marx makes the point that wage labor turns the worker into "a fragment of a man."[40] On the other hand, racial slave labor turned human beings into objects in which a private domestic sphere was often minimal. The slave was a slave—he or she was property in its totality. For Du Bois this meant that black workers were positioned in a special location in the Americas. With his eyes firmly fixed on how race operated in the interstices of American life, Du Bois remapped the story of capitalist evolution. Racial slavery and oppression were not peripheral to the world system; they were an organic part of it with enormous political and social consequences. This was important not only for Marxist theory but also for American history. Investing the category of labor with some new meanings, Du Bois then offered a different narrative about the nature of labor in the West.

This led Du Bois to think about the nineteenth-century American debate surrounding wage slavery, racial slavery, and free labor. Michael Sandel observes that the rapid increase of factory life in nineteenth-century America was in part the occasion for a debate about the relationship of freedom to wage labor.[41] However, Sandel follows the normal pattern of studying this debate in American political thought as one that involves only fierce arguments about the perquisites of economic independence and its relationship to human freedom. So although he notes that some participants in the debate raised the arguments which compared wage slavery to slavery, absent from his work is any discussion by the ex-slaves themselves about the nature of freedom.[42] This silence is the norm for discussions in political philosophy about freedom in the Americas. For

Du Bois, wage labor and slave labour were both exploitative systems, but slavery was *both* a system of property ownership *and* labor exploitation. It was thus a special form of human domination:

> There was in 1863 a real meaning to slavery different from what we may apply to the laborer today. It was in part psychological, the enforced personal feeling of inferiority, the calling of another master; the standing with hat in hand. It was the helplessness. It was the defenselessness of family life. *It was the submergence below the arbitrary will of any sort of individual.*[43]

The consequence of this theorization of slavery was the possibility of alternative conceptions of freedom. This emerged as a central focus of the book as Du Bois wove the historical narrative. His category of black workers now opened new terrain both for analysis and for vindication. Thus, for example, black workers in the period of the Civil War were engaged, he argued, in a general strike—the mass movement of slaves from the plantations to the Union Army. He describes this movement thus: "This was not merely the desire to stop work. It was a strike on a wide basis against the conditions of work. It was a general strike that involved directly in the end perhaps a half million people. They wanted to stop the economy of the plantation system, and to do that they left the plantations."[44]

By calling this movement a general strike, Du Bois, like James, made the slaves into a different social category. In Du Bois's case this stance was consistently maintained. Thus in the end Du Bois calls Reconstruction a period that was in part a "dictatorship of labor." Obviously such an appellation destabilized the intellectual practices of Marxists at the time. James Allen rushed to the defense of American Marxism, quickly publishing *Reconstruction: The Battle for Democracy* (1937), in which he made the point that while *Black Reconstruction* was praiseworthy in its "spirited defense of the Negro in Reconstruction, Dubois's failure to grasp the bourgeois character of the revolution leads him to mistaken notions."[45]

But at the core of Du Bois's representation of Reconstruction were other purposes than being an orthodox Marxist. First, Du Bois wanted to demonstrate how racial slavery had created racism and how this racism would bedevil any alliances between white and black labor. Second, Du Bois wished to demonstrate that in the nineteenth century black ex-slave labor had constructed in the South an effort at radical democracy which should be placed alongside the efforts of the Parisian working class of the time. He writes, for example, that Reconstruction was an "extraordinary experiment in Marxism that the world had seen before the Russian revolution." Like James, Du Bois was opening new spaces for the interpretation of radical history. The consequence of locating these two events in radical historiography would raise new questions about political practice and offer possible alternative insights into old political ideas. Du Bois was at the same time refuting the nature of the social memory of the Civil War and Reconstruction that held sway in America.

At this point it might be important to indicate another Marxist opinion of *Black Reconstruction.* William Gorman, in a 1950 article on Du Bois, observes that in *Black Reconstruction*

> Du Bois . . . far outdistances his contemporaries. . . . A great work of this kind is always a climax of historical accumulation. Everything was poured onto its writing: the slave system, the slave insurrections, the murder of abolitionists, fugitive slave rescues, the last letters of John Brown . . . and if the prosperity of European imperialism was built on the massacre of the Paris Communards, America's rise as a participant and leader in world plunder was built on the unbridled deceit and terror which broke Black Reconstruction in the South.[46]

Du Bois was more successful than James in writing about the social mind of the slaves. James makes the point that while he had set out to prove the humanity of the slaves, Du Bois took it for granted. Because of this, James says, Du Bois "opened out the historical perspective in a manner I didn't know."[47] The narrative of *The Black Jacobins* stops at the victory of the revolutionary army led by Dessalines. Du Bois, on the other hand, pursued another set of questions. What was the nature of the ex-slaves' project as it unfolded in the late nineteenth century? How did they make emancipation? James stopped at vindicationism—the revolutionary "transformation of slaves, trembling in hundreds before a single white man, into a people able to organize themselves and defeat the most powerful European nations of the day."[48] Du Bois's probing of the ideas of the ex-slaves about freedom and their attempts to construct democratic communities in the South takes *Black Reconstruction* out of the realm of history and into that of political theory.

The Mapping of Transformation

In probing the ideas of the slaves about freedom, Du Bois points us to the slaves' political language of this freedom. In exquisite lyrical prose he describes this freedom as "the coming of the Lord":

> There was to be a new freedom! And a black nation went tramping after the armies no matter how it suffered; no matter how it was treated, no matter how it died. First, without masters, without food, without shelter, . . . they prayed; they worked; they danced and

sang; they studied to learn; they wanted to wander. . . . they were consumed with desire for schools. The uprising of the Black man, and the pouring of himself into organized effort for education in those years between 1861and 1871, was one of the marvelous occurrences of the modern world; almost without parallel in the history of civilization.[49]

But as is usual in radical historical studies, when one excavates a different archive, alternative categories are opened up. Much of radical Western radical political theory, following Enlightenment secularization, regards religion as "opiate" irrationality or the sighs of the oppressed. However, the grammar of the freed slaves suggested another interpretation. Du Bois writes again:

> . . . the mass of the slaves even the more intelligent ones, and certainly the great group of field hands, were in religious and hysterical fervor. This was the coming of the Lord. This was the fulfillment of prophecy and legend. It was the Golden Dawn after chains of a thousand years. It was everyday miraculous and perfect and promising."[50]

Du Bois then makes the point that the world did not understand the nature of this freedom:

> The world at first neither saw nor understood. Of all that most Americans wanted, this freeing of the slave was the last. Everything black was hideous. Everything Negroes did was wrong, if they fought for freedom, they were beasts; if they did not fight, they were born slaves. If they cowered on the plantations, they loved slavery; if they ran away, they were lazy loafers. If they sang, they were silly; if they scowled, they were impudent. . . . And they were funny, funny-ridiculous baboons, aping man.[51]

While *The Black Jacobins* does not spend a great deal of time reviewing the political program, the social and economic activities of the Haitian Revolution, *Black Reconstruction* does probe these areas. In scrutinizing the government of South Carolina, Du Bois elaborates an evolutionary theory of democracy. For Du Bois, democracy evolved from notions of rulership of the chosen few to the idea that most "men had capabilities, except the Negro." Clearly, for Du Bois, in this frame democracy was linked to conceptions of citizenship. What is interesting here is that for Du Bois, citizenship did not include a notion of politics which concerned itself primarily with duties, something very common in political philosophy. In Du Bois's political thought, democracy was a function of freedom. It was the practices of a body politic in which freedom was not separate from social and political equality, and where questions of justice were resolved around the issues of political economy, what he called "industrial democracy." In the Du Boisian paradigm, within the historical domain there were two key questions that faced the American emancipation process: freedom and democracy. On the other hand, I would suggest that for the Haitian Revolution and the ex-slaves the key questions were freedom and social equality.

In Du Bois's historical schema, the defeat of the Reconstruction reverberated throughout the world and established the ground for the quality of the "American Century" and the intensification of colonialism in the late nineteenth century. Du Bois argued that if a popular form of democracy and of citizenship had won out in the Reconstruction period, world history would have been different. It is here, I think, that we can better appreciate Du Bois's aphoristic statement, "The problem of the 20th century was the color line."

We know that by the end of the nineteenth century, America had begun its external expansion and was now what Du Bois called in *Darkwater* "a modern industrial imperialism." This form of imperialism was different from that described by Lenin, Rosa Luxemburg, and the English political economist John Hobson. For Du Bois this kind of imperialism could not be called only the economic stage of monopoly finance capitalism, because it created a world of racialized labor and subjects. Modern imperialism, Du Bois argued, depends upon a "modern discovery of whiteness." What we have here from Du Bois is an early theorization of the nature of race and its functions in the modern world. For Du Bois, race was a post-Enlightenment invention: "Even up into the 18th century we were hammering our national mankinds into one, great Universal man, with fine frenzy which ignored color and race, even more than birth."[52] However, Du Bois recognized that the American Century would have to reckon with the meaning of race both externally and internally. In 1900, after the Cuban war for independence, he wrote:

> What is our attitude toward these new lands and toward the masses of dark men and women who inhabit them? Manifestly it must be an attitude of deepest sympathy and strongest alliance . . . We must remember that the 20th century will find nearly twenty millions of brown and black people under the American flag, and . . . that the success and efficiency of the nine millions of our own number depends [upon] the ultimate destiny of Filipinos, Puerto Ricans, Indians and Hawaiians.[53]

Du Bois links the fate of African Americans to that of other nonwhite, non-European peoples. As things stood, however, by the 1930s the defeat of the

Reconstruction project and the consolidation of Jim Crow meant that a new basis had been found for the continued domination of people on the basis of skin color.

It is perhaps not an accident that in the nineteenth century, "race" became a popular word. Centuries of racial slavery had removed all inhibitions from Western thought about the supposed true nature of the African. In his 1896 *Sunshine and Storm in Rhodesia*, F. C. Selous captures this current in Western thought well:

> Therefore Matebeleland is doomed by what seems a law of nature to be ruled by the white man, and the black man must go, or conform to the white man's laws, or die in resisting them. It seems a hard and cruel fate for the black man, but it is destiny which the broadest philanthropy cannot avert . . . the law which has ruled upon this planet ever since, in the far-off misty depths of time, organic life was first evolved upon the earth—the inexorable law which Darwin has aptly termed the "Survival of the Fittest."[54]

It was in this context that Du Bois sought to propagate an alternative historical possibility. He painted a picture of radical world history that had been made invisible because of the nature of Western historical knowledge. In the end he bemoaned the fact that "A great human experiment was present in Reconstruction, and its careful scientific investigation would have thrown a world of light on human development and democratic government."[55]

Heresy, Double Consciousness, and Black Radicalism

We are now at the final stage. Here it might be useful to summarize Du Bois's and James's connections to Marxism, and to extract from this relationship and their writings some understanding of the elements of black radical intellectual production. James, as we have stated before, was a Marxist by 1934. His sojourn on the terrain of Marxism took him by 1948 to an independent Marxist stance critical of the Soviet Union and the Leninist party, into activities with a group then called the Johnson-Forest Tendency.[56] By the mid-1960s, after failed participation in the Caribbean nationalist movement and federal projects, James wrote his famous *Beyond a Boundary*. He never again participated fully in any Marxist movement, and by the late 1960s had become a political mentor for the new generation of radicals. In a 1980 interview he remarked that he thought that his major contributions to political theory were his book on Hegel and Marxism,[57] and his work that attempted to reconfigure Marxism as a doctrine for the self-emancipation of the working class. In many of his later interviews James spoke as an independent Marxist—one who had attempted to use Marxist categories in a creative way.

In what ways can it be said that James was a heretic thinker? James's heresy was rooted in the black radical intellectual tradition, and in his efforts to speak and write a political language reflective of the conditions of the racialized black subject. This did not mean that his thought and political practice were bereft of tensions. He himself stated in 1972 at a lecture to students at Tougaloo College, in referring to Africa: "I was twice your age before I began to understand . . . [its] juridical systems, political systems, philosophical systems and its great artistic achievements in plastic arts and its music."[58]

For Du Bois, the situation was more complicated. Du Bois had recognized as early as 1903 the feature of "double-consciousness" as part of African-American life. Drawing from Hegel's *Phenomenology of Mind*, and William James's and Ralph Waldo Emerson's conceptions of double life, he had, as we stated in an earlier chapter carved out both a poetic and a social insight into the intellectual and political practices of African Americans. He writes in *The Souls of Black Folks*, "It is a peculiar sensation, this double-consciousness, this sense of always looking at oneself through the eyes of others, of measuring one's soul by the tape of the world that looks on in amused contempt and pity."[59] But this "double-consciousness" was not a Hamlet-like condition of existential anguish and indecision. It produced a "second sight" into American life that then formed the basis for a critique of both dominant discourses and radical critiques. So while Du Bois formally embraced orthodox Marxism in the last years of his life, he conducted a political practice that critically engaged Marxist theory. It is a misnomer to call the most radical sections of his oeuvre simply black Marxism. This leads us to a discussion about the political intellectual in the black radical intellectual tradition.

It is the heresy developed in the political and historical writings of these two men that profoundly marks the shape of twentieth-century black radical intellectual production. James's and Du Bois's engagement with the Western intellectual tradition represents a study of conflictual discursive practices and creative tension. By the time James and Du Bois became mature political writers, they had digested the major intellectual practices of the West. As late as the 1940s in his biography *Dusk of Dawn*, Du Bois would note his relationship to the Western intellectual tradition and its ramifications for his work. In his 1963 semi-autobiography, *Beyond a Boundary*, James would make the point that by the age of ten, he was a "British intellectual with a literary bent." For the stream of the black radical intellectual tradition that these two men represented, the conflicts and tensions with the Western intellectual tradition would be great, and the

Western epistemic erasure of Africa and Africans was painful. As in all heretical practices, these two writers began with orthodoxy and a sense of limits. However, as Pierre Bourdieu points out, heretical practices occur when the social world does not appear self-evident or natural. There is no *doxa* in the political practices of the black radical intellectual. Engagement means criticism and the exercise of heretical power, what Bourdieu calls "the strength of the sorcerer who wields a liberatory potency."[60] This "liberatory potency" begins with black radical intellectual production correcting historical knowledge, reversing its silences in a practice of *discursive representation*. In this sense we can say that both *The Black Jacobins* and *Black Reconstruction* represent the coming to the fore of subjugated historical knowledge.

The emergence of this form of subjugated knowledge in the fields of history and politics requires two things: a new way of thinking about the political intellectual, and reviewing the forms of political knowledge. Much ink has been expended on the concept of the intellectual. In Western conceptual history, the emergence of the intellectual as part of a group, with a public face, was coterminous with the needs of secular political power and the creation of new instruments of legitimacy and knowledge.[61] Thus, in sixteenth-century Europe there was a shift in the keepers of knowledge from clergy to members of the laity who became knowledge officers. The need for the European state to gather experts to carry out its disciplinary functions and to elaborate the ideology of its existence required the creation of a trained group of men of ideas. The rapid emergence of schools and universities in tandem with the growth of the modern state in Europe is testimony to this relationship. So intellectuals emerged first as priests, keepers of knowledge, and then, over time, as legitimators of the state in the transformation of what Foucault calls "pastoral power." By the time of the French Enlightenment, intellectuals, organized in the "republic of letters," were the embodiment of reason.

The "kingdom of reason" became the lifeblood of intellectual life. Within this kingdom of reason, intellectuals shared a similar vocabulary, a common world, and a community of interests and meanings. But the "kingdom of reason" also allowed for criticism. Two streams developed within the fold of intellectuals: the critic and the expert. The expert was the keeper of knowledge; the legitimator of the status quo, while the critic "spoke truth to power." However this representation of the conceptual history of the intellectual is highly problematic when dealing with the radical black intellectual. Racism is not only a relationship of power and domination with social consequences; it is also a way of knowing, of shaping ideas and thoughts. Racism fixes the boundaries of what can be studied and how it should be studied. It creates categories of hierarchy and is not simply reducible to personal prejudice or false consciousness. As a mode of thought, Etienne Balibar has suggested, racism connects words with objects, and words with images, "in order to create concepts."[62] To fully understand racism, therefore, one has also to deal with the questions of knowledge.

Although the radical black intellectual sociologically falls in a stratum that is superficially similar to that of the Western intellectual and is educated in the same way—to master the conventions and vocabulary of the West—she or he is engaged in a discursive practice that pits learning and education against the ontological self—Du Bois's "double-consciousness." So as a consequence, as we stated earlier, the radical black intellectual becomes both a critic and a heretic. Michael Walzer suggests that the social critic is primarily engaged in an internalist argument, that she or he, using Gramsci's formulation, initiates a process of "differentiation and change in the relative weight that the elements of the old ideologies used to possess."[63] In other words, the social critic calls forth the contradictions of the regime by exploding its ideological conceptions of social life. This might mean the expansion of new concepts and political knowledge, but this form of criticism operates within an already defined discursive field.

We have already established that for the radical black intellectual there is the performance of a double negative—there is a double critique that makes possible a different form of criticism. Extending Gilbert Ryle's distinction between thick and thin descriptions, I want to propose that the kind of internal criticism which Walzer suggests is a "thin" form of criticism. This "thin" criticism is enclosed within the discursive framework. Its force is to open the dominant ideology to its own hypocrisy. "Thin" criticism does not destabilize the epistemic field of the dominant discursive order. So, for example, in Western political philosophy the critics of bourgeois equality argue that equality is primarily a political good, which ignores the way market property relations stymie social equality. These critics argue that equality in such situations becomes a foundational procedural claim. However, in a profound sense the grounds for the argument are already established as the argument continues the dichotomy between different political values, in particular that of freedom.[64] The genealogy of this debate is grounded in the intellectual and political practices of liberalism. On the other hand, if we step outside of the historical practices of liberalism and its rationalities to examine the history of rebellions and movements against racial slavery/oppression and colonialism, it would suggest that the dichotomy between these political values is a false one.

Thus "thin" criticism remains within the established boundaries, seeking to radicalize political values rather than to create new meanings. For black radical intellectual, criticism challenges the knowledge framework and categories of the discursive order. It does this in three steps. The first is the call for *discursive representation.* The second is the *rewriting* of history. The third is to establish *different values* for the practice of politics. This form of criticism, then, has the potential to create new radical practices; it is "thick" criticism, which troubles the waters. Because the black radical intellectual practices this form of criticism, she or he is a heretic.

Conclusion

Michel de Certeau makes the point that modern European history began as an exercise in self-reflection at the time of the European voyages.[65] History as the rendering of an account of self is both heuristic and imaginative. Historical meanings, we know, are present constructions. In other words, the questions of history are not posed by the past but by the present. It is from this standpoint that we should begin to grapple with the historical methodologies of *The Black Jacobins* and *Black Reconstruction.* In the last chapter of *Black Reconstruction,* Du Bois flays the American historical profession for what he calls the "propaganda of history." Detailing the historical works of the period, he queries whether or not history as practiced by American historians can be scientific. At first blush it seems that Du Bois is reaching for a Rankean formulation of history as "objective truth." But I wish to suggest that that for Du Bois, truth is not a quality external to human action and subjectivity, but instead is the correction of the racist propaganda with which the American historical profession was engaged at the time. Du Bois asks how far truth is ascertainable, and goes on to speak of the moral wrongs of slavery, which are neglected by American historians. The "propaganda of history" is, then, racist historical knowledge.

Du Bois, like James, seems to have had a conception of historical writing in which the reesearch was the search for facts akin to formal science, and the writing was an art. For Du Bois, history was also about interpretation. He proclaims in *Black Reconstruction,* in a note to the reader: "This book will seek to tell and interpret."[66] It is of interest to note that in one of his last major works, *Black Flame* (1957, 1959), Du Bois revisited the issues of historical knowledge: "After action and feeling and reflection are long past, then from writing and memory we secure some picture of the total truth, but it will be . . . imperfect with much omitted, much forgetting, much distorted. . . . There is but one way to meet this clouding of the facts and that is by the use of the imagination where documented and personal experience are lacking."[67] For Du Bois, when he was writing *Black Reconstruction,* the documentary evidence was there for the writing of *historical truth.*

Black Reconstruction and *The Black Jacobins* set out to challenge forms of historical knowledge. In doing so, they expanded our understandings of human social and political knowledges. They attempted to confront the *epistemic erasure* of the Western intellectual tradition. Their example offers humanity hope not only for reflective self-understanding but also for a renewal of the logic of the African slaves' fight for freedom. In the final analysis, we have to ask ourselves what issues these two theorists raised that are still relevant to the present world. I suggest that the most obvious ones surround the issues of race and the legacies of colonialism. But there is something more. If many radical critiques of modernity focused on questions of exploitation, human alienation, and politics as involving issues of political obligation, sovereign self, and citizenship, the works of black radical theorists like James and Du Bois shift our gaze to questions of domination, oppression, and politics as a practice of freedom. They offer a different optic on the possibilities of human emancipation.

CHAPTER **4**

Julius Nyerere
Radical African Humanism, Equality, and Decolonialization

Mtu ni Watu. A human being is a human being
because of other human beings.
—KiSwahili precept

There is no nation in the world which can teach
the Africans how to liberate themselves.
—The Mwongozo-TANU Guidelines, 1971

Introduction

During the 1970s two political texts animated much debate and controversy within the twentieth-century African anticolonial tradition: *Ujamaa*
(1962) and *The Arusha Declaration* (1967). Both texts are deeply embedded within the politics of Tanzanian society, yet they became exemplar anticolonial writings, read and studied in many parts of the anticolonial
world outside of Africa. C. L. R. James, whose life and political work
spanned much of the anticolonial moment in twentieth-century world
history, remarked in the revised edition of his *History of Negro Revolt*, originally published in 1938, that *The Arusha Declaration* was "something new
in the history of political thought."[1] In spite of this, neither political document is found in any discussion of general political thought. One reason
obviously lies in the way in which the academy continues to reflect on and
think about Africa, relegating the African experience to the bottom of a
totem pole of hierarchical knowledge. This has meant, in political thought
and theory, the utter neglect of any serious study of the political thought of
individuals involved in the anticolonial movements or of the movements
themselves.[2]

The anticolonial movements (African, Caribbean, and Indian) organized in what has been loosely called the Third World shattered the empires of the Old World and reordered the Westphalian political order of nation-states. If the late nineteenth century was in Eric Hobsbawm's phrase the "Age of Empire," then political logic would suggest that the collapse of these empires was a central feature of world politics in the mid-twentieth century, having profound meanings not only for the structural relationships of nation-states but for political thought as well. Julius Nyerere put some of these matters well in a 1998 interview. Asked what he thought was the significance of the twentieth-century anticolonial movement, Nyerere stated:

> There are two fundamental things that the anti-colonial liberation movement contributed to humanity. The first is simply that the suffering of a whole chunk of human beings through the actions of others was halted. The arrogance of one group of people in lording it over the human race . . . was challenged and discredited . . . that was a positive contribution made by the liberation struggle to all humanity.[3]

But all of this seems to be lost on contemporary political thought and theory.[4] One might argue that one possible reason for this lacuna has been the collapse of many radical anticolonial projects, and that the stories of these "failures" are far important things to think about than examining what was being attempted. But the study of political thought and theory has never been only about success or failure. However, there is a way in which the "failed" anticolonial projects are studied that gives succor to the theses about Africa as a "dark continent" in dire need of rescuing by the programs of multilateral agencies.[5] From this stance in the field of comparative politics, the key frame for African political studies is democracy. Not a form of democracy in which the mass of the population exercises control over their lives, but forms of Western representative democracy in which political equality, namely the vote, is the apex of democratic values. From such frames there is no real examination of African political thought or African political philosophy as the general position seems to be, what on earth can we learn from the "dark, hopeless continent"?[6]

It is the contention of this essay that many of the radical national liberation movements in the mid-twentieth century were important moments both in world history and in the *history of political thought.* Using the political thought and practices of Julius Nyerere, and focusing on the two political documents *Ujamaa* and *Arusha,* with some reference to a third, *The Rational Choice,*[7] we will attempt to explore three central ideational features of the African anticolonial movements: African humanism, African nationalism, and African socialism. In conducting this exploration, we will see how each of these systems of political thought reflected upon the African political experience, and their connection to a larger intellectual tradition that we have been calling the black radical intellectual tradition.

In the study of African political thought, we encounter the paradigms of tradition versus modernity and political theory versus political ideology. We now turn to examine some of these ideas and their relationship to the issues of tradition.

Tradition and Modernity

Epistemic erasure means, of course, that no real weight is given to African ideas and theories because political theory and philosophy are the subjects of the rational West.[8] The basis of this argument is the idea that there exists no worthwhile African intellectual history or history of ideas from which fruitful political abstract ideas can be gleaned. Thus, African political thinkers only copy Western political thought or, at best, adapt various elements of modern Western thought to specific contexts. The argument further runs that African ideas, if they exist, are "traditional," primarily excavated by anthropological methods and thereby having no intrinsic value for political thought or theory. When combined, these two arguments result in the conception that African political thought is derivative, and can be understood only within some paradigmatic framework of "tradition" and "modernity." In this frame, twentieth-century African intellectual history is then read as a contestation between the forces of "tradition" and those of "modernity." In the words of Robert July, "Was modern Africa to be cast in the mould of the West or would she emerge unmistakably African, an ancient culture reborn in the modern idiom?"[9]

This modernity/tradition paradigm is pervasive in studies of African thought. When Western political categories are used to think about Africa, they squeeze Africa into this frame of polarity without any investigation of the baggage of the paradigm This has deleterious effects upon our understanding of Africa. One problem with the paradigm is its roots in modernist sociological and anthropological discourses and practices. Within this paradigm, tradition is often viewed as static, frozen, and unchanging, compared to modernity, which is marked by constant change, the dominance of science and rationality. With reference to Africa, tradition then comes to mean not just a past but *the unchanging past*. Terence Ranger has ably demonstrated how the invention of this particular view of tradition creates profound misunderstandings about African societies. Using one element of political symbolism to make his point, Ranger argues:

> European invented traditions were marked by their inflexibility . . .
> [while African societies] had certainly valued custom and continu-
> ity but custom was loosely defined and infinitely flexible. . . . More-
> over, there rarely existed in fact the closed corporate consensual
> system which came to be accepted as characteristic of "traditional"
> Africa.[10]

Thus one so-called paradox to sort out in the study of African political
thought and theory is what, if anything, is the role of "traditional." It is a
crucial issue. Many African political thinkers refer to "traditional" African
democracy or, in the case of Nyerere, to "traditional" African socialism.
When they do this, what does it mean? Does the political language of "tradition" refer to a return to the precolonial past or an intellectual excavation of
ideas that shaped precolonial Africa? Is this excavation a process of historical vindication or an attempt to grapple with the specific features of African
society before colonial conquest? Or is the political language of "tradition" a
speech act in which the political speaker and thinker engages an audience in
a political voyage in which the reclamation of a legitimate African past becomes an integral part of the search for a postcolonial future?

Debates in contemporary historiography have made us aware that our
discussions of the past are animated by present questions,[11] so there is no
authentic and definitive recovery of the past nor any unchanging "tradition." Thus, what we have to grapple with in this hermeneutical exercise is
not so much the *accuracy* of the representations of the past offered by these
African political thinkers in their texts and speeches, but rather *how* the
past and the conception of tradition functioned in their political thought.
Finally, we should remind ourselves that the polarities of "modernity" and
tradition were deployed by colonial political practices. By the early twentieth century, colonial powers had developed theories of modernization on
the African continent. Central to these theories was a kind of education
that would form a particular kind of character and, therefore, colonial subject. The British colonial policy for education in Africa, published in 1925,
stated in part that one of its objectives was "the formation of habits of
industry, of truthfulness, of manliness, of readiness for social service and
of disciplined cooperation, [as] the foundation of character."[12] This idea
of creating a certain kind of African subject has never quite left Western
thought.

In intellectual history one examines a tradition both for the questions it
asked and for the answers given. Inside an intellectual tradition, questions
are asked from within the framework of lived experiences, and certainly
political questions are asked within the context of the problems of political
life. This makes for a direct relationship between political life and political

knowledge, but the two are not the same thing. Political knowledge as answers to political questions has been, in many cases, given autonomous room in Western political theory, but against a concrete background. William Kymlicka has accurately observed that "Most Western political theorists have operated with an idealized model of the polis."[13] This idealized model of the polis is one that James Tully describes as "the ways in which modern subjects (individuals and groups) should be treated as free and equal and cooperate under the immanent and regulative ideals of the rule of law and constitutionalism on the one hand and popular sovereignty and democratic self-determination on the other."[14] The unproblematic site of the "idealized polis" is a normative liberal state, the "unseen hand" that scripts the template for modern Western political theory.

On the other hand, many twentieth-century anticolonial African thinkers lived under a "command" colonial state.[15] Their angle of approach and the questions they ask of political theory are therefore different. This different angle is rooted in the nature of colonial power, polity, political economy, and episteme. V. Y. Mudimbe has described well the multilayered nature of the colonial project. He argues that its organization meant three things: "the procedures of acquiring, distributing and exploiting lands in colonies; the policies of domesticating natives; and the manner of managing ancient organizations and implementing new modes of production."[16] Radical anticolonial politics in the postindependence period therefore had to grapple with how to reverse all the above processes while organizing political power; to negotiate new modes of production, all the while considering what political knowledge could accomplish these things. This is what led to the situation whereby there was often a close fit between political theory and political practice in the anticolonial movements.

Political Theory and Ideology

Today much of Western political theory continues to operate from the stance that theoretical political knowledge does not have to be integrated into political practice. However, for African political thinkers, political practice is central. This feature of African political thought has led many commentators to argue that African political thought and theory are really ideology.[17] Such a view is reflective of an established hierarchy of political reason. In its present form this hierarchy draws its substance from three mid-twentieth-century sources: Leo Strauss's lecture "What Is Political Philosophy?";[18] the arguments generated by Peter Laslett's pronouncement of the death of political theory, and Isaiah Berlin's 1961 essay "Does Political Theory Still Exist?"[19] At the heart of these debates were issues surrounding the relationship of empirical political science to positivism and

the response of political philosophy to the dominance of analytical philosophy. In the end, this debate made distinctions (some of them dubious)
between what became known as ideology, political ideas, political theory,
and political philosophy. In particular, Strauss made two distinctions, one
between political thought and political philosophy, and the other between
political theory and political philosophy:

> Political thought [is] the reflection on, or the exposition of, politi-
> cal ideas . . . all political philosophy is political thought but not all
> political thought is political philosophy. Political thought is . . . in-
> different to the distinction between opinion and knowledge . . . but
> political philosophy is the conscious, coherent and relentless effort
> to replace opinions about political fundamentals by knowledge re-
> garding them.[20]

In this hierarchy of political reason, the study of political philosophy is
the study of the classical Western thought in a manner that Quentin Skinner has called "conceptual parochialism."[21] While for Skinner "conceptual
parochialism" does not allow for interpretative detail of the meanings of
political language used in different contexts, he limits himself to the historical periods of Western thought. On the other hand, I would argue that
the epistemic narrowness of Western thought in general leads to an overall
"conceptual parochialism" which then passes for political universalism.
The hierarchy of political reason alongside this kind of "conceptual
parochialism" renders twentieth-century African political thought primarily as political discourses of nationalism or Marxism . . . therefore as ideology.[22] The only credence allowed for the generation of a distinctive African
political thought is given to the discourses about Negritude, and again this
is seen as ideology, not rising to the level of political theory in coherence or
sophistication.[23]

In summary, then, Western political thought examines African political
thought not as theory but as ideology. From this position, African political
thought might be studied for what it can tell us about the relationships between institutions, ideas, policies, and politics in Africa, but is of no relevance to the larger questions of political knowledge and the complex problems of political life.[24]

But perhaps the narrow episteme is only one foundational difficulty
with Western political theory. Another, I would argue, has been identified
by Hannah Arendt. She has argued that a major difficulty with the Western
political canon is the way in which it splits philosophy from the activity of
politics. She remarks that from its inception, Western political thought developed a "dichotomy between seeing the truth in solitude and remoteness
and being caught in the relationships and relativities of human affairs."[25]

Although in Arendt's analysis much of the "authoritative dichotomy" in Western political thought begins to be broken with the thinking of "Kierkegaard, Marx and Nietzsche," I would suggest that in the current discipline of political theory this dichotomy has been further formalized. The recognition of this has led to calls for the "politicizing of theory."[26] These calls operate from the fruitful perspective that there should be links between politics as practice and politics as theory, and that perhaps political theory in part should be critical reflections on these practices. If we think about politics as a form of relational activity where speech, words, language, and action are central in the human labor to construct modes of living, then the general systematic ideas that emerge from this activity, and that oftentimes have a dialectical relationship to each other, can indeed be called political theory.

From this ground I want to offer an examination of some of the dimensions of the political thought of Julius Nyerere. The effort here is not an attempt to command universalism for Nyerere's thought. Instead, it is to open one possible door for us to think about the study of political theory as a practice.

African Socialism

Commentators on radical African political thought typically begin their discussions with a review of Marxist and socialist figures. Conventionally, these include Amilcar Cabral, Frantz Fanon, Samora Machel, Eduardo Mondlane, and Léopold Senghor. Kwame Nkrumah straddles the socialist and Marxist currents, but his 1970 text, *Class Struggle in Africa,* finally locates him in the latter. Julius Nyerere is typically considered as belonging to the socialist wing of this movement. In mid-twentieth-century Africa the ideological configuration of African socialism was a very complex one. Such was its complexity that Walter Rodney suggested that "When 'African Socialism' was in vogue early in 1960s it [was] comprised of . . . interpretations ranging from a wish to see a socialist society in Africa to a desire to maintain the status quo of neo-colonialism."[27]

This elasticity of "African socialism" requires us to probe its particular expressions before we formulate political judgment. There are two moves involved in this operation. The first is to explore the meaning of the African appellation. The questions here are: Was the appellation used to demonstrate a unique vision of socialism while signaling affinity with the main tenets of Marxist political theory? Or was it a nomenclature that expressed a form of African nationalism which was then ideologically manipulated to maintain the status quo? In other words, was "African socialism" a form of politics that the Jamaican political scientist Louis Lindsay has called "the politics of symbolic manipulation"?[28] The second move requires us to grapple with the different elements that precisely constituted African socialism in its different sites. In the case of Nyerere this will allow us to understand how he interpreted socialism, and whether or not that understanding, along with its African inflection, created a distinctive anti-colonial political theory. In performing these moves, we will of necessity take into account some of the critical voices who were part of the wider political and intellectual milieu established in Dar-es-Salaam during the first period of Tanzanian political independence, for both *Ujamaa* and *The Arusha Declaration* had very sharp critics.

Nyerere's Political Thought

Nyerere developed a coherent theory about the nature of politics and the ways in which a polity should be organized. At the foundation of his political theory was the conception that the overarching good of a human polity was that of equality. One unusual feature of this theory was its inter-active development as part of a larger political dialogue between elements of Tanzanian society.[29] This dialogue created a situation that is not often seen in the history of political thought. It is one whereby a thinker's theory becomes a central element of the ideology of the society through a series of debates and political actions. Some might argue that forms of Marxism also became institutionalized after the 1917 Russian Revolution under the leadership of the Bolsheviks, or that all states entrench a state ideology. However, I want to point to a much more fluid process here, one in which an explicit political theory is being shaped by the cut and thrust of a rich societal political discourse. This factor has contributed to studies of Nyerere's thought as ideology.

Given this rich dynamic of political conversations and dialogue, two other things come to the fore. First is the importance of the word and, alongside that, language. In this regard it is important to note that KiSwahili becomes not only Tanzania's national language but also the pre-ferred language of political speech and discourse. If, as argued earlier, politics is a practice in which speech and language are foundational, then the very fact that the chosen language of political speech and discourse is different from those of the two colonizers, German and English, means that words and their political meanings take on a special import. Certainly it means that the political thinker has to perform a set of alternative linguistic and theoretical operations in order to express a radical theory different from the hegemonic order. The linguistic operation to express a theory of a polity based on equality in a colonial order requires tapping into an order of the symbolic and linguistic world different from the ones created by the colonial power. The second matter is the recognition that the close relationship in a dialogue between a thinker and the society often requires that we make distinctions between what is of lasting theoretical value and what is of tactical value. In studying aspects of the political theory of Nyerere, since it is clear that his strategic objective was the creation of a polity based on human equality, it is this strategic objective which will allow us to distinguish between the tactical and theoretical concerns. With these caveats we can now proceed.

Julius Nyerere published many political texts.[30] One of these documents, *Ujamaa: The Basis of African Socialism*, fundamentally changed the terms of Tanzanian mainstream political discourse. It was the first in a long series of political documents produced by Nyerere in the period 1962–1974. Next came *The Arusha Declaration, Socialism and Rural Development, The Varied Paths to Socialism,* and *The Purpose Is Man,* all in 1967. These were followed by documents on the relationship between freedom and development, the nature of the postcolonial development process, and, in 1974, *The Rational Choice: Capitalism or Socialism.* The texts we have chosen to examine are the central elements of his thought that have been characterized as different strains of African socialism and African humanism.[31]

Ujamaa begins with a declaration. "Socialism," it says, "like democracy, is an attitude of mind."[32] There are a couple of things that strike one here. In the first place, Nyerere is not using the words "socialism" and "democracy" to describe political patterns or systems. Second is his focus on the subjective. These two things should alert us that what is being attempted here is not a conventional description of socialism. The document goes further, stating that socialism does not have anything to do with wealth creation, and proclaims, "Destitute people can become potential capitalist-exploiters of their fellow human beings. A millionaire can equally well be a socialist."[33] Later in the document Nyerere clarifies this point by suggesting that a socialist millionaire is "a contradiction in terms."[34] Then the document makes one of its most distinguishing comments: "The basic difference between a socialist society and a capitalist society does not lie in their methods of producing wealth, but in the way that wealth is distributed."[35]

At this point I am not concerned about the differences between conventional socialist or Marxist arguments about modes of production, and whether or not Nyerere is really following Marxism. Rather, I want to draw our attention to two things. First are the ways in which Nyerere is setting up the arguments, his emphasis upon the subjective element and his statement that the inequities of wealth are not a problem of production but of distribution. The second feature is Nyerere's reference to capitalism and how, even though he is drawing some contrasts, these are not in the realm of economics but of the ethical: "There must be something wrong in a society where one man, however hard working or clever he may be can acquire as great a 'reward' as a thousand of his fellows can acquire between them."[36] I want to suggest that in this early section of the text, Nyerere is laying the basis for his chief political argument and concern—How does one establish a society of human equality in an African postcolonial context? It is his search for the conditions of a polity of human equality that leads him to introduce the idea of *ujamaa*.

This preoccupation with a polity of equality leads Nyerere to argue that "traditional" African society was constructed along the following lines: "Both the 'rich' and the 'poor' individual were completely secure in African society . . . the capitalist or the landed exploiter [was] unknown to traditional African society."[37] From this standpoint Nyerere then suggests that one possible basis for a polity of equality was for the members of the society to recover this "traditional" attitude:

> Our first step, therefore must be to reeducate ourselves; to regain our former attitude of mind. In our traditional African society we were individuals within a community. We took care of the community, and the community took care of us. We neither needed nor wished to exploit our fellow men.[38]

It is now obvious what Nyerere is doing here. By beginning with the definition of socialism as a mental attitude, he recognizes that colonialism was a knowledge regime which attempted to create new subjects, so his call for reeducation is a call for the decolonialization of the political mind. At this point it is not so important if his descriptions of African society are accurate (he later gives more elaborate descriptions, and we will discuss these); what *is* important is that in this political statement Nyerere establishes two grounds for a polity of equality. The first is intellectual decolonization, and the second is the relationship between the individual and the community. Nyerere then suggests that colonialism brought into Tanzania a different set of concepts which changed some of the ways in which property and wealth were understood. For example, he opines that colonialism changed the African concept of land, making the "concept of land . . . a marketable commodity."[39] He calls historical African society "tribal socialism," and argues that while European socialism was born out of the conflict between what he calls the "Agrarian Revolution" and the "Industrial Revolution," "tribal socialism," on the other hand, was able to emerge because of the absence of classes: "It did not start from the existence of conflicting 'classes' in society. Indeed I doubt if the equivalent for the word 'exists' in any indigenous language . . . the foundation, and the objective, of African socialism is the extended family."[40]

There is one other aspect of this first enunciation of "African socialism" that we might find instructive, Nyerere's distinction between worker as proletariat in the Marxist sense and the ethic of work:

> In traditional African society everybody was a worker. There was no other way of earning a living for the community. Even the elder, who appeared to be enjoying himself without doing any work and for whom everybody else appeared to be working, had, in fact worked hard all his younger days. . . . I do not use the word "worker" simply as opposed to employer.[41]

In this section of the statement Nyerere is attempting to get at the nature of work that had been created under British colonialism, one in which there was a huge chasm between the educated elite and the mass of the population, partly centered on distinctions between manual and mental labor. Sensitive all the time to this fact, Nyerere used the occasion of this first political statement to signal the necessity for change in the relationship between the elite and the mass of the population.

In *Ujamaa,* Nyerere advances a theory of African societal evolution distinct from that of Europe. At the same time, while engaging with European socialist thought, he is attempting to locate socialism as a universal feature of human polity—but doing so while suggesting that there are distinctive paths to this political objective. In this regard Nyerere argues that Africa can draw from its "traditional" heritage and develop its own form of socialism—*ujamaa.* Since *ujamaa* means "family" in KiSwahili, it is clear that Nyerere was engaged in a quest for an indigenous African political and social tradition which could be reclaimed in the postcolonial period. At this point Nyerere was operating under an understanding of precolonial African society as one in which social groups formally organized themselves around extended families. From this position *ujamaa* was not just a set of political ideas, but a call for the revitalization of what he considered to be a unique feature of African society. However, there were many problems with this conception, as we shall see.

Nyerere's preoccupation with human equality allowed him to translate socialism as primarily a doctrine of equality, not of class struggle, or a dictatorship of the proletariat, or a mode of economic production. In a 1967 speech at Dar-es-Salaam University, he declared:

> Socialism . . . is not simply a matter of methods of production. They are part of it but not all of it. The essence of socialism is the practical acceptance of human equality. That is to say, every man's equal right to a decent life before any individual has any surplus above his needs; his equal right to participate in Government; and

his equal responsibility to work and contribute to the society to the limit of his ability.[42]

I wish to suggest that this definition of the relationship between socialism and human equality was not just a result of Nyerere's religious beliefs,[43] but also an expression of a sentiment that had become very pervasive in radical anticolonial thought: the primacy of the human. This concern with the human and the setting forth of a new man was a central ingredient of radical anticolonial thought, and later we will need to probe how this "humanism" was similar to or different from Europe's. For now we need to note that it is this notion of the primacy of the human, deeply embedded within African cosmologies, which animates Nyerere' political thought.

In 1968, when he reflected on *ujamaa*, Nyerere proclaimed:

> The word "ujamaa" was chosen for special reasons. First, it is an African word and thus emphasizes the African-ness of the policies we intend to follow. Second, its literal meaning is "family-hood," so that it brings to the mind of our people the idea of mutual involvement in the family as we know it. By the use of the word "ujamaa," therefore we state that for us socialism involves building on the foundation of our past, and building also to our own design.[44]

As an attempt to develop an indigenous political discourse *ujamaa* attracted both critics and supporters. For the Marxist left, the denial of class struggle was particularly annoying, and the idea was criticized as belonging to the current of nineteenth-century prescientific socialism. Walter Rodney, however, took up the cudgels in support of *ujamaa*. In his 1971 article on the subject, Rodney suggests that it was possible to identify "Tanzanian *Ujamaa* with Scientific Socialism in certain ideological essentials."[45] He goes on to argue that a nondogmatic reading of Marx and Lenin would demonstrate that it was possible for socialism to be arrived at without having to go through extensive capitalist industrial production. He cites as his example Marx's discussion of nineteenth-century Russian society, and asserts that Marx's and Engels's understanding of historical materialism was much more flexible than that of contemporary Marxists: ". . . they were implying a single mechanical line of historical progression and they actually deny this in the course of the discussion. . . . Marx explained that his description of the historical inevitability of the foundation of the capitalist system was expressly limited to the countries of Western Europe."[46] The second leg of Rodney's argument is that the Tanzanians were attempting to find what he called "the principal motion" of their own society. For other left critics, *ujamaa* ignored the development of social classes during colonialism and drew a far too romantic picture of the African past.

These critics suggested that Nyerere's "tribal socialism" was really the Marxist definition of the stage of primitive communalism, and that he was seeking to resuscitate a past which never quite existed.[47]

In general, it is fair to say that the critiques of Nyerere's thought at this time were focused on the applicability of *ujamaa* to Tanzanian society. Today those critiques have been bolstered by writings that demonstrate how the implementation of the project as it translated in large-scale, planned villagization was flawed.[48] What I wish to focus on at this point is the ways in which Nyerere raises a fundamental point in the construction of any polity, the relationship between the individual and the community. It is true that Nyerere thinks about this issue within the framework of his own understanding of the nature of an African past. However, by raising it in the first major promulgation of *ujamaa*, he is signaling that questions of human equality are not separate from this issue. Part of the reason for this may reside in the ethnic composition of the country, with its more than 120 ethnic groups and the subsequent political requirements of national unity. Another part was his early attempt to erode the ground for the emergence of a native middle class who would then use state power as a vehicle for capital accumulation. But whatever the reason, this particular problem stayed with him for some time. In the end, during the 1970s Nyerere developed a set of ideas about the political party, its role, and the highest good of the individual in which the community always trumped the individual. For postindependence Tanzania, attempting to come grips with the legacies of colonial rule, this kind of political thinking was contrary to the political knowledge of colonial rule.

Colonial political rationality was rooted in coercion and "omnipotence." Achille Mbembe makes the point that colonial rule did "not rest on any covenants. . . . It does not compromise on its rights; on the contrary, it plunders its object and deprives it of what used to be its own."[49] This means that colonial political rationality shattered stable communities, and then attempted to reorganize the subjects of these communities. In postindependence Tanzania, Nyerere was concerned about the unity between individual and community in two senses. In the first he focused on restoring an African self that was able to destroy the harm and prejudices against the native which colonialism had wrought. And second, he wished to create, in sharp contradiction to the colonial regime, a notion of the common good. This notion of the common good was to be a way of life, not a search for private gain. Nyerere did not think that there was neutrality in an individual's relationship to society, particularly, he would argue, in any society that was not wealthy. In Nyerere's thought, the human self was deeply embedded in society:

> Man's existence in society involves an inevitable and inescapable conflict—a conflict of his own desires. For every individual really

wants two things: freedom to pursue his own interests . . . at the same time he wants freedoms which can only be obtained through life in society. . . . This means that neither the good of the individual as such nor the group as such, can always be the determining factor in society's decision. Both have constantly to be served. Yet underlying everything must be a consciousness that the purpose of society . . . must be individual man. . . . It is not any particular man who is the justification for society . . . it is every man, equally with every other man. . . . Thus the ideal society is based on human equality and on the combination of the freedom and unity of its members.[50]

From this perspective, the common good to be pursued was human equality. "Traditional" African society, then, functioned in Nyerere's thought as a site where human equality was present. In his efforts to develop an indigenous African political thought, this was an advantage. In 1967, five years after the promulgation of *ujamaa,* and pushed by his critics, Nyerere redefined the character of what he had earlier called "tribal socialism." Pointing to what he called "inadequacies of the traditional system," he stated that in this system at least one form of inequality prevailed: "Although we try to hide the fact, and despite the exaggeration which our critics have frequently indulged in, it is true to say that women in traditional society were regarded as having a place in the community which was not only different, but was also . . . inferior."[51] The other feature of concern to him was the economic poverty of the traditional African system. He remarked in the same speech, "The other aspect of traditional life which we have to break away from is its poverty. Certainly there was an attractive degree of economic equality, but it was equality at a low level. The equality is good, but the level can be raised."[52]

How does Nyerere's thought compare with the other streams of "African socialism," particularly the theories of Kwame Nkrumah? Nkrumah's and Nyerere's ideas about "African socialism" run along similar lines, but with two main differences. In the first instance, Nkrumah's conception of "African socialism" is a continental one, focused on what he calls the "African personality." The "African personality," in Nkrumah's words, is "defined by the cluster of humanist principles which underlie the traditional African society."[53] Thus both thinkers are concerned with the "traditional." Nkrumah goes on to say, "When socialism is true to its purpose, it seeks a connection with the egalitarian and humanist past of the people before their social evolution was ravaged by colonialism."[54] The second difference is the attention that Nkrumah pays to Islamic and Euro-Christian influences. For Nkrumah, these cultural and ideological influences constituted a second and third ideational plank of African society, and any theory of decolonialization had to take them into account. In writing about his conception of "philosophical consciencism," he states:

> Such a philosophical statement will be born out of the crisis of African conscience confronted with three strands of present African society. Such a philosophical statement . . . will give the theoretical basis for an ideology whose aim shall be to contain the African experience of Islamic and Euro-Christian presence as well as the experience of the traditional African society, and by gestation, employ them for the harmonious growth and development of that society.[55]

Nyerere did not include these influences in his political thought. His major concern was since colonial conquest had created a society of inequities, he was required to focus on creating a polity of human equality in the postindependence period. Nkrumah, on the other hand, saw socialism as the end result of a political and economic process that would harmonize the different elements of African society. However, we would do grave injustice to Nkrumah if we did not point out that the development of "philosophical consciencism" adumbrated in 1964, was dramatically altered in his *Class Struggle in Africa* (1970). Rethinking his "African socialism" in 1970, after he had been deposed, Nkrumah writes:

> For too long social and political commentators have talked and written as though Africa lies outside the main stream of world historical development—a separate entity. . . . Myths such as "African socialism" . . . implying the existence of a brand or brands of socialism applicable to Africa alone have been propagated: and much of our history has been written in terms of socio-anthropological and historical theories as though Africa had no history prior to the colonial period.[56]

Here Nkrumah, now being profoundly influenced by Marxism, discards "African socialism" not only on practical political grounds but on theoretical grounds as well. In his eyes, Africa did not have an enclosed social system that was not influenced by capitalist modernity. Nyerere's political text, *The Rational Choice* (1974), also indicates a shift to a more conventional Marxist framework, though there are still differences between Nkrumah's Marxism and Nyerere's African socialism. Nyerere argues that while there were inequalities in precolonial African society, the colonial contact between Africa and the West occurred in the historical period when Africa was in a period of primitive communalism. He admits that colonialism created classes, and agrees that "In the modern world there are two basic systems of economic and social organization—capitalism and socialism."[57] Here it seems to me that Nyerere was being moved both by the internal debates in Tanzania and by the debates then occurring in the non-aligned movement.

We should also observe that while both Nyerere and Nkrumah argued about precolonial Africa in terms of classes, Amilcar Cabral, the Guinean revolutionary theorist, posed the problem in another way. In an extraordinary political statement delivered in Cuba at a Tricontinental Meeting, Cabral declared that "Whatever the formulas adopted on the level of international law, it is the inalienable right of every people to have its own history."[58] From this position he went on to suggest that if one argues that the class struggle was the motive force of history, then some groups of people would have no history. As a consequence, he advanced the position that perhaps the motive force of history, "of each human group is the *mode of production.*"[59]

This theoretical innovation, I would suggest, goes part of the way toward solving the knotty dilemma that faced radical African thinkers— What was the precise nature of precolonial Africa? Anthropological and historical studies of African society were still being conducted in the 1970s from the stance of Africa as a site of "primitive" man.[60] For the radical African thinker, attempting to synthesize African experiences with the theoretical tenets of Marxism or socialist thought, there was always a conundrum—what weight to give to precolonial African society. How much of African historical forms had been erased by colonial conquest? Did the institutions of customary law keep precolonial practices intact? And finally there was the question that African thinkers were forced to face, what Mahmood Mamdani calls "history by analogy."[61]

All these issues were critical to constructing a political theory about African society. One result of this set of circumstances was an "Africanist solution [that placed] Africa's age-old communities at the center of African politics."[62] This attempt was partly guided by the desire to seek local foundations for radical political practice. Senghor puts this conundrum well when he writes of "African socialism" that "A third revolution is taking place: a reaction against capitalistic and communistic materialism that will integrate moral, if not religious values with the political and economic contributions of the two great revolutions. Here the colored peoples, including the Negro African, must play their part and help construct the new planetary civilization."[63]

One preoccupation of African radical political thinkers was to define the precise nature of this contribution, and the different formulations of "African socialism" were attempts in this direction. In the case of Nyerere, it is clear that his conception of "African socialism" was guided by the overarching theme of human equality. It suffused his thought, and he always returned back to it. It was this preoccupation that led in 1967 to the *Arusha Declaration,* perhaps one of the most important documents about political life in the postcolonial world.

The Declaration

If *Ujamaa* established the theoretical framework for Tanzanian postindependence political discourse, the *Arusha Declaration* became the concrete ground on which the polity of equality could be built. The writing of the document had its origins in intense party discussions and mounting internal societal concern about the rapid emergence of a bureaucratic political class. In his discussion about the document's origins, Issa Shivji makes the point that "The Arusha Declaration was the most decisive turning point in the struggle between the petty bourgeoisie and the commercial bourgeoisie, leading to the latter's disintegration."[64] The first draft seems to have been written by Nyerere, following extensive party discussion, before it was translated into English. Reflecting in 1998 on the document, Nyerere noted:

> Maybe I would improve on the Kiswahili that was used but the Declaration is still valid. . . . Tanzania had been independent for a short time before we began to see a growing gap between the haves and have-nots in our country. A privileged group was emerging from the political leaders and bureaucrats who had been poor under colonial rule but were now beginning to use their positions in the Party and Government to enrich themselves. . . . The Arusha Declaration was what made Tanzania distinctly Tanzania . . . we made mistakes—and when one tries anything new and uncharted there are bound to be mistakes.[65]

The postindependence Tanzanian context that saw the emergence of a dominant native political class has been a major feature of all postindependence societies. The anticolonial nationalist movement was not a homogeneous one, as Amilcar Cabral points out. The colonial state was a highly bureaucratic and authoritarian one that was not dismantled by the anticolonial nationalist movement. Indeed, in many instances the political objective of the movement was to capture the colonial state and use its structures and practices to govern. Only part of the radical anticolonial movement sought to transform the state, and oftentimes this was attempted under unfavorable circumstances. If the colonial state inflated might, then in the postindependence period this might was combined with practices of accumulation. Five years after political independence, Tanzania faced this common feature of postindependence society, and since it ran in the opposite direction from the common good of human equality, it is not surprising that political discourses about human equality provoked such intense debate.[66]

The *Arusha Declaration* is divided into five sections: a review of the basic party beliefs, a discussion of the meaning of socialism, a discussion of the concept of self-reliance, a section on party membership, and a section on the leadership code. Taken together, they form a document that is a significant breakthrough in modern radical political thought. It is a comprehensive document that weaves together and integrates politics, economics, and issues of political leadership. It begins with the declaration that the objective of the party, the TANU (Tanzanian African National Union), is to build a socialist state. Of the nine political precepts that constitute TANU's meaning of socialism, six have to do with questions of equality, human dignity, the relationship of citizen to government, and individual freedoms. The remaining three have to do with economic questions and the relationship of the state to economic resources. These latter three precepts suggest that Nyerere's political thought had moved more in the direction of mainstream socialist thinking. The consistent reference in the document to "means of production" and "state ownership" confirms this point. However, the document goes on to make the point that state ownership does not constitute socialism:

A state is not socialist simply because its means of production and exchange are controlled or owned by the government ... for a country to be socialist, it is essential that its government is chosen and led by the peasants and workers themselves. If the minority governments of Rhodesia or South Africa controlled or owned the entire economies of these respective countries, the result would be a strengthening of oppression.[67]

The focus of the document's definition of socialism is the primacy given to ordinary persons and their relationship to government. The *Declaration* advocates that socialism is a belief and a way of life, and that within the African context it involved a set of political practices which supported general African liberation. In addition, the document raises the issue of the basis and meaning of development, staking out a position in the intense international debates of the period. The modernization theories of development posited notions of "stages of development." In response to this, many radical political economists argued that development required not only an assault on poverty but also the creation of a modern industrial society.[68] The *Arusha Declaration* attempted to carve out an alternative path. Noting that the country was at war with poverty and oppression, one section of the document focuses on self-reliance and points out that one of the elements of conventional development strategy is its reliance upon money. Since the country was poor, this meant that for development projects, Tanzania had to turn to external funding. However, the document observes that "Independence cannot be real if a nation depends upon gifts and loans from another for its development."[69]

Noting that previously too much emphasis had been placed on industrial and urban development, "where the real exploitation in Tanzania is that of the town dwellers exploiting the peasants,"[70] the *Declaration* proposed shifting the basis of economic development to that of the peasantry and agriculture, in recognition of the fact that Tanzania was a predominantly agricultural country. Obviously such a position was in opposition to the conventional Marxist position about the role of industrial development and modernity, and the centrality of the industrial working class. Thus, even when the *Declaration* seems to run along Marxist lines, when it comes to describing the concrete Tanzanian situation, it moves in another direction. The privileging of the peasants, the eschewing of massive industrialization, and the continuing emphasis on a definition of socialism as a way of living marked off Nyerere's political thought from Marxism.[71]

When the declaration is discussed in terms of anticolonial political thought, what is often referred to is its final section, the leadership code. The code is comprised of six elements. They range from the fact that no TANU leader associated with capitalism or feudalism could be a leader, to restricting the leadership from owning shares in companies, serving as directors in private enterprises, receiving two salaries, or being a landlord. Accustomed as we are to the porous relationships between political leadership and the economic domain, this code may seem quaint and strange. It may also might seem strange in any discussion about political thought, with some persons thinking that the code represented a concrete political detail rather than political ideas. But if we reflect upon the fact that political thought has always engaged questions of rule, who should rule, and what should be the relationship between those who rule and those who are ruled, then is not the *Arusha Declaration* an attempt to guarantee that this ruling relationship becomes one of accountability? Political rulers in general are not philosopher-kings (although we should note that Plato did speak to the corruptibility of the rulers, and required that the philosopher-king have training which would limit the potential for corruption). In the postindependence context, where the state could combine might and accumulation, political thought had to face this political problem. In Tanzania the answer to this dilemma was the *Arusha* leadership code.

As was by now the norm in Tanzania, one response to the codes and the *Declaration* was extensive debate. From the Marxist left, the analysis provided was that the *Declaration* was a "populist" one which "declares the society of workers and peasants by proclamation . . . it hates the development of the productive forces and seeks to control the distribution of commodities instead of developing production of commodities."[72] Those on the left who were less critical argued that the declaration was the "prevention of a political-economic elite dominated society, and the radical reconstruction of the power structure of economic decision."[73] Walter Rodney's article in the journal *Maji Maji* offers another assessment, arguing that the most decisive contradiction in Tanzanian society was the relationship of its economy to international capital, and thus the internal struggles were related to this fact.[74] Others of course opposed the *Declaration,* and at the international level, consternation was the order of the day because it was quickly followed by a spate of nationalizations. However, from whatever standpoint, the *Arusha Declaration* marked a watershed in Tanzanian political life and was a high-water mark in African political thought.

In what senses can we say that it contributed to African political thought? In the first instance, the *Declaration* posed the central questions of African political life in the postindependence period. If political freedom and political equality were the overarching concerns of the nationalist anticolonial movement, then in the postindependence period the questions of political life revolved around human equality and economic transformation. How to transform economies that were colonial appendages and to construct polities of human equality animated political life for the radical anticolonial thinker. These were questions of a different order than those facing western Europe and America, although the issue of human equality was, and remains, an overarching one. Both *Ujamaa* and the *Arusha Declaration* contributed to African political thought, not just because they spoke in African terms or developed a history of Africa different from that enunciated by the colonial powers, but also because they sought to answer the questions concretely posed by African political life. We have attempted to show how much the answers in these two texts revolved around human equality, so at this stage it might suit us to briefly examine how the conception of equality in *Ujamaa* and the *Arusha Declaration* was similar to or different from those which have been developed in Western political thought.

Equality, the West, and Africa

Equality and liberty are two of the most discussed political values in Western political thought. The definitions of equality are wide-ranging, and so, too, are the debates about what should constitute practices of equality. Equality has many usages and, as political language, conjures up many different things. The dominant strain of Western political thought, liberalism, organizes equality around two concepts. The first is a formal foundational equality that gives persons rights under the rule of law, rights of free practice of religion, rights of speech, and a general set of individual rights. The major purpose of these rights, it is argued, is that each person should be free to pursue his or her individual good. The second form of equality is the right to vote, political equality. However, the language of equality triggers other concerns than these two formal grounds of liberal equality. The political language of equality raises issues of social and economic inequities that recent liberal political theory has spent some time attempting to answer.[75] What is interesting about the debates is that the question of equality is more often than not raised against the ancient Greek question of the relationship of equality to justice. Aristotle states in *The Nicomachean Ethics* that "The just is equal, as all men suppose it to be, even apart from argument, and since the equal is an intermediate, the just will be an intermediate."[76] John Rawls, the most celebrated academic political philosopher in the late twentieth century, announces in his *Theory of Justice* (1971) a theory of equality that rests upon conceptions of justice. Kymlicka accurately sums up Rawls's theory thus: "Rawls ties the idea of justice to an equal share of social goods, but adds an important twist . . . inequalities are allowed if they improve my initially equal share, but they are not allowed if, as in utilitarianism, they invade my fair share."[77]

Thomas Nagel eloquently puts the problem that faces liberal theories of equality when he writes: "Modern political theories agree that society must treat its members equally in some respects . . . the natural question is how far it is desirable or possible to extend the rule of equality into the areas of social and economic relationships."[78] Nagel goes on to suggest that the real problem in political theory which shapes this dilemma is what he calls the "question about each individual's relation to himself."[79] Nagel poses the question as one of ethics, and argues for amicable resolution of the conflict between morals of personal conduct and those of social and political institutions.

Historically, in political theory this conflict has been the so-called irreconcilable dilemma between personal liberty and equality.[80] In this view, the problem is not foundational equality but the extent to which equality as distributive justice interferes with so-called individual liberty. However, like much of Western liberal political theory, the unseen hands in this debate are the overriding economic market relationships and the notion that the state stands in an adversarial relationship to the market and the free, unique desires of individuals to pursue their own good. For the Marxist, the conception of equality is based on two things. First, that foundational equality is a sham, given class relationships and power, and second, that distributional equality, even if it is achievable, does not deal with the real problem of capitalist society—the exploitation of labor. For Marx the distributional dimension of equality does not reside with any theory of egalitarianism, but rather in a context where the principle "to each according to his needs" operates.

How does all of this relate to Nyerere's theory of equality? In the first place, the assumptions are different. Although Nyerere pays a great deal of attention to the individual, he argues that what constitutes the individual is not so much his or her bundle of needs and desires but the fact that human beings are first and foremost social beings. Thus for him, the important thing is the social relationship with which individuals enter into society. Those relationships, he would argue, have to do with family, work, and the larger community. Within each of these relationships, Nyerere argues, while the individual is important, it is the social that must dominate, since it is the social that creates the conditions for full individual realization. In this sense, Nyerere sees equality not as one element in a polity but as *the* element that answers the question of all politics—How and why shall we live together? It would be fair, I think, to argue that his conception arises partly from his understanding of some of the political and social ideas of precolonial Africa, in particular the elements that constitute a human being and personhood.[81] Nyerere's understanding of equality is one reason why he does not pay great attention to questions of production. For Nyerere, wealth is a secondary feature; he focuses more on distribution than on wealth creation:

> If the pursuit of wealth clashes with things like human dignity and social equality, the latter will be given priority . . . the creation of wealth is a good thing and something which we shall have to increase. But it will cease to be good the moment wealth ceases to serve man and begins to be served by man.[82]

International Equality

Nyerere's preoccupation with human equality was the foundation for his wide-ranging advocacy of the New International Economic Order (NIEO) and the special role that the nonaligned movement would play in the midtwentieth century during the cold war. Commentators on the NIEO have observed that a primary concern of the nonaligned movement was economic equality. Political leaders like Nyerere argued that colonialism had produced three kinds of inequality: "between the colonizer and the colonized; between the races; and between the rich and poor."[83] The interna-

tional program developed by the nonaligned movement sought to reform
the world economy, again focusing on the way distribution and commodity exchange was organized. The NIEO program demanded:

1. The establishment of producer associations in "third world nations" to argue for better commodity prices
2. Local ownership of the natural resources that resided in Third
   World nations
3. Equitable transfer of technology and broader democratic control
   over multilateral and multinational organizations.[84]

I want to suggest that while Western political theory has focused on political life located within nations (although early modern political theory—for example, the work of Kant—attempted to develop what today is
being called cosmopolitanism), radical anticolonial thought ruptured the
divide between the nation and the global community as a unit of analysis.
The reason for this is not mysterious. Although the colonial project rested
on different empires, and thus each would have different historical
specifics, there was an *overall* colonial project. The General Act of the Conference of Berlin (1885), signed by all the colonial powers, including those
which did not possess any African colonies (e.g., Austria-Hungary, Swe-
den, and Norway), after agreeing that the act was a "mutual accord, to reg-
ulate the conditions in certain regions of Africa, and to assure to *all* nations
the advantages of free navigation on the two chief rivers of Africa flowing
into the Atlantic Ocean,"[85] goes on to proclaim its other objectives. The act
states that colonial powers would "without distinction of creed or nation,
protect and favor all religious, scientific or charitable institutions, and un-
dertakings created and organized for the above ends, or which aim at instructing the natives and bringing home to them the blessings of civilization."[86] This was a *global* colonial project. Anticolonial political thought
recognized this. The consequences of this agreement meant that at the
level of episteme, one has to think about colonialism in terms not only of
the colony but also of the ideational relationships between the colony and
the mother country. And certainly at the level of economic and international political relationships, what Rodney called the "disengagement from
imperialism" was not just a local act but one that required international
political action.

Nyerere's political thought demonstrated all these elements. Not only
was he committed to the NIEO and central to its initial conceptualization,
but he was very active and a leader in the African frontline states against
the South African apartheid regime. He also attempted a unity of East
African states (Uganda, Kenya, and Tanzania) in recognition of the fact
that the logic of radical anticolonialism in Africa results in Pan-Africanism.
All these elements point to a Nyerere who should now be studied within a

tradition of African political thought and that thought's contribution to general modern political theory. To establish the last leg of this point, I now want to turn to Nyerere and humanism.

Humanism and Radical African Thought

The savageries of colonialism conducted in the language of civilization and modernity stirred up a complex set of ideas about the nature of man in African anticolonial thought. This focus on "man" has been called a form of humanism. This strain of thought can be seen in the writings of Aimé Césaire when he declares in *Discourse on Colonialism* (1972): "And that is the great thing I hold against pseudo-humanism: that for too long it has diminished the rights of man, that its concept of those rights has been— and still is—narrow and fragmentary, incomplete and biased and all things considered, sordidly racist."[87] Of course we cannot forget Fanon's eloquent call: "Let us decide not to imitate Europe; let us combine our muscles and our brains in a new direction. Let us try to create the whole man, whom Europe has been incapable of bringing to triumphant birth."[88]

In the late twentieth century this call for a human was taken up by the Caribbean critic and writer Sylvia Wynter.[89] Humanism has unstable meanings ranging from its association with the "European Renaissance" to its representation as the apex in the practices of human freedom. This is not the place to unravel humanism's many tangled meanings; but I wish to focus on the Western claim that modernity inaugurated the "human" or man. The claim is an important one because what the radical anticolonial thinkers have argued is that this inauguration was a "false" start and that "man" has yet to be invented. In trying to answer the question of whether the radical anticolonial thinkers invested humanism with new meanings, it might be useful to say a few words about the relationship between Marxism and humanism. Accepting the notion that there was a human which had been invented in the period of early European modernity, Marx makes the point that "Every emancipation . . . is a restoration of the human world and of human relationships to man himself." He also makes the point that human emancipation occurs when "individual man reabsorbs in himself the abstract citizen."[90] For Marx, the invention of the human was a constant process of restoration of a wholeness to man, since exploitation, particularly the exploitation of labor, had shattered man through alienation and fragmentation. For Marx this wholeness was impeded by a series of blockages that mediated the self-realization of human qualities. In other words, like all forms of humanism that center on man, for Marx the invention of man—or, better yet, the restoring of man—is an act of emancipation which overturns obstacles. This conception of humanism within radical

Marxist thinking has a long lineage. It includes the writings of Georg Lukacs, Maurice Merleau-Ponty, and E. P. Thompson. The 1957 journal, *New Reasoner*, subtitled *A Quarterly Journal of Socialist Humanism*, tells the tale of one side of this current.[91]

However, I want to suggest that within the anticolonial intellectual tradition, the preoccupation with man was not quite the same. In Nyerere's thought, as well as in that of other thinkers, the concern is not to "restore man," but to create something new. Acts of emancipation in radical anticolonial thought set out both to overthrow the existing conception of man and to set the ground for a new one. Césaire confirms this point when he announces, "I felt that the emancipation of the Negro consisted of more than just political emancipation."[92] Césaire is making the point here that one central concern of Marx's view about the abolition of politics beyond bourgeois society and the replacement of politics by "the administration of things" was not adequate to encompass black and anticolonial liberation. So while the Marxist tradition focused on the abolition of the political and of wage labor, for the radical anticolonial thinker another set of concerns operated. One of these concerns surrounds how we think of ourselves as human. For the radical anticolonial thinker, the "man" that Europe proclaimed was implicated in a series of barbarous practices which included not only colonial conquest but also Nazism. Césaire makes the point, "At the end of formal humanism and philosophic renunciation, there is Hitler."[93]

Therefore, in attempting to construct a new basis for humanism, radical anticolonial thinkers attempted to shift some of the discursive grounds for the debate. This is clearly seen in Nyerere's view on the meaning of being a human being and the grounds he tries to establish for an African polity. When Nyerere states that the "purpose is man," or in his political statement "Freedom and Development" announces, "Development means the development of people ... [that] development brings freedom, provided it is the development of people ... [and therefore] roads, buildings, the increase of crop output, and other things of this nature, are not development,"[94] is he not implicitly elaborating a new concept of the human? This concept goes beyond what Sylvia Wynter has identified as a "bioeconomic conception of man."[95] In other words, the "man" that was invented by Europe is not only male, but a certain kind of male. He is a male in which human needs and desires are organized around a bioeconomic paradigm. What Wynter and the earlier radical anticolonial thinkers argue is that this conception of the human is deeply flawed and cannot emancipate human beings.

In the end it would seem that many radical anticolonial thinkers attempted to overthrow the conception of "bioeconomic man" by the ways in which they refigured questions of science, the economic and the human.[96] If colonialism destroyed the colonized as human, the radical humanism of the anticolonial thinker was not only about the centering the human but also, in the words of Fanon, it was also to "introduce invention into existence."[97] Thus, to talk about the humanism of radical anticolonial thinkers without any reference to these above understandings is to miss some of the complexities of radical anticolonial thought. What the conceptions of humanism in radical anticolonial thought establish is another instance of heresy that occurs in the dialectical dialogue that takes place when the anticolonial thinker enters into a relationship with Western thought.[98]

In Nyerere's humanism is a preoccupation not just with man but also with human equality. Nyerere's political praxis facilitated many reconfigurations of his political thought and it was complicated by the added dimension of the translation of many of his ideas from KiSwahili. With this said, we can now turn to the final leg of our exercise: an examination of the discursive practices that shaped Nyerere and his location within the black radical intellectual tradition.

The Shaping Influences

The critical question that faces us when we examine Nyerere's political thought is the extent to which he was influenced by the social ideas of the ethnic group into which he was born. This is a knotty question because even though one can point to the political and social forms that would have clearly influenced him, the issue of degree is an important one. We will attempt to answer this question in two ways. First, we will see the similarities in the political and social forms of Nyerere's ethnic group, the Zanaki, to his ideas of "African socialism." Second, we will pay some attention to the other influences, and then ask the admittedly imprecise question about possible ideational weighting.

Research on the Zanaki group, who lived on the eastern shore of Lake Victoria, paints a picture of a group based on a mixed economy of agriculture and cattle raising. People were grouped in homesteads, with several homesteads forming a distinct community. Central to the social life of these distinct homesteads was *erisaga,* a form of "voluntary association for mutual aid established in order to deal with recurrent conditions of uncertainty."[99] Notions of private property ownership were absent, and

> The elders of various descent groups were entitled to allocate land use, that is, they determined which individuals had the right to cultivate specific pieces of land. Individual ownership in the western sense, including the right to sell land ... for cash, was unknown among the Zanaki.[100]

Observers noted the absence of centralized governments organized around so-called chiefly authority, and the existence of a group of persons collectively called *hamati*. This group consisted of "traditional male elders . . . who had distinguished themselves by exceptional debating skills, [and] served as leading mediators and judges."[101] It seems also that for this group the preferred method for solving disputes was "lengthy and exhaustive discussion among the elders, the object was a consensual resolution of the problem."[102] Therefore, central to this group was a socially defined gerontocracy. Among the Zanaki one important social value was generosity. An anthropological study noted that "The highest form of social prestige and *nyangi* can be obtained only through generosity—voluntarily parting with a portion of one's wealth."[103]

It is clear from these descriptions that Nyerere's conceptualization of precolonial African society was rooted in his own existential experiences. German colonialism, accustomed to centralized state rule, upon conquest established individual chiefs in eastern Africa. Nyerere comments, "If you study the sociology of the population in the Lake Victoria region, the tribes to the south and to the west have chiefs, but the tribes to the east traditionally had no chiefs. But the Germans came and they had [the] fixed idea that every tribe has a chief."[104] However, the entire Tanzanian society was not of that ilk. Therefore, what Nyerere seems to have done was to extrapolate primarily from the Zanaki social and political experience, and to frame this as a Tanzanian experience. The myriad groups and societies that comprised precolonial Africa had different forms of social and political organization, and therefore different political and social ideas. There was no single "authentic" precolonial Africa that could be seized upon. So although there is no doubt that the Zanaki social principles profoundly shaped Nyerere's political thought, the question one has to ask is whether or not those social principles applied to all the ethnic groups of Tanzania. Did all of the more than 120 ethnic groups have the same historical memory? The evidence suggests that this was not so, which means that even though there was robust debate about the ideas of *Ujamaa* and *Arusha,* there were instances in which the debate might not have resonated with other ethnic groups.[105]

Nyerere makes the point that when he was in teachers college, he came across the writings of John Stuart Mill, particularly his work on the subjugation of women. Mill's work on women's subjugation struck a chord in Nyerere's thought because even though women in many cases were diviners in the Zanaki group, the outstanding feature of that group's inequality was the common oppressed position of the women who did not belong to the diviner group. Nyerere came to the attention of Tanganyika's colonial education authorities when his essay on the subjection of women won a prize. He himself admits that Mill's work influenced him in another way as well—the notion of individual rights. However, it is clear that Nyerere did not place individual rights above the questions of the social, and sought to integrate them into a theory about human equality. Certainly his conception of politics and the role of the political party was different from that of Mill. Thus, we have to conclude that the influence of Mill was limited.

The other major intellectual and political influence on Nyerere was Fabian socialism. The Fabian Colonial Bureau was formed in 1940 under the leadership of a British Labour Party member of Parliament, Arthur Creech-Jones. Its main purpose was to "collect and coordinate information concerning activities in the dependencies and to foster popular demand within the home office for the dissolution of the Empire."[106] The dissolution of the empire was based on the liberal reform notion that an empire based upon mercantilism was at an end and should now be replaced with a British commonwealth of self-governing states. However, the pace of self-government was to be determined by the colonial power. Thus, for example, when a left-wing member of Parliament, Fenner Brockway, argued in 1956 that Tanganyika was ready for independence, the Fabian Bureau retorted that this statement was premature.[107] The influence of Fabianism, I would argue, lay more in the realm of political tactics.

Many times during the period 1958–1959 the Tanganyikan nationalist movement appeared before this committee, seeking support in its struggle for decolonization, and there is no doubt that over some issues alliances were made. What is interesting to note in Nyerere's political career is that six weeks after independence was gained on January 22, 1962, he resigned from the leadership of the government and spent nine months in rural Tanzania. It was in the aftermath of these nine months that *Ujamaa* was produced. Even though there seem to have been tactical matters that led to his resignation, it would also appear that, on the cusp of political independence, he himself was unclear on the direction in which to proceed. The nine months in the rural areas seem also to have refocused his political ideas.

The final political and intellectual influence on Nyerere was his education at Edinburgh University. His course of study included political economy, moral philosophy, British history, and English literature. Importantly, Nyerere was part of a group of anticolonial Africans and West Indians who were excited in the aftermath of the 1945 Manchester Pan-African Congress and the constitution of independent India.[108]

Nyerere seems to have picked up on the ideas of socialism that were swirling around the anticolonial movement during that period. However, I wish to suggest that his primary concern while a student was political independence, and that only at the moment of decolonialization did he face an entirely new problem—how to build a new society after the withdrawal of the colonial power. It is this problem that led him to a set of theoretical understandings about politics, the good, and human equality.

Conclusion

So how do we locate Nyerere? It is clear that Nyerere belongs to the line of Africana thinkers who in the postcolonial period grappled with the nature of politics in African and colonial societies, carried out a set of political practices, and wrote political documents that promulgate visions of a new society. One characteristic of these thinkers was the way they engaged their societies in a series of political discourses. This was political thought and theory being developed in direct relation to the practices of decolonization. Such a move required two things on the part of these thinkers—a willingness to question the orthodoxy of political thought and the capacity to begin to understand their own societies on their own terms. This was not an easy venture, because one had to operate at the daily level of political life and also engage in reflection and political work. Thus political discourse was being continuously reshaped. In this, Nyerere was an outstanding figure. His elaborated political theory today stands as the result of a heretic practice that attempted to overthrow the Western framework about the natural nature of the human, one in which individual material wants trump the social. In the end his heresy made him a consistent theorist of the Swahili precept that a human being is a human being because of other human beings.

CHAPTER 5

Walter Rodney
Groundings, Revolution, and the Politics of Postcoloniality

> *We*
> *Fight the "mimic men"*
> *Who fill the seats*
> *Of those who were*
> *Our masters*
> *Sugar so sweet*
> *Its working so bitter.*
> —Evelyne, in *Walter Rodney: Poetic Tributes*

Introduction

Writing about Walter Rodney evokes many things. For many African and Caribbean radicals, he was the iconic revolutionary of the 1970s. His revolutionary spirit was deeply admired. The way he was able to "ground" with ordinary people, his links with and profound understandings of the African liberation struggles of Tanzania, Angola, and Mozambique became for many an inspiration to radical action. For some he embodied Che Guevara's new man, a revolutionary intellectual whose every fiber was honed to revolutionary practice.[1] However, as I began to think about this essay, rereading Rodney's writings and speeches and thinking of the times in which he lived out his revolutionary commitment, a subtle, more nuanced Walter Rodney emerged—a black revolutionary intellectual who in the postindependence period of the black world (1960s and 1970s) posed central questions that then haunted, and continue to haunt, the ex-colonial world. Walter Rodney considered himself a "black Marxist." In 1975, five years before his assassination, he adumbrated this self-view: "At this particular time, for this era, I believe that our history imposes upon a black Marxist the necessity to operate almost exclusively, certainly essentially, within the black community."² The operative phrase here is "black Marxist." What did it mean? What were its revolutionary ideographical implications? What did being a "black Marxist" mean for questions of history, and of political and social knowledge, and for the black radical intellectual tradition and its different engagements?³

The temptation in any study of Walter Rodney's thought is to limit textual analysis to his more "formal" academic writings, and in particular his two pathbreaking books: *How Europe Underdeveloped Africa* (1972) and *A History of the Guyanese Working People, 1881–1905* (1981). In this essay I want to shift to a different set of texts, ones that were interactively elaborated with audiences—in other words, speeches or "reasonings" constructed by Rodney in dialogue with audiences, where the terrain was the political debate about crucial questions which faced the international black liberation struggle: the issues of class, race, the nature of the revolutionary intellectual, and the character of history. Overarching these issues was the question that Rupert Lewis posed so well in his moving study of Rodney—"Rodney tried to understand why the moment of independence was also a moment of recolonisation."³

It is this question that animated Rodney's theory of politics and revolution. In the end it made him a postcolonial revolutionary theorist following in the wake of Frantz Fanon. (Fanon died at age thirty-six, and Rodney was murdered when he was thirty-eight.) If Fanon diagnosed the colonial revolution, highlighting the agency of the "wretched of the earth" and suggestively pointed out the dangers of false independence, then Rodney gave body to the workings of the double transformation of colonialism into postcolonialism, then into neocolonialism.

The term "postcolonialism" is a contested one, and I do not wish to enter into an exhaustive debate about it.⁴ However, I want to agree with David Scott that the major achievement of postcoloniality as a discourse of criticism is its "demand for the decolonization of representation."⁵ Scott goes on to bemoan the fact that this achievement has come at the cost of suspending the political, "a deferral of the question of the renewal of a theory of politics."⁶ Postcolonial criticism oftentimes becomes a form of "discursive radicalism"⁷ that folds back upon itself in self-referring discourses of disappearing subjects while the site of the human world, the human subject, is being dominated and subjugated in myriad ways. Therefore, to call Walter Rodney a postcolonial theorist is to place squarely on the agenda of early twenty-first-century radical discourse a theory of politics and revolution. It is one of the reasons why I want to shift textual emphasis from the two standard works and focus on the following texts: "Marxism in Africa" (1975), "Tanzanian Ujamaa and Scientific Socialism" (1972), "Some Thoughts on the Political Economy of the Caribbean" (1972), *The Groundings with My Brothers* (1969), the mediations collected in *Walter Rodney Speaks* (1990), and Rodney's final public speech before his assassination, "A Sign of the Times."

In calling Rodney a revolutionary postcolonial theorist, one is also pointing to elements of the Caribbean radical intellectual tradition.[8] This tradition has its literary genesis in the English-speaking tradition in the nineteenth century. Beginning with the work of J. J. Thomas (1840–1889), the radical Caribbean intellectual tradition mastered the protocols and conventions of the Western intellectual tradition and then critiqued the ways in which the writers and thinkers in the latter tradition either made Afro-Caribbeans invisible or portrayed them as objects without human features and history. What was central to this tradition in the late nineteenth century, from Thomas through Theophilus E. Samuel Scholes (1856–1935), whose two-volume *Glimpses of the Ages or the "Superior" and "Inferior" Races, So-Called, Discussed in the Light of Science and History* (1905) is a marker in black twentieth century intellectual production, was the preoccupation with constructing histories of the New World African that demonstrated achievement and civilization. What characterized Rodney's intellectual labor was his focus on the concrete radical links that could be constructed between the intellectual and the mass of the population. In other words, while one central radical element of the Caribbean intellectual tradition was historical vindicationism, Rodney raised the issue of the purpose of this vindication. In large measure his political thought was shaped by his responses to this question. By his political and theoretical practices Walter Rodney opened a new space in radical Caribbean political thought, one that is important for the Caribbean radical political intellectual tradition.

The Caribbean political novelist George Lamming, in his novel *Season of Adventure,* does an unusual thing. In the last third of the novel he places an author's note that starkly brings to the fore the critical issue which has always challenged the radical Caribbean intellectual. Lamming writes that he and Powell, one of the main characters in the novel, attended school together, grew up together, and then "the division came. I got a public scholarship which started my migration to another world . . . it had earned me a privilege which now shut out Powell and the whole *tonelle* right out of my future."[9] This feature of the Caribbean intellectual tradition—the ways in which the workings of the division of labor, complicated by colonialism, created an educated group who were both distant and contemptuous toward the ordinary people—has been a major problem in radical Caribbean political thought. At the heart of the nationalist elite's anticolonial political practices was the invisibility of the agency of the African and Indian masses. This invisibility resulted in part from the contempt that the anti-colonial Creole nationalists and the black nationalists of the early twentieth century had for what they perceived to be non-Western forms.

In the Jamaican Creole nationalist anticolonial newspaper, *Public Opinion,* we find the following discussions about Jamaican culture—the culture of the slaves was "on too low a plane," and only the "educated classes could produce a proper culture."[10] In remarks about the social and cultural conduct of a section of Kingston's poor, Marcus Garvey, a towering figure in twentieth-century black radical political practice, stated, "These people indulge in pocomania and in the practices of most ruthless and horrible barbarities."[11] The construction of Caribbean and Jamaican class vocabulary with its layered meanings of "outside" and "inside" was the framework for the political language and practice of Caribbean politics.[12] Such discursive representations were adapted from the colonial/imperial constructs of the New World black, and became the normative frames for analysis of Caribbean society and politics.

Walter Rodney attempted to break from this practice in two ways. First, he attempted to elaborate a radical historical and political theory about Guyanese and Caribbean society, by decolonizing the political language and categories of the radical tradition—what one can call his efforts to "Caribbeanize Marxism." Second, he attempted to create an alternative approach to another central issue in Caribbean politics—the role of political leadership. However, on both of these matters I will argue that the old way created tensions in Rodney's political writings and political practice. The debates that still swirl around his assassination some twenty years ago are indicative that in the end they were never fully resolved.

Rodney's major works, in particular *How Europe Underdeveloped Africa,* break the strictures of mainstream academic historical practices, and are the result of engagements about the nature of the African revolution in the early 1970s. However, I think that the texts chosen for this essay will demonstrate deeper insights into the issues of revolutionary political and theoretical practice that faced the radical Caribbean intellectual.

Groundings

In *Dread Talk, the Language of Rastafari* (1994), Velma Pollard posits that the new meaning for "ground" within the language of Rastafari is the concept of the sociable.[13] Within Jamaican nation-language,[14] "ground" means a cultural, physical, and legal space that had been created by the slaves to grow their own food for consumption and local trade. In the postemancipation period, the word came to mean a small plot of land that was owned or controlled by the ex-slaves. Beginning as a noun, the word became an adjective to describe fruit, animals, or plants that stayed on the ground. For example, as Cassidy and Le Page point out, "ground dove" was the name for "the smallest of the Jamaican doves, which feeds and is usually seen on the ground."[15] "Ground" therefore represents, in Afro-Jamaican language, a master noun that then develops into an adjective. In Rastafari language and wordplay, "ground" became the site of sociality. Obviously drawing from the sense of "ground" being a special place that was controlled by the black population, Rastafarians used the word as participle, "groundings." There was also the verb "to ground," which in addition could be used as an adjective to describe persons ... such a person is a "grounds person," which meant someone who comported himself or herself without the traditional class, color, or race prejudices so common in Jamaican society. In the discursive practice of Rastafari, when "grounds" became "groundings," the meaning was layered. Not only did it mean sociality—an equal meeting that breaks socially constructed barriers of race, class, and education—but the nature of such an encounter was marked by "reasonings"—a form of discussion in which each person contributed equally to the discourse without any prior hierarchical claims of knowledge. For Walter Rodney, therefore, to engage in the political practice of "groundings" meant that he shattered the conventional intellectual and political practices of the Caribbean radical intellectual. For Rodney, to think, to speak, to write through a political practice of "groundings" was to collapse the distance between the object of his thought and his political practice. Thus his political practice was a drama that transgressed the normality of the postcolonial intellectual. It was the success of this dramatic political practice that first bought him to national and international public attention. Rodney first came to the notice of the general Caribbean public in 1968, when he was prohibited from reentering Jamaica by the Jamaica Labor Party (JLP) government. By the time this had happened, Rodney had completed a doctorate in African history at the University of London's School of Oriental and African Studies (SOAS). He had also taught at the University of Dar es Salaam and had been teaching African history at the Mona campus of the University of the West Indies.[16]

Rodney's banning catalyzed a set of events that have come to be called the "Walter Rodney Riots," a watershed moment in postcolonial Jamaican political history. In 1962 Jamaica had received political independence "gratis."[17] The Jamaican decolonization process was a classic one following Harold Macmillan's "Winds of Change" speech. The form and substance of political independence did not fundamentally reorder Jamaican society, and as a consequence engendered social movements that opposed the politics of the national elite. One major social force involved in this was the

Rastafari (see chapter 6 for a detailed discussion of the discursive practice of Rastafari and its meanings for Jamaican politics and the black radical tradition). The late Jamaican political sociologist Carl Stone reports that the early postindependence period was one in which "strong feelings of black solidarity within the black working and lower class in Jamaica"[18] existed. In such a milieu Walter Rodney began the teaching of African history.

There were two things about Rodney's teaching. First was the subject matter, because for the new Jamaican national elite, with its hegemonic Creole political constructions embodied in the national motto "Out of many, one people," Africa and African history were taboo. Second was the manner in which Rodney taught this history. He had come back to the Caribbean via Africa. In London, while studying at SOAS, he was a part of a Marxist study group led by C. L. R. James and his wife, Selma James. This group was an important source for his political formation. Writing about this period of his life, Rodney states: "Getting together in London and meeting over a period of two to three years . . . afforded me to acquire a knowledge of Marxism, and a more precise understanding of the Russian Revolution, and of historical formulation."[19] He continues, "It was not enough to study Lenin's *State and Revolution*. It was important to understand why it was written and what was going on in Russia at the precise time."[20] The attention to concrete historical context and its nuances, and grappling with human creativity in the political domain, would become central ingredients in Rodney's efforts to develop a form of Marxism that was applicable to Africa and the Caribbean.

But there was something else that the James study group would reinforce—the understanding that emancipatory politics was the action of the oppressed group itself. These two strands, the self-activity of the oppressed and the attention to the details of historical contexts, positioned Rodney to break the traditional mold of the radical Caribbean intellectual. Individual members of the oppressed classes recognized this. Here is how one participant in those "groundations" viewed Rodney's activity:

> Dr. Walter Rodney, Bro Wally to the sufferer. He identified himself to be a man from the working class, who was not afraid to use the education that Babylon had given him for the good of the Ordinary man. Bro Wally did not hesitate, he let the sufferer know what he stood for, Black people should all know about Mother Africa, Africans must reject white culture imperialism and black people must mobilize and unify themselves to act in their own interest. To the Ja. Sufferer an educated man is always a man looking for some personal gain, yes the Ja. Sufferer is the most reluctant man to ground with a so-called educated man because of his history of de-

ceit. But Bro. I and I accepted Wally as a man as an equal, as an African.[21]

In his earliest radical political practice, Rodney therefore began by raising the issues of the relationship between the intellectual and the ordinary person. These issues are the overarching frame that shape the text *The Groundings with My Brothers*. Published one year after his banning from Jamaica, the text is a collection of some of Rodney's major speeches during his Jamaica sojourn plus an essay that sums up his perspective on his political practice at the time. This essay is an important one in the political and intellectual elaborations of Rodney because it succinctly marks out a threefold position for the radical black intellectual in the postindependence world. The language and imagery of the title form an essential part of the text. The political conditions of its production—Walter Rodney's banning and the subsequent riots—give the book an iconic status in Caribbean radical political culture and history. One result is that the text now forms part of the historic practice of radical Caribbean politics which upholds the agency of the subaltern. It represents in early postindependence Caribbean politics a practice that combines several elements of the Caribbean radical intellectual tradition: race, history, and a new dimension in the critique of elite nationalism. It broke new ground within the Caribbean tradition with its emphasis on the creativity of the black masses on their own terms and reordered the role of the radical intellectual in the Caribbean. If C. L. R. James's *The Black Jacobins* was the historical work that demonstrated the revolutionary capacity of the Haitian slaves, then *Groundings with My Brothers* became the model text for radical postcolonial political praxis in the Caribbean. The reason was clear.

The Text

A small booklet (sixty-eight pages), *Groundings* elaborated a global perspective on black struggle, yet it was rooted in the struggles of radical urban unemployed Caribbean youth. *Groundings with My Brothers* begins with a statement on the Jamaican situation that reviews the aftermath of the riots which occurred after Rodney's banning. The statement identifies the nature of the Jamaican postindependence economy, defines the black political elite as "lackeys of imperialism," and places emphasis on the "creative social expression on the part of the black oppressed masses."[22] Singling out the Rastafarian group as central to the emergence of black power in Jamaica, Rodney suggests that his meetings with this group gave him a sense of humility. He breaks with the Jamaican class conceptions of race and color when he writes about the local middle-class views of poor black

Jamaicans: "The system, says they have nothing, they are illiterates, the dark people of Jamaica . . . but with the black brothers you learn humility because they are teaching you."[23] Rodney then makes a point that is still being ignored in the discussions about and analysis of Caribbean culture: "You know that some of the best painters and writers are coming out of the Rastafari environment. The Black people in the West Indies have produced all the culture that we have, whether it be steel band or folk music. Black bourgeoisie and white people in the West Indies have produced nothing."[24] Such a statement in 1968, six years after independence, was remarkable.

However, there were three other things about the text: first, its attempt to give a race/class analysis of the postindependence Caribbean; second, its exposition of the relationship between historical studies and revolutionary practice; and third, its detailing of a position on the relationship of the revolutionary intellectuals to mass activity and revolutionary politics in general.

In explaining the workings of race and class in the Caribbean, Rodney identifies a white economically powerful class, a brown (mulatto) and a black middle class who were the beneficiaries of the 1938 workers' rebellions that swept across the English-speaking Caribbean, ushering in the modern Creole Caribbean nationalist movements. In his effort to break down the ethnic barriers that exist between the Indian and African populations in Trinidad and Guyana, Rodney locates the arrival of both groups in the policies of British colonialism and racial oppression, making the point that the Indian population arrived in the Caribbean as indentured servants. Here I might suggest that if the Caribbean was conceived through the genocide of the native Amerindian population, it grew up through the horrors of racial plantation slavery and came of age with Indian servitude, making the region a laboratory of racial oppression and colonial servitude labor.

Rodney observes that Afro-Caribbean persons often view the Indo-Caribbean population through the lenses of white normativity, and in turn are viewed by the Indo-Caribbean population in like manner. Given the racial context of Guyana, Rodney was not blind to the position of the Indo-Caribbean population. Therefore, in *Groundings with My Brothers* he applied the term "black" in a political sense to describe the nonwhite oppressed population of the region. Thus the Indo-Caribbean population was both oppressed and an ally in the social struggle against neocolonial rule. In this, his first major political text, Rodney locates the Caribbean middle class and its members as the major obstacle to radical struggles. This was a theme he would consistently return to—the transformation of the native nationalist elite into the dominant political group and its meanings for politics in the postcolony. In this regard he would take up Fanon's idea about the nature of anticolonial nationalism and fully explore it with regard to the Caribbean and Africa.

The second theme that Rodney explores in the text is the relationship of history to revolutionary struggle. We have already explored how history is a central theme in the black radical intellectual tradition and how it operates as a vehicle for human validation. In the 1960s, with the rise of the international anticolonial movement and the emergence of black nationalism, the nature of black historical vindicationism shifted to focus on Africa. In this focus many questions were posed along traditional European historical lines. A crude schema of the ways in which this form of historical narrative was written went something like this: Europe had kings and queens, and so did Africa; Europe invented important things, and so did Africa; Europe had great civilizations, and so did Africa. In Rodney's mind this form of vindication did not question the terms on which the vindication process was conducted, and could lead to cultural essentialism about African people.

Aware of this, he attempted to shift this model of history. In a talk given outside the confines of the university lecture hall, he confronted this question. Speaking to a group of persons who had come to hear from him the typical things about African history, the nature and the splendor of African civilization, Rodney used the first part of his talk to outline the major civilizations of precolonial Africa, their importance not only to Africa but also to Old World trade in the fifteenth century. Then subtly he shifted the parameters of the discussion and asserted: "What is most fundamental is an attempt to evaluate the African contribution to the solution of the problems posed by man's existence in society."[25] The purpose of historical vindication for Rodney, therefore, was to establish the basis for contemporary radical struggle: "If there is to be any proving of our humanity it must be by revolutionary means."[26] This "revolutionary means" was linked to the role of the black intellectual.

And so we come to the third major theme in *Groundings with My Brothers*. Using the language of Rastafari, Rodney posed the issues of the black radical intellectual in the colonial context thus: "How do we break out of this Babylonian Captivity?"[27] In responding to his own question, Rodney suggested three ways, all of which still resonate within the field of radical black political practice. The first was the work of the intellectual/academic, whose function was to "to attack those distortions which . . . white cultural imperialism has produced in all branches of scholarship."[28] In the present moment we would see this as deconstructing the episteme of eurocentrism and its false universalism. However, while it is important to deconstruct the false universalism of the Western intellectual tradition, it is equally important to engage in the constructivist project of mining black intellectual production and its meanings for human society. This obviously requires establishing the contours of the tradition and then plumbing its depth and figures, not for the sake of historical curiosity or for making analogies, but for grappling with some of the critical elements that face human society. In his brilliant study of Muhammad Ali, Mike Marqusee puts it well when he writes: "the African-American freedom struggle, in all its metamorphoses, is a resource for all humanity."[29]

The second dimension of Rodney's injunction to radical black intellectuals was that it was important for the black intellectual to "move beyond his own discipline to challenge the social myth."[30] Here, Rodney is calling for the black intellectual to be a social critic. Certainly within the neocolonial zone of the Caribbean or Africa, being a social critic had profound consequences. We recollect here that Rodney was speaking against the background that many of the intellectual critics of the Jamaican neocolonial state had found themselves deported (Clive Thomas, an economist from Guyana) or had their passports seized (George Beckford, who is viewed by many as the major contributor to a theory of Caribbean society through his book *Persistent Poverty* [1972]) or were blacklisted from jobs. In Africa, the social critic in the neocolonial state often disappeared, was murdered, or was forced into exile. So for the black intellectual in the neocolonial world, social criticism often demanded personal courage.

Such a context meant that once the radical black intellectual was a social critic in these neocolonial spaces, he or she often operated as an "organic" intellectual. This intellectual spoke "truth to power" but was rooted in organizational and institutional relationships with the oppressed. The functioning of such an intellectual did not depend upon state or mainstream institutions giving space for intellectual activity. On the contrary the neocolonial context forced the radical black intellectual into a "return to source" and, as we have already explained, such a journey required rethinking the political and social categories in which we explain social and political life. To state that Rodney's conception of the role of the radical black intellectual was slightly different from that of Gramsci requires us to examine Rodney's statement that the primary task of the radical black intellectual was to "attach himself to the activity of the black masses."[31]

Now at first blush it might seem that Rodney is arguing for a typical Gramscian intellectual who is integrated into, and represents, the ideational activity of that class. However, there is a difference here. For Rodney the masses were already in motion, and were not in need of any political party through which the intellectuals were organized as representative of the class. Rodney felt that the black intellectual had to learn from the masses, a point he made about learning from Rastafari. We note that Cabral calls for the intellectual in the colonial context to commit what he calls "class suicide," and it is appropriate here to suggest that this notion also seems to have functioned in Rodney's thought. Cabral had also made the point that "national liberation is an act of *culture*."[32]

I want to suggest that Rodney himself held similar views, and that his penchant for historical specifics carried him in that direction. In the end, Rodney's Jamaican political sojourn in the late 1960s at the height of the decolonization movement in Africa and the Caribbean and of the black movement in America, shaped some of his insights into questions of political knowledge. This process was surely facilitated by his involvement in the James's study group in London. Also important were his skills as a historian who grasped the nature of historicality. In *Groundings with My Brothers*, Rodney broke with the discursive political practice of rendering invisible the interiority of the Afro-Caribbean population, which had been carried forward by the nationalist Creole politicians of the Caribbean. In an insightful essay on the radical intelligentsia of the period in the Caribbean, Rupert Lewis argues that "Issues of self-respect and racial dignity, so important to the construction of personhood in postcolonial societies, tended to be ignored by the left, and were seen as soft issues, while economic questions were the hard issues that contained the key to liberation."[33]

Rodney stepped out of that mold. His first major intervention in Caribbean politics established a new marker. It was an effort to integrate the issues of class, race, history, and political economy into a radical praxis that would change Caribbean society. From this platform he would seek to probe the nature of the middle class in the region and its role in postcolonial society. Also, it was from this ground that he would attempt to examine how Marxism could be applied to the African context and would make efforts to build a revolutionary organization in Guyana. With regard to building a revolutionary organization in the Caribbean, Rodney was again breaking with one segment of the Caribbean radical political tradition. He put it this way in a 1976 interview: "We have tended, through force of circumstance, to become involved in what we may broadly call the international revolution or Pan-Africanism . . . however the present generation recognizes much more that it is difficult to make any of these ideas come to fruition except in a Caribbean context itself."[34] So if the radical Caribbean political tradition in the colonial era focused itself outside the Caribbean—Garvey, James, George Padmore, Henry Sylvester Williams, and others—Rodney wished to "return to the source" to make revolution. As we will see later, there was an important theoretical reason for his action. The reason was so important that even when the Forbes Burnham government made it impossible for him to be appointed as the head of the history department at the University of Guyana, Rodney insisted on returning home to Guyana and, under severe conditions, began his archival work for

The History of the Guyanese Working Class. But before we run ahead to the end of our story, we need to retrace our steps. In the next section we will turn to Rodney's attempts to "Africanize" Marxism and his analysis of the major features of postindependence oppression.

Black Marxism

As we observed in the "Opening Chant," in *The Wretched of the Earth,* Fanon makes the point that "Marxist analysis should always be slightly stretched every time we have to deal with the colonial problem."[35] It is, I believe an accurate statement. Colonialism bought with it the entire knowledge regime of the West, so when the native intellectual engaged in radical thought, he or she generally found that Marxism was one available system of thought which encouraged revolt. In many instances, however, Marxism did not take into account the specifics of the colonial context. The result was that many radical black intellectuals, although not abandoning some tenets of Marxism, renounced their membership in Communist parties and began to search for alternative radical political frameworks.[36] In the immediate postindependence period, for many ex-colonies the relevance of Marxism as a ideological practice that would usher in liberation once again became a cause of contention. This time around there was a major difference. While in the early twentieth century the debate about Marxism in the colonies did not have to face the requirements of making revolution, this time it did.

Walter Rodney was very conscious about the history of this debate. As a child growing up in Guyana during the 1950s, he was aware of the ideology of Marxism, because he had distributed pamphlets for the Marxist/nationalist party then led by Cheddi Jagan, the People's Progressive Party (PPP). In England, as we stated before, he was a member of one of the study groups that met under the wing of C. L. R. James. While in Dar es Salaam, Rodney had come into contact with leading members of the African liberation movements and engaged in debates about the nature of Tanzania's *ujamaa* and its relationship to Marxist theory. At the Sixth Pan-African Congress, held at Dar es Salaam in 1974, Rodney's position paper critiqued the absence of clear class analysis in many of the conference proceedings. In his conference statement, "Pan-Africanism and Neo-Colonialism in Africa," Rodney makes the point that "The questions posed at the outset of this analysis in relation to the class content of nationalism suggested that one identifies the leading class, assesses its revolutionary capacity, and evaluates the manner in which subordinate classes are handled."[37] He goes on to identify the African middle class as the blockage in the struggles of African liberation and calls for contemporary pan-Africanism to be an "internationalist, anti-imperialist and Socialist weapon."[38]

All of this demonstrates that Rodney's intervention in the debate about the relevance of Marxism was conducted with a sense of history and an understanding of the character of the political moment he inhabited. There are two other presentations in which the nature of the intervention is clearly spelled out. The first was a speech delivered in March 1975 at Queens College in New York City, and the second was a series of reflections made at the Institute of the Black World in Atlanta, published in 1990. In the March 1975 speech, Rodney began by acknowledging that the debate about Marxism inside the black world was a historic and important one, and suggested that it was narrow to perceive the debate as one in which race and class were organized as opposing poles. For Rodney the critical issue was one of thought and how to counter what he called the "dominant mode of reason."[39] Marxism, Rodney said, was a body of thought, and therefore could be divided into two distinctive parts—methodological and ideological. This division was critical to Rodney's thinking because the former could be applied universally, while the latter did not have such a status.

In speaking about methodology, Rodney poses the question of the applicability of Marxism across time and place even though it was promulgated as a nineteenth-century European body of thought. He admits that it is a valid question for black people to ask "whether an ideology generated within the culture of Western Europe in the 19th century is, today, . . . still valid for another part of the world, namely Africa, or the Caribbean or Black people in this country?"[40] For Rodney, Marxist methodology allowed an affirmative answer to this question. In answering the question, Rodney argues that Marxist methodology was one which "begins its analysis of any society, of any situation, by seeking the relations which arise in production between men . . . that production is not merely the basis of man's existence, but the basis for defining man as special kind of being with a certain consciousness."[41] For Rodney, Marx's methodology was akin to the practices of natural science and was a theory of human science:

> People have no difficulty relating to electricity but they say, "Marx and Engels" that's European . . . they genuinely believe that they are making a fundamental distinction, whereas, in fact, this is obscuring the totality of social development. And the natural sciences are not be separated from the social sciences. Our interpretation of the social reality can similarly derive a certain historical law and hence scientific law of society which can be applied irrespective of its origins or its originators.[42]

Rodney concludes this section of his speech with a caveat. "Any ideology" he says, "must be applied with a thorough grasp of the internal realities of a given African society."[43] In this part of his speech Rodney demonstrated two things. First, as we said before, he is wedded to a current in

Marxist thought that sees Marxist theory as scientific laws akin to natural sciences, a kind of "social physics." However, this is only one dimension of Rodney's thought, because when he becomes "interpretivist," Rodney is sensitive to the fact that differences within each social context require revolutionaries to think hard about their own condition. For Rodney, therefore, ideology was something that grew out of concrete circumstances. Here he was not interested in debating the nature of ideology as false consciousness, but seemed more concerned that there was a local dialect which would shape the Marxist dialectic. As a black Marxist, Rodney was preoccupied with creating a revolutionary ideology and theory that would emerge from the historical specific, the particular conditions of the black world. This preoccupation he called "making sure that Marxism does not appear as the summation of other people's history, but appears as a living force within one's history."[44] There was a sharp tension in Rodney's thought that revealed itself in his separation of Marxism into ideology and methodology. Later on in the speech, Rodney was unable to sustain the distinction and cast it aside, making the point that the ideology is itself revolutionary in all conditions, even while advising caution.

This tension in Rodney's thought became even more acute in his subsequent reflections on the same topic at the Institute of the Black World. Starting from the perspective of his extensive contacts and engagements with different segments of black struggles around the world, Rodney enunciates a form of politics that eschews universal answers. He announces that it is politically uncreative to ask somebody "what is *the* answer in that very global sense of the word."[45] Because he thinks there are no global master keys, Rodney makes the point that even though political language might sound familiar, the contextual differences created when we pay insufficient attention to the unique details of a situation could easily be carried over into overgeneralizations.[46] He asserts that revolutionary practice and theory require that individuals look:

> . . . at each specific history and the context in which certain concepts and terms originate . . . one has to be careful that what comes out of the last most successful revolution doesn't become the dictum for everybody else . . . it can sometimes act as a constraint upon creativity. You can only break with it when you make your own revolution.[47]

Turning to Marxism and Marxists, Rodney argues that "Marxism is not just the study of some classic texts . . . very few of them have an awareness of how misleading it can be to take an understanding of someone else's theory and just imagine that it can be projected on to your situation."[48] Turning to the context of the African-American community, he proclaims:

"At this particular time, for this era, I believe that our history imposes upon a black Marxist the necessity to operate almost exclusively, certainly essentially, within the black community."[49] This position sounds heretical to Marxism but was based on the American context and what we recognize today as "white privilege." Rodney further develops his position into one that recognizes the need for a "new terminology in order to apply the Marxist methodology to a completely new situation."[50] What is clear is that Rodney's preoccupation with the concrete pushes him to seek new categories in the examination of a local reality. However, what he did not ask was, what if the methodology did not allow one to see the new? To recite Fanon, if one has to stretch Marxism, then when does stretching Marxism make it no longer Marxism?[51] For Rodney, I want to suggest, this tension between the creative concrete and a universal methodology was never quite resolved. In his 1976 interview with the journal *Race and Class,* Rodney, reflecting on a "Caribbean Marxism" that was able to expose the "pseudo-socialism" of Caribbean governments at the time, called for a "a certain localization of the revolution."[52]

This was related to two things. First, it was the reversal of a tendency of Caribbean revolutionaries to participate in struggles away from the Caribbean, what he referred to as the "international revolution or Pan-Africanism." The second meaning was the creation of concrete categories. For Rodney, revolutionary theory without specific references to revolutionary struggle was meaningless. To be a "revolutionary intellectual," he observed, means nothing if there is "no point of reference to the struggle of those who are more directly engaged in production."[53] In the end, therefore one feature that makes Rodney's life and theoretical work of contemporary relevance was this preoccupation with the nature of revolutionary theory and practice. It was his stress on the concrete, as the living force in radical political knowledge, that framed his *How Europe Underdeveloped Africa.* It was the concrete, the search for local knowledge, that inserted him in the revolutionary imagination of the Caribbean, making him the iconic figure of his generation. In reaching for local political and social knowledge, Rodney recognized two things—limit and circumstances. It is why he insisted:

> Some people who have been talking about Marxism for some while and who have a grasp of the theory, in my opinion, don't seem to want to break loose from previous categories. . . . In Africa and Latin America, people . . . recognize that when new phenomena appear on the scene, you must recognize them to be new and not imagine that you are simply speaking of an extension of something that was going on in the 19th century.[54]

What factors could possibility account for this focus on the concrete? Perhaps part of the answer lies in the ways in which many Marxist historians have had to negotiate historical materialism. The English Marxist historian E. P. Thompson, in thinking about the writing of radical history, and continuing one form of historical materialism noted:

> Men and women are . . . not . . . autonomous subjects, "free individuals," but as persons experiencing their determinate productive situations and relationships, as needs and interests . . . and then "handling" this experience within their consciousness and their culture . . . in the most complex . . . ways, and then . . . acting upon their deterministic situation in their turn.[55]

I want to suggest that Rodney was very focused on the nature of human experience. This focus made him think hard about what a different set of human experiences would mean for revolutionary theory. Getting inside these experiences meant, for Rodney, a turn to the concrete.

Rodney's interest in looking for the new led him to develop a theory of radical politics for the neocolonial condition. C. L. R. James makes the point that while he (James), along with "Aimé Césaire, George Padmore, Dr. Du Bois and others . . . had established some Caribbean foundations or foundations for underdeveloped peoples, *Walter did not have to do that.*"[56] In James's view, the radical political and intellectual foundations had been laid in the anticolonial struggles. The issue that faced someone like Walter Rodney in this period was not how to create a anticolonial movement but what was the nature of the postindependence moment. In other words, was there a new phenomenon that had emerged with the collapse of the colonial empires? Rodney's wrestling with these questions is what makes him a theorist of postcolonial revolution.

A Theory of Postcolony

Obviously, Rodney's political theoretical work was not influenced only by Marxism there were other influences as well: the African liberation movements, the Cuban Revolution and in the early period of his political growth, the Black Power movement in the United States. All these combined to serve as a platform from which Rodney's major political theoretical contribution about the nature of neocolonialist politics was launched. Rodney's theory of neocolonialism rested on his capacity to combine elements of political economy and infuse them with an understanding of the new social and political categories of the postindependence period. In constructing his theory of neocolonial politics, he flayed many Third World Marxists: "Many third world intellectuals are very fascinated by models,

models that were historically applicable to societies outside their own . . . [one must] have the courage and a lot of energy to deal with their own situations and to come up with relevant answers."[57] Focusing as usual on the concrete, Rodney announced that forms of economic control which once were deemed progressive in many Third World countries were now not so:

> The new colonialism is sometimes so difficult to decipher . . . take nationalization as an example. There was a time . . . when people who nationalized were automatically regarded as progressive . . . and imperialism moved against them to squash them immediately. But now nationalization has become a technique that can just as well be used by the enemy as by progressive Africans, Asians and Latin Americans.[58]

This new response to nationalization signaled to Rodney that major shifts had occurred in the structure of the international system. He identified this shift as one in which the global ruling elites were now prepared to turn the "Third World" native elites into junior partners. This meant that in terms of radical social change, one now had to pay attention to the ways in which this relationship would develop, and how it would influence one's understandings about a particular society. In developing his analysis of the native elite, Rodney drew extensively from Fanon. With regard to Africa, he made the following point:

> The national government of the petty-bourgeoisie has little control over production, and is endowed with a feeble political base. They of course have the police and the military forces . . . we find also that the petty bourgeoisie in . . . third world countries are not as capable as the bourgeoisie in the metropoles when it comes to playing certain kinds of political games. They are not capable of granting to their own population participation in bourgeois democracy.[59]

Within the Caribbean context, what was one to call this new feature? In an early 1970s talk titled "Some Aspects of the Political Economy of the Caribbean," Rodney announced that while some Marxists called this petite bourgeoisie a "comprador class," he felt that this grouping was more accurately called an "overseer-group": "I see the West Indian middle-class as essentially playing the role of over-seers, a term after all that is much rooted in our historical experiences on the plantations."[60] The dominance of this group meant that there were "continuities between pre-independence and post-independence." However, even within these continuities, there were new features that were reflected in what Rodney called a "pattern of politics." Using Fanon's notion of "a process of retrogression," Rodney developed seven features of Caribbean and African postindependence politics:

1. The concentration of power in the hands of the petite bourgeoisie
2. The destruction of popular political expression and participation
3. The manipulation of race and other divisions among the people
4. The institutionalization of corruption
5. The extension of political repression and victimization
6. The vulgarization of "national culture" as a tool for class rule
7. The deliberate distortion of revolutionary concepts.[61]

In Rodney's political thought, some combination of the various elements above solidified to create the basis for neocolonial politics. Given his experiences in Guyana and eastern Africa, particularly in Uganda, Rodney used his polemical energies to expose what he understood as "pseudo-socialism." In the Caribbean, he felt that Guyana under Forbes Burnham and Jamaica under Michael Manley were typical examples of "pseudo-socialism." Rodney argued that in general, "neo-colonial politics have entered into a new operational phase in which pseudo-socialism as means of maintaining control over working people . . . is intended to and partially succeeds in giving a new lease of life to neo-colonialism."[62]

Rodney's theory of neocolonial politics was rooted in a set of concrete understandings about the failure of the independence project and the ways in which seeking the "political kingdom" did not lead to liberation. If Fanon with foresight understood the reactionary potential of the Third World native elites in the aftermath of independence, then Rodney attempted to show how this expressed itself in the politics of the period. What is distinctive in Rodney's thought at this time is that he eschewed the orthodox Marxist interpretation of the nature of radical Third World developments. Much of orthodox Marxist analysis of these developments was conducted through a theoretical paradigm then called "non-capitalist path of development." This path of political, social, and economic development for the newly independent nations was seen, in the words of a leading theorist at the time, as "a transitional period, an extremely complex combination of socio-economic and political processes opening up new prospects for progress and socialism."[63]

In Rodney's thought such a characterization missed the ways in which the native elite behaved politically. His argument was that the native elite used "pseudo-socialism" to bolster "its image abroad."[64] If the main Marxist orthodoxy at the time focused on political leadership and state relationships governed by the dictates of the cold war, Rodney's gaze was elsewhere—the relationships of rule inside the postcolony. This angle of vision led Rodney to a position in which radical democratic forms became a central principle of his political thought. We saw this angle of vision when we examined his political style of "groundings." Although some would argue that this practice was really early Rodney, they make the typical cast-iron divisions which are often made in studies of a political thinker's praxis. Rodney's political gaze on radical democracy can be discerned in much of his activity. Rupert Lewis's view that "The role of the masses in the making of history and in government and their political education became central issues in Rodney's academic research, writing and political practice"[65] is therefore an accurate assessment. A further demonstration of Rodney's angle of vision on democracy is that while supportive of the revolution in Grenada, he disagreed with its leadership about the banning of a major newspaper and advocated the holding of elections, contrary to the views of many in the Caribbean left.[66]

Rodney's organizational perspective on radical politics was predicated on three grounds. First, he had an antipathy to vanguardism developed from his association with C. L. R. James. Second, his experiences around the African Liberation movements, particularly the armed wing, gave him an organizational sense that revolution was both about the overthrowing of the old regime and the establishment of zones of liberation in that process. Third was the way in which the July 13 Movement, led by Fidel Castro, had seized power. All these elements combined with his open and democratic leadership style. Within the context of dominant and often authoritarian party leadership styles in the Caribbean,[67] Rodney attempted to forge a politics of organizational leadership that reflected his focus on the concrete and his understanding that the liberation of the oppressed masses resided in their own activity. Therefore, it is an ironic twist of political fate that the sharpest critique of Rodney's political practice should come from someone who was acknowledged as the most important twentieth-century Caribbean thinker on radical democracy—C. L. R. James.

On the Taking of Political Power: James and Rodney

In March 1981, nearly a year after the Rodney's assassination, C. L. R. James wrote a letter to Robert Hill.[68] In the letter he proclaims:

> This is one of the most important letters that I have ever written. It is about the Life and Death of Rodney. Walter was the most advanced of the West Indian intellectuals. But he faced and failed to conquer the last responsibility of revolutionary West Indians: he was not a master of the seizure of power.[69]

In August 1980, a Trinidad newspaper carried a story that in part stated: "Noted author and historian CLR James has warned leaders of the Guyana Working People's alliance to be on the alert for people who may attempt to assassinate them in the current struggle in the cooperative republic."[70] It is against that background that we will examine James's critique of Walter Rodney's political practice.

In a lecture commemorating Rodney's achievements, James argues that Rodney's political practice did not take into account two central elements of revolutionary politics. In the first instance, James states, Rodney did not properly prepare for insurrectionary activity. He claims that while Rodney understood the nature of Forbes Burnham's authoritarian political power, he organized wrongly against it:

> A revolution is made with arms, but a revolution is made by the revolutionary spirit of the great mass of the population. And you have to wait for that. . . . Walter saw that his WPA had many good things about it but he realized that Burnham was ready with the police and the army. . . . and Walter became too nervous, too anxious about it. He did not wait for the revolutionary people and the revolutionary class to be in conflict with the government before he could start the question of the insurrection.[71]

The second aspect of Rodney's political practice that was problematic, James insisted, was Rodney's conception of political leadership. His conception of leadership meant, James said, that he "did not [ask] anybody to do anything that he would not do himself."[72] In James's mind, this was contrary to the revolutionary conception of political leadership, particularly as it related to insurrection and the seizure of power. James suggested that Rodney's conception of leadership demonstrated that he had not seriously studied the question. This, he argued, was a fatal political flaw.

Some commentators have suggested that James's critique of this dimension of Rodney's political practice was based on James's Leninism.[73] However, I want to suggest a different way of seeing this conflict. In the first place, James made the point that the business of taking power is a question a thousand years old, and does not depend upon the "knowledge of Marxism."[74] Although James littered his lecture with references to Lenin and the 1917 Russian Revolution, his main point was that it is not individual political leaders who make the revolution, but the mass activity of the oppressed classes. Also involved in his analysis was his Marxist notion of the revolutionary conjuncture. In this perspective there were two things necessary for revolution—the appropriate revolutionary moment and the political leadership to seize political power. What James failed to realize, however, was not that Rodney did not understand these two questions, but that he was more *preoccupied* with defining a new kind of revolutionary political leadership in the Caribbean. Under that leadership the gap between the highly educated and the mass of the population would not be reproduced in a political hierarchy where the educated did the thinking about political programs while members of the oppressed class did the doing, the mundane work which sometimes placed their lives in danger. In authoritarian political systems, political leadership is an overweening command political presence and the dominant political culture is typically organized around it. Rodney was very aware of this, and his theory of neocolonial politics required him to break that mode of political practice. A clearer understanding of this point can perhaps be gleaned from a brief analysis of his last major public speech.

A few days before his murder, Rodney addressed a public meeting in Georgetown, the capital of Guyana. The focus of his address was the proposed new Guyanese constitution, which would have entrenched the power of the political leader to the extent of granting him legal immunity on personal matters not only while he an officeholder but even when he no longer held political office. Rodney proclaimed to his audience that such a constitutional formulation was in a very real sense monarchical. He called the president of Guyana "King Kong," and suggested that the constitution was being made by a "self-proclaimed monarch." In opposition to this kind of political leadership in postindependence Guyana, Rodney made the following point:

> In many ways, Brother Rupert Roopnarine, Brother Omawale and myself owe to you, the Guyanese people, a word of thanks. The Working People's alliance as an organization, all the members, owe to you a word of thanks for the immense solidarity and support which is developing. . . . But while offering this word of thanks, we also want to make it clear that the solidarity which we have seen is itself an indication that the people are struggling for their own rights.[75]

Rodney was keenly aware that the old relationship which the novelist George Lamming describes so eloquently had a logic in Caribbean postcolonial politics, which had been central to anticolonial politics and would continue to plague the movement unless it was confronted. The most prescient anticolonial thinkers, Cabral and Fanon in particular, had also identified this problem. Fanon made the point in *Wretched of the Earth* that the native anticolonial intellectual, when he returns to the population, oftentimes "only catches their outer garments . . . merely the reflection of hidden life."[76] The translation into concrete radical political praxis of a different mode of return—again to use Cabral's phrase, "return to the source"—was a very difficult one. In Rodney's case I want to suggest that he attempted to negotiate a different mode of return. In negotiating these new practices, Rodney developed a political style of connection to the life of the Guyanese ordinary person. Rupert Lewis reports that not only did

Rodney lead study groups in political economy and comparative revolutions as part of his political work, but he listened and learned as well. The foundation of this mode of Rodney's connection was his political conception that the emancipation of the oppressed classes required their own action.

In an assessment of Rodney's contribution to Caribbean radicalism, Lamming wrote:

> Caribbean scholars have, on the whole, concentrated on the intricate arguments and provisions made by those who ruled the land. . . . This is an important contribution, but Rodney was engaged in illuminating our understanding from a different perspective. Working people of African and Indian ancestry in Guyana have had a history of active struggle, which it has been our habit to omit or underestimate in political discourse about the past.[77]

Therefore, while James's critique focused on questions of seizing power, he missed Rodney's efforts to change aspects of Caribbean political culture. James is accurate to point out that Rodney stood on the ground which he and others had planted. But if the early segment of the black Caribbean radical tradition laid some of the intellectual foundations for social change in the Caribbean, Rodney's generation was focused on developing the theoretical and political work which would effect that change. In doing this, they were aware of a style of politics that had emerged in the early anticolonial struggle and that now overshadowed Caribbean politics. Rodney's efforts to break this mode should be considered as part of the complex of events that led to his assassination. It was another dimension to his "groundings" practice that returns us once again to his conceptions of the revolutionary intellectual.

The Radical Intellectual

We have seen that in 1968, Rodney had developed a conception of the revolutionary intellectual. This conception was to be further elaborated after his political experiences on the African continent. For Rodney the revolutionary intellectual was someone who was organically connected to the struggles of the oppressed groups and to what he called "points of struggle." However, the question arises of how one characterizes radical intellectuals who are not organically connected to these "points of struggle," particularly those who remain in the academy. Using the American academy as his example, Rodney suggested that the increasing opening of academic positions to blacks was the result of "developments in the black struggle," and was only a concession "designed to incorporate us within the structure."[78] To resist this and to shape a progressive agenda, Rodney suggested that the radical black intellectual in the American academy should function like a "guerrilla intellectual."[79] In Rodney's view, the "guerrilla intellectual" wages struggles on the intellectual terrain:

> The major and first responsibility of the intellectual is to struggle over ideas. We didn't create the artificial distinction between mental and manual labor but it is there, and if it is to be transcended, it isn't simply to be transcended by a so-called progressive intellectual going out to be a manual laborer. . . . The "guerrilla intellectual" is one who is participating in this whole struggle of transformation within his own orbit . . . we have to find ways of mastering knowledge from a different perspective . . . the petite bourgeoisie is a service class, a managerial class, with respect to ideas and administration. It is that struggle to which I am trying to refer when I use that concept of the "guerrilla intellectual."[80]

What is animating Rodney here is his concern about the class that assumes political leadership. It seems that in the context of the African-American, struggles he also felt that this social group was an important one. The question he raised was therefore a central one. Perhaps Rodney's *How Europe Underdeveloped Africa* was the example of the work of a "guerrilla intellectual." It was an interventionist text that, while rooted in deep scholarship and research, in many ways eschewed some of those conventions. He states in the book's preface: "The purpose has been to try and reach Africans who wish to explore further the nature of their exploitation, rather than to satisfy the standards set by our oppressors and their spokesman in the academic world."[81]

In thinking about Rodney's elaboration of a "guerrilla intellectual," it is accurate to point out that the terrain of ideas is one of the "points of struggle" in social transformation, and that revolutionary intellectuals should confront dominant knowledge regimes, tracing their linkages and their foldings into structures of domination. At the same time there is the business of theoretically developing alternative knowledge, writing a history of the practice of thought that reflects the human, not man or Eurocentrism. This has become extraordinarily important because in our contemporary world we do not live by bread alone, but by bread and the word—the latter playing a great role in shaping our conceptions of our life world. As we engage in the labor of understanding ourselves, the "guerrilla intellectual" engages in a praxis that shifts and decenters reason. For this kind of intellectual activity there are three moves. The first locates reason firmly in the black world—a geographical move. The second seeks to understand the categories and thoughts of the women and men who once stood outside the bounds of reason. In making this second move, Rodney's conception of the "guerrilla intellectual" is a useful place to begin.

The third is critical. Rodney's radical intellectual project attempted to reposition the location of theory. For Rodney the opposition of theory and practice was one which could not be sustained in the process of making a revolution, since revolution was a complex rupture primarily rooted in local conditions. In this regard revolutionary theory was to be developed in conjunction with the making of revolution. In the end, what can we make of Rodney's conceptions of the revolutionary intellectual and the guerrilla intellectual? Do they add to our understanding of the complexities of the category of revolutionary intellectual? Rodney himself has often been called an "organic" intellectual.[82] Again that category is useful, but not sufficient, to grasp the conceptions that Rodney was attempting to elaborate. What Rodney was searching for was a mode of operating for the revolutionary intellectual in neocolonial circumstances. Taking seriously the notion that one had to be engaged in order to change the social world, Rodney extended "groundings" to a substantive political praxis. It is this effort that continues to inspire the radical political imagination of those who read him.

Rodney and Fanon: The Radical Politics of Postcoloniality

Why the above comparison? We have already noted the great influence that Fanon's work on colonialism and decolonization had on Rodney. There is also the fact that both Rodney and Fanon were from the Caribbean, and that they both participated in the continental African revolution.[83] It is also important to observe that the most important theoretical work of both these radical thinkers focused on questions which arise from the African revolution. *The Wretched of the Earth,* while having global significance for all anticolonial and radical movements, was written from the heart of the African experience and in the first instance was a call for the radical militants engaged in that struggle at the moment of decolonization. In the case of Rodney, in the postindependence period two questions, among others, faced the radical movement: what economic and social paths it should follow and, in determining that path, what had been the nature of Africa and Europe's economic relationship. *How Europe Underdeveloped Africa* was Rodney's response to these questions.

There is, however, another link between Fanon and Rodney other than the Caribbean/African connection: similar intellectual concerns—one was a theorist of anticolonial struggle and decolonization, and the other was a theorist of neocolonialism; both were theorists of revolution. Oftentimes we neglect the fact that Fanon was a revolutionary. His second book published in English, *A Dying Colonialism,* in its earlier French edition was titled *Sociologie d'une révolution* (Sociology of a Revolution). But apart from the book title, Fanon's political practice was that of a revolutionary. His major political and theoretical preoccupations were the social transformations necessary for the decolonization process and the political processes required for such a task. He makes the point in *Wretched of the Earth* that decolonization can be described "in the well known words: 'The last shall be first and the first last.'"[84] In elaborating this position, Fanon did not point just to the obvious revolutionary violence entailed in such a condition,[85] but to the organization of social forces as well. It is why he paid attention to the role of the peasant, the urban unemployed, the worker, and the role of the national middle class—he was attempting to gather social groups that would effect social change. Fanon's theory of revolution is at the same time rooted in both a materialist view of society and a sociogenic one. In this instance revolution is both deed and word. It is not only the overturning of old social and political relationships but also the establishment of a "new man," inventing the new history of man with the understanding that "the nation's spoken words shape the world while at the same time renewing it."

A couple of things are interesting here. First is Fanon's difference with the offerings of Marxist historical analysis and its calls for a human freedom. Fanon does not divide human history into prehistory and human history; instead he recognizes that humanity has made history but that the issue is the nature of that history. In this regard the "new man" is something to invent and make discoveries about. This is one reason why the revolution he calls for is a richer understanding of freedom than that which others have posited. The second thing of note is that while Fanon places some emphasis on the nation as the unit of political analysis, his call for a radical humanism is a global one. In Rodney's case there is also the attempt to identify the social forces that would make the revolution. In the case of Guyana, Rodney paid very close attention to the ethnic divide between Indo-Guyanese and Afro-Guyanese. Second, he also pays attention to the unemployed urban youth, to the extent that one of his colleagues, Andaiye, remarked: "For me what Walter misread wasn't Burnham. What worried me was his misreading of that category of person called the lumpen."[86]

If, as Theda Skocpol argues, social revolution entails "rapid, basic transformations of a society's state and class structures, accompanied and in part accomplished through popular revolts from below,"[87] then Rodney was preoccupied with advancing the popular from below. This required that the social structure of both colonial and neocolonial society be interpreted concretely as designations and roles given in other social contexts that, although looking similar, may mean different things. In Rodney's political thought, revolution was also deeply connected with questions of culture. This is clearly seen in his efforts to theorize a form of political practice that we have called "groundings." If Fanon wished to expose "false decolonization," then Rodney wished to expose false socialism in the neo-colonial context.

Therefore, both Fanon and Rodney were seeking forms of authentic liberation. This search links them in a mode of being. One cannot read about the attempts on Fanon's life, his travels on behalf of the Algerian national liberation movement, or his personal code enunciated at the end of *Black Skin, White Masks*—"Make me always a man who questions"—and not see the similarities between his mode of being and Rodney's. Walter Rodney traveled extensively throughout the black world, speaking and writing on political subjects of concern to that world. As he did this, one of his constant refrains was that he was still developing his Marxism. In Guyana he was consistently arrested by the regime, and in the end he was murdered. Every fiber of Rodney's being was organized toward the liberation project. Both Fanon and Rodney were therefore *engaged*. Their personal politics was an ethics of self, organized around a radical immersion in the social and political world they inhabited.

Ngugi wa Thiong'o observed in 1985 that perhaps one difference between Rodney and Fanon was that the former placed revolution in a world context.[88] I would disagree. Both called for a self-emancipation. While they were concerned with the colonial or neocolonial world, both implicitly recognized that a new world had to be born. For Rodney this new world was born in the vortex of the struggle to understand and change the neocolonial world. His political theory and practice were founded on the effort to integrate the local dialect with the dialectic.[89] That was the fountain of his heresy. Of all the figures we have examined so far, it is Rodney who by his political praxis of "groundings" most forcibly turns our gaze toward the other stream within the black radical political tradition—the prophets. It is to them that we turn now.

THE PROPHETS

CHAPTER 6

Rastafari
Babylon, Dread History, and the Politics of Jah

Hear the words of the Rastaman say . . .
Babylon Throne burn down, Babylon Throne burn down . . .
—Wailers, "Rasta Man Chant" (1973)

Slave Driver . . . The table is turned
—Wailers, "Slave Driver" (1973)

Ethiopia shall soon stretch out her hands unto God.
—Psalm 68, verse 31

If you know your history
Then you would know where you are coming from
—Bob Marley and the Wailers, "Buffalo Soldier" (1979)

Introduction

Rastafari is a central phenomenon of twentieth-century black radicalism. Its genealogy is linked to the following features of the black radical intellectual tradition: the emergence of late nineteenth-century Ethiopianism as an explicit manifestation of black radicalism in continental Africa and the African diaspora; the mode of black protest that privileges the counterformation of alternative systems of sociocultural symbolic practices and meanings; and the way in which prophecy functions as an alternative source of resistance to colonial knowledge regimes both in Africa and in the West. In its nearly seventy-year history, Rastafari, in whatever mutated forms, has remained an ontological site of resistance to the West's efforts to make the black subject into an *object* stripped of everyday ordinariness and humanness. The resilience of Rastafari—its capacity to renew itself in different forms—in various parts of Africa, in America, and in urban

Kingston—is indicative that the struggles for human emancipation from the colonial and racialized episteme of the West, as well as from the political economy of imperial oppression, are yet to be achieved.

As an expression of twentieth-century black radicalism, Rastafari engages the most fundamental question of the black body and the African person: *Who am I?* This question is reducible neither to issues of difference nor to identity politics. Instead, it is related to what Umberto Eco calls the "Magic word which helps us define everything."[1] Frantz Fanon and others have pointed out that the black colonized native is located in the zone of the nonbeing. As a consequence, one central dimension of the antiracist and anticolonial struggle is to annihilate this zone, to construct a new being. This construction and its accompanying search for a language in which to enunciate the event have been a distinctive marker of Rastafari since its inception in Jamaica in the 1930s.

We know that oftentimes human beings tend to draw a distinction between the thing and the nature of the thing, between the "ontic" and the ontological. What is interesting to observe about the ontological quest of Rastafari is that these distinctions are collapsed. Rastafari's ontological practice is a frontal assault against colonial and racial knowledges and practices that makes the African human a thing, a Caliban, a savage, who then becomes a problem, a pathology, a native, a nigger, a Kaffir, and at best a Negro. To rescue black being, to restore humanity, to answer the question *Who am I?* means that the black subject must collapse dichotomies. The reason is very straightforward.

Being is constituted by constant interaction with the world. Since in Western thought the black subject in an anti-black world is acted upon, has an empty self, is a nothing, and thus is incapable of agency, there is no magic of being. Rastafari establishes the black as *being* in one move that has a most important consequence. In one fell swoop Rastafari makes God and man the same being. The divine in Rastafari theology is human, as Robert Marley makes clear when he sings, in "Get Up Stand Up," "We know and understand almighty God is a living Man." The consequence is that this move defines Africans as humans by announcing in Rastafari theology that a black human is God. For many, this proclamation of the late emperor of Ethiopia, Haile Selassie, as God sounds like a bizarre flight of fantasy. Selassie is dead; when alive, he was in the main a reactionary ruler; and any radical materialist analysis should shatter illusions and mythical semiotic creations. These strictures and caveats are well-known aspects of traditional materialist analysis. However, I wish to insist that if we do not grapple with the creations of the oppressed on *their* own terms, we will miss insights that are critical for the construction of an emancipatory political philosophy. Also, we will continue to reproduce theories and political practices that negate the lived experiences of African people. On such a path we will continue to ignore the Fanonian injunction that when "Ontology leaves existence aside . . . it does not allow for the understanding of the Black."[2]

It is against this background that I will review some dimensions of Rastafari. In this examination I will pay attention to the nature of prophecy and redemptive politics in the work of two paradigmatic figures of early Rastafari, Leonard Howell (the central founding figure of the movement) and Claudius Henry. Then I will attempt an elaboration of one central question that emerges from Rasta's political ontology and the practices of redemptive prophecy: the nature of historicality.

Ethiopianism, Prophecy, and Leonard Howell

We begin our narrative in Africa. In 1872, in South Africa, a white observer commenting on the growth of independent black churches stated that this movement was the "beginning of that pernicious revolt against European *guidance*."[3] The anthropologists John and Jean Comaroff have detailed white colonial South Africans' anxieties over the growth of this "Ethiopian" movement. They describe how in 1893 the Cape Parliament expressed concern, and an editorial in the *Cape Times* commented on the "racial . . . ecclesiastical, and political character" of such movements.[4] The authorities in the British colonial empire were aware of what John and Jean Comaroff have called the "domestication" of Christian Protestant practices in the Caribbean and African colonies. An integral part of this "domestication" was the creative reinterpretation of elements of the Christian doctrine and the invention of practices anathema to colonial rule. These practices were an empirewide phenomenon that constructed religious-political practices ranging from Myalism in late nineteenth-century Jamaica to Zionism in nineteenth- and twentieth-century Africa.

This is not the place to conduct a comparative analysis of the nature of religious-political practices in the African and Caribbean colonies. However, we should note the growth of black independent churches in these colonies and the way "Ethiopia" functioned on both sides of the Atlantic as a founding myth of the origins of Christianity, as well as a site of historical vindication for black humanity.[5] Bengt Sundkler, in his 1961 study *Bantu Prophets in South Africa,* recommends a typology for Ethiopianism. He makes the point that the word oscillates between two sorts of meanings. The first was "a general reference to the program Africa for the Africans with a corresponding aversion to White domination." Second, Sundkler claims that because "Ethiopia is mentioned in the Bible [it] gives antiquity to the claim of the African Church . . . [and] on the other hand the word

'Ethiopian' can be more specific referring to a particular African country."[6] Ken Post adds to this general typology Jomo Kenyatta's description of the Watch-Tower Movement in Central and Eastern Africa.[7] For St. Clair Drake, "'Ethiopianism' became an energizing myth in both the New World and in Africa itself for those pre-political movements that arose while the powerless were gathering their strength for realistic and rewarding political activity."[8]

As a movement, Ethiopianism drew on many currents in nineteenth-century black thought. These included the "domestication" of Christianity, Ethiopia as a founding mythical geographical site for black existence, a Pan-African impulse, a racial understanding of the nature of colonial oppression, and a historical understanding of black suffering as the result of Africans' being the last chosen children of God before final judgment. It is important to note the differences in the black redemptive tradition between Exodus as a story of liberation and Ethiopianism as a practice. While both utilized modes of prophecy, the Exodus story functioned, as Eddie S. Glaude, Jr., writes, as a narrative that:

> ... empowered Christian slaves and free persons to look beyond their condition and envision a future in which they were truly free. . . . the narrative structure of the story accounts for this transformation. . . . Exodus, then, is not only a story of these people but their history—a political history about slavery and freedom . . . the march, with its linear progression, its movement from beginning to end provides a key to understanding the historical and political significance of African American dramatic reenactments of the story.[9]

On the other hand, Ethiopianism functions as an explicit counterpractice that reverses symbolic orders. It draws from both biblical sources and indigenous African practices. However, there are elements of overlap in both movements, particularly in the African diaspora. For example, Rastafari combines an exodus notion of exile, and therefore of return, with a theological conception of a black human God. Part of the reason for these overlaps and similarities is that both the Exodus narrative and Ethiopianism were constructed in part from a "domestication" process. From within the Ethiopianist "domestication process" emerged the prophet figure—an amalgam of healer, diviner, political authority, and often resistance leader who inhabited African religious and political practices.[10]

In the "Opening Chant" we noted that Michael Walzer had observed that "Prophecy is a special kind of talking . . . prophecy aims to arouse remembrance, recognition, indignation, repentance."[11] Within the African tradition in the late nineteenth and twentieth centuries, prophets performed all these functions while engaging in many others. Gerhardus

Oosthuizen's, work on South African Afro-Christian churches describes prophets in the African context as having a "wider designation"[12] than in the Old and New Testaments, and links the gift and function of prophecy with healing.[13] The case of Nontetha Nkwenkwe of South Africa is clear evidence of this. She was a Xhosa woman whose dreams revealed that her duty was "to preach the bible, . . . warn that Judgment day was imminent, and to stress the unity of African people."[14] As Nkwenkwe built her following, the South African authorities twice charged her with seditious activities, and then in 1922 placed her in the Pretoria Mental Hospital. There she joined the catalog of prophetic anticolonial leaders in late nineteenth- and twentieth-century Africa who were placed in mental hospitals by colonial authorities.[15]

Across the Atlantic in colonial Jamaica, a similar situation existed. Certainly in late nineteenth-century Jamaica, Alexander Bedward's reported healing skills were a critical element that fostered the growth and emergence of the Bedwardite movement.[16] The historian Robert Hill reports that Leonard Howell had "excellent hands with sickness and helped many people, even well-to-do-people, too."[17] Howell was twice charged in the 1930s with sedition by the colonial state. In his continued skirmishes with the Jamaican colonial state, he was sent to the mental asylum in October 1937 and February 1938. By placing prophets in the mental asylum, the colonial authorities were reacting to a set of political activities that were outside the normal political practices of modernity—political party, trade union, mass demonstrations, and strikes. They confined the leadership of alternative movements in which "revolution is revealed" to the mental asylum, for in the colonial eyes such revelations were truly abnormal.

Two things were at work here. First was the way in which the colonial mind understood the "native" as a different species, and second was the social meaning of "madness" under colonialism. As the colonial regime strove to organize a polity and develop racial and colonial knowledge about the "native" subject, a key question became how to develop within the "native" an embodied consciousness that privileged Western ideas, Western modernity, and "civilization." Doing this required the construction of an episteme in the Foucauldian sense of "the fundamental codes of culture—those governing its language, its schemes of perception, its exchanges, its techniques, its values, the hierarchy of its practices."[18] The success of this dimension of the colonial project meant that in the final analysis the colonial power (certainly in the British case) was able to develop models of tutelage.[19] Ethiopianism, with its panoply of prophets, was outside the colonial episteme. It created a symbolic order in which the colonial masters oftentimes were missing or eradicated. In a context where human domination was essential for the extraction of commodities and reorganization of societies, no inch could be given to those who struggled against

158 • Black Heretics, Black Prophets

the colonial symbolic order. Therefore, those who went against the grain were "socially insane" to the colonial regimes. This was one of the central features of the colonial condition that shaped the emergence of Leonard Howell to prominence in the colony of Jamaica.

Howell's Emergence

Robert Hill notes that the early twentieth century in Jamaica was a period of religious revival. He also comments on Marcus Garvey's anxieties about the character of the revival, which he saw as "[A] large number of the people are leaving the established churches to join these religions—religions that howl, religions that create saints, religions that dance to frantic emotion."[20] Ken Post carefully documents how the political and social climates of the time were shaped by the political practice of Ethiopianism, and argues that "Ethiopianism emerged as an ideology, as a general explanation of the fate of the black man in Jamaica and throughout the world."[21] In any survey about the nature of ideology, we need to pay attention to the catalytic events that stamp an ideology's hold upon the human imagination. In the case of Ethiopianism, it was the crowning of Selassie as king and emperor of Ethiopia.

Leonard Howell was born in the parish of Clarendon, Jamaica, in June 1898. His father was an independent small farmer and his mother, an agricultural laborer. Howell had a varied career. Like many other Jamaicans from his social class, he migrated to Central America in search of a better life, and then to the United States.[22] In America he seems to have been on the fringes of radical black politics, and had some acquaintance with the leading black Communist of the period, George Padmore. It is noteworthy that in a 1940 interview Howell, when asked about the establishment of the Rastafarian camp at Pinnacle in the Jamaican parish of St. Catherine, stated that he was attempting to lead a "socialistic life."[23] When Howell returned to Jamaica in 1932, he made contact with Marcus Garvey and the Universal Negro Improvement Association (UNIA). Garvey refused him permission to sell photographs of Emperor Haile Selassie at mass UNIA meetings, and Howell began to develop his own platform. Selling the pictures at a shilling apiece, he established the King of Kings Mission and proclaimed himself the ambassador of the emperor. Within a short time he shifted his base of operation from Kingston to the eastern parish of St. Thomas, where his activities came to the attention of the colonial authorities and the Jamaican elite. In April 1933, it was reported by the island's major newspaper, *The Daily Gleaner,* that the language and content of Howell's speeches in Trinityville, St. Thomas, were seditious. One consequence of this was that the colonial state instructed the police to watch him. Late in the year, the newspaper carried a front-page feature story on

Howell, accusing him of engaging in a major swindle in the parish. The report stated in part:

> During the last few months largely attended meetings have been convened at which seditious language and blasphemous language is employed to boost the sale of the pictures of "King Ras Tafari" of Abyssinia . . . devilish attacks are made at these meetings, it is said on the government, both local and imperial and the whole proceedings would tend to provoke insurrection. . . . There are some already 800 followers of this new teaching. "King Rasta" according to the pictures, has the face of a Turk, and the said sleek young Jamaican is saying that the spirit of our Lord has returned in this mystical figure.[24]

In above newspaper report there are three things that should make us pause. First, the report makes it clear that while it thought Howell was engaged in sedition, this was a sedition that turned on language. Second, it suggested that Howell had begun to make divinity claims for Emperor Selassie, and third, that the movement seems to have grown. From the newspaper report Howell also appears to have been engaged in a common practice of many religious figures: garnering financial support from their congregation. Making the front page of the colony's major newspaper was a sure way of attracting attention, and in January 1934, Howell and his assistant, Robert Hinds, were arrested and charged with two counts of sedition. The trial judge was Sir Robert William Lyall-Grant, the same justice who had presided over the trial of John Chilembwe in what is now Malawi in 1915, an act for which he was honored and knighted.[25] The charges against Howell, read by Lyall-Grant, are worth quoting in full:

> A seditious speech in which he abused the Sovereign, Queen Victoria, the Governor of Jamaica and both the governments of Great Britain and this island thereby intending to excite hatred and contempt for His majesty the King . . . and to disturb the public peace and tranquility of this island.[26]

We should note that Lyall-Grant did not charge Howell with swindle, but instead focused on sedition. The legal proceedings of the case constituted the clash of two rationalities—the colonial one and the black "native" efforts to overthrow the symbolic order that governed the ideological space of the colony and ordered the lived experience of black Jamaicans.

Seditious Rationalities

On Tuesday, March 13, 1934, in the St. Thomas Circuit Court, Howell, described in the newspaper report as an "athletic figure in black, with a beard not dissimilar to that worn by the King of Abyssinia . . . took with him into the dock sheaths of documents and a few books of unusual proportions."[27] This presence must have struck the colonial justice system as odd . . . a black man with documents and books defending himself! The prosecuting attorney, H. M. Radcliffe, opened the colonial state's case by carefully defining sedition:

> A subject was at liberty to criticize Government once he did so constitutionally. That was to say so long as kept within the bounds of honest and fair criticism, founded on fact. When one however went beyond that limit and uttered language liable to stir up hatred between classes and bring the Sovereign into contempt, and Government and those administering it into hatred that was altogether a different thing.[28]

The kernel of the colonial state's charges came in Radcliffe's next statement, when he proposed to the jury that "While they might pass over some of the references as being untrue and nonsensical, those references were nevertheless brought within the realm of utter contempt and ridicule for the Sovereign."[29] For the colonial state, the problem was twofold: the symbolic dislocation of English sovereignty and the resulting consequences. The displacement of the English sovereign in symbolic terms had concrete political and social consequences. It meant that the payment of taxes and the political obedience of the colonial subject were threatened. Months after the trial, in August 1934, the editorial writer in the *Daily Gleaner* recognized this:

> Silly persons of the small producer and laboring classes in eastern St. Thomas who have allowed themselves to be saturated with a dangerous cult that has been labeled "Ras-Tafari" . . . have become passive resisters. They have been informed by some one, a trickster no doubt, that the instructions sent to them by Emperor Ras-Tafari from the Abyssinian capital prescribe that those who own holdings in the parish must not pay taxes to the Government, neither must others who rent lands from the Government and property owners pay rent for plots on which they squat and cultivate. Their belief is that the land belongs to the black people: no longer are they accountable to Government or property owner.[30]

The colonial authorities therefore were deeply concerned about a growing movement that might in time challenge their political rule. They were never sure when the symbolic could spill over into mass public disobedience. So in the court case the colonial state was attempting to erode the symbolic challenges that Howell had laid out. The successful challenge of the colonial symbolic order meant the creation of a subject whose mental horizons were no longer dominated by the colonial regime. Howell responded to the colonial state's charges by arguing that the king of England had acknowledged both the kingship and the divinity of Haile Selassie. He also proclaimed to the court that "Christianity was only idolatry."[31]

At this point in the court proceedings, Howell performed three moves. First, Howell was thinking in the mainstream political language of another period. His location of Haile Selassie in a special place that linked divinity and kingship drew from language about the divine rights of kingship. This move integrated the political language of a current of "domesticated Christianity" with the mainstream political discourse of empire at the time. However, in his third move, while drawing from the Bible, the principal text of Christianity, Howell flayed Christianity as idolatry. Here his key argument was that if God is a living man, then any ritual which puts God outside of both human affairs and the world worships the wrong God. This obviously was a radical criticism of some of the central aspects of Christian doctrine.

Cross-examined by Radcliffe, Howell responded that Rastafari was the Messiah who had "come back into this world . . . and that his kingdom shall have no end . . . that all kings of the earth had to bow down as he was the only King in the world as an ancient king."[32] In this enunciation Howell turned the colonial symbolic world upside down. First, if Selassie was the most important king on earth and had divine properties, then the existing colonial world of the British empire no longer had any legitimacy. Second, that illegitimacy broke the bonds of political obedience, thereby shattering the subject/sovereign relationship. Then there was a third element. Howell centered on Africa. Defending himself, Howell reiterated his statement to the people of St. Thomas: "People, you are poor but you are rich, because God planted mines of diamond and gold for you in Africa your home."[33] The report continues, "He told them that 700 billion pounds had been sent from Africa to England, and urged them to go back to Africa, the home of their forefathers."[34] Howell declared to the court, "I told them that our king had come to redeem them home to their Motherland, Africa."[35]

These statements are early enunciations of Rastafari theology, and it is accurate to say that Howell was following a stream of black radical thinking which centered on Africa. What was different about Howell's perspective is that African repatriation became *the* central demand of the movement he founded. Raising Africa in the symbolic order of the colonized in Jamaica was an achievement that would reverberate throughout the trajectory of Rastafari. In the end it would serve as the counterweight to the creation of a false multiracialism in the Jamaican nation-state, and of its Creole nationalism at the moment of the country's decolonization. The discursive practices around the centering on Africa would in postindependence Jamaica make Rastafari the ideological ground from which radical postcolonial politics could be launched.[36]

Howell was of course found guilty and sentenced. On his release he continued his work before being arrested again, and this time sent to the mental asylum. On his second release he went to the parish of St. Catherine, where he founded the Rastafari community, Pinnacle. It did not last. Robert Hill and other scholars of Rastafari have suggested that Howell's text, *The Promised Key*, should be regarded as one of the founding texts of the movement. In 1998, the text was placed in the public domain through the efforts of the editorial team involved in developing the first Rastafari reader, *Chanting Down Babylon*.[37]

The Promised Key

The text is divided into seventeen sections on subjects ranging from Ethiopia to healing, fasting, Eve as the mother of evil, and an appeal for black people to "arise and shine." It blends history, religion, politics, and healing practices. It also includes commentary on male/female relationships, marriage, and dietary habits. There are four contextual frames: the Italian invasion of Ethiopia, the centering of Ethiopia in the social mind of the black world, the discursive practice finely developed by the black radical tradition—the reinterpretation of the Bible, and the relationship of the text to two other written works in the early twentieth century: Athlyi Rogers's *The Holy Piby* (1924) and Fitz Ballantine Pettersburgh's *Royal Parchment Scroll of Black Supremacy* (1926).

Some contemporary Rastafarians have argued that *The Promised Key* was a "slight carbon copy of *The Holy Piby*.[38] What is clear is that the texts of Pettersburgh and Rogers profoundly shaped early Rastafari thought. For example, given the fact that Garvey was hostile to Howell—he turned him away from UNIA meetings and, as the Garvey scholar Rupert Lewis states, "challenged Leonard Howell's claim that Selassie was divine"[39]—it has been a puzzle how Garvey then turns up as a prophet in the Rastafari worldview. If *The Holy Piby* was one foundational text that shaped Rasta thought, then it might be that chapter 7, which "declared Marcus Garvey an apostle of the Lord God for the redemption of Ethiopia and her suffering posterities"[40] is a partial explanation for this apparent puzzle. While it is obvious that Howell drew some ideas from the *Holy Piby,* his text is a much richer one. Rogers wrote an explicitly religious text that attempted to contest the conventional Bible. Howell's text, on the other hand, not only was divided into sections but had several themes—questions of civilization, government, and the role of women—that are not found in *The Holy*

Piby. Some of *Promised Key* themes were found in Pettersburgh's text. However, the real point, I think, is that there existed in the early twentieth-century African diaspora, at the level of the subaltern, a series of writings about Ethiopianism which circulated throughout the Americas. So when Howell wrote *The Promised Key,* he was participating in a well-established discursive practice.

The Promised Key begins by identifying Ethiopia as a mystery country that is "populated by Black people whose attitude towards this so called Western civilization has not changed within the last six thousand years."[41] These people are, in Howell's eyes, both Christians and "primitive," and "extraordinarily blended into a refined fashion that cannot be met with in any other part of the world."[42] Howell's attraction to Ethiopia is based upon the fact that it was not colonized. This was combined with the recognition of the country's historic Christian tradition as well as a fallacious view, developed in the West, that the somatic features of Ethiopians made them some how different from other Africans. Following the pattern of reordering the symbolic order, Howell's text speaks about white laborers building a road for the emperor, and flays traditional Christian churches and the papacy. His language continuously refers to Europeans as "Anglo-Saxon white people," and posits that Ethiopia is the "succeeding Kingdom of the Anglo-Saxon Kingdom." A great deal of the text's politics revolves around establishing an alternative system of monarchy that usurps the European model. Within this history and politics of the rise and fall of kingdoms is embedded an attempt to explain the enslavement and colonial condition of Africans, and their eventual redemption. The appearance of Haile Selassie, in the eyes of the prophet Howell, meant that judgment had finally come and that evil would soon befall the Anglo-Saxon Kingdom: "They showed us no mercy therefore evil shall come upon them suddenly."[43]

This dimension of the text resembles many other prophetic texts in which God acts through history in what Paget Henry has felicitously called "providential historicism."[44] But Howell's narrative of history posits a new twist, since for him God works through history only at the moment of judgment. For Howell the rise and fall of kingdoms is the work not of God but of human action. However, the time of judgment that ushers in the new dispensation which would redeem blacks *would* be an act of God. Finally, there was a major difference from Henry's "providential historicism": the God of Howell was now human.

When the text turns to healing and balm yards it repudiates obeah. Howell makes distinctions between different healing practices, calling one set "the Royal" work of healing, which can be done only by the Holy Spirit, and the other, healing that is done for the "cleansing and healing of the nations."[45] The second form of healing is conducted by the prophets, the "consecrated men and women that the holy spirit moves,"[46] and is called balming. This balming is very similar to the healing practices of the independent Zionist churches of which we spoke earlier.

The text also argues for what it calls "Black Supremacy." This notion appears in the text in both religious and political guises.[47] In its religious dimension "Black Supremacy" is conceived of as recognizing the power of full baptism and being linked with the rise of a new religion. In its political aspect Black Supremacy is counterposed to white supremacy. Howell writes, " Black Supremacy has taken charge of white supremacy by King Alpha and Queen Omega, the King of Kings. Instead of saying Civilization hereafter we shall say Black Supremacy."[48] In Howell's symbolic world, however, whites would be allowed to live with equality *if* they supported this black government and deity/king. Howell's order of "Black Supremacy rested upon open acknowledgment of the idea that by oppressing people, white governments had failed, and needed to be destroyed. He argued that as a consequence of white governments' failure, they no longer deserved to rule. On the other hand, Howell claimed that "Black Supremacy will promote the mortals of every shade according to our power . . . the Black museum will be opened day and night for life. Education will be free and compulsory to all mortal beings, if you are not an enemy of Black Supremacy."[49]

Howell's perspective is based on reordering the world through the establishment of another kingdom. Politics in such a kingdom are tied to sovereign/subject relationships. Howell's text also calls for race-based marriages and establishes a patriarchal perspective on the role of women. In the text Howell suggests a narrative in which the Klan and lynchers of America raped black women in what he calls "Advance Rate."[50] This "Advance Rate" created in Howell's mind another race of people. However, he gives no special weight to these mixed offspring, and continues to operate from within the framework of the existence of two main races. Thus he sees the political and religious history of the world climaxing in the overthrow of white supremacy by "Black Supremacy." Sensitive to the issues surrounding lynching in America, Howell calls for "both the perceived rapists (meaning black men who were purported to have raped white women), mob lynchers and the Klu-Klux-Klan . . . to be shot down from off the face of . . . beautiful earth."[51] He ends the text with an appeal: "Black people, [to] Arise and Shine."[52]

At its core this text makes the first last and the last first, but does so without any fundamental reorganization of hierarchical structures. In other symbolic reorderings of black prophets, the proposed new order is one of equality. Not so in Howell. His new symbolic order maintains sovereign monarchical rule and, as a consequence, while he overturns the colonial symbolic order, brings Africa to the fore, and creates the conditions for its embodiment within the Afro-Caribbean commonsense consciousness, he does not create a revolutionary world order. So what we have here are the different streams of symbolic reorderings that are contained within the black radical tradition. Some reorderings are shaped more than others by the political ideas of the period, while others distance themselves and invent new political language. In the case of Howell, it is clear that he developed a religious/political doctrine which reversed the historic claims of white supremacy, racism, and colonialism. However, in doing this he paid no attention to questions of equality. His validation of the black being was therefore on terms that were strikingly similar to the criteria of the human subject at the time: masculinity and a subject relationship to nation-state and king. In radical political discourse and practice, such a form of validation is highly problematic, and in the end leads to disastrous political consequences. In Howell's case this was not a danger, primarily because what he was concerned with was *symbolic displacement* and the historical reclamation of Africa for the African diaspora.

It should also be observed that during this period in Jamaica, Rastafari was not the only stream of Ethiopianism. Ken Post, in his magisterial volume on Jamaican society in 1930s, *Arise Ye Starvelings,* has carefully documented other streams and their influences in helping to create the conditions for the major labor rebellion of May 1938, which shook the colonial system.[53] What was distinctive about Rastafari during this early period of its history was its preoccupation with creating what Barry Chevannes has called a "community of believers"[54] and the construction of a worldview.

But worldviews do not remain static. Over time new prophets appear who appropriate and refashion their components. Such refashioning is critical for the renewal of the worldviews and their survival. It is in this regard that we must now review the work of Claudius Henry and the only guerrilla movement in twentieth-century colonial Jamaica. But before we leave Howell, we should note that in 1941, when his camp was raided by the colonial state, the *Jamaica Times* attempted to do an investigative story on Pinnacle. It is worth quoting one of the inhabitants of the camp who was interviewed at the time. This woman stated that she had "disposed of all her worldly possessions when preaching convinced her that Ras Tafari was truly the Kings of Kings." She also thought the economic benefits of joining the camp would mean that "There would be no need to worry about the day's meal, the landlord or the bill collector; as a matter of fact there would be nothing to worry about at all."[55] What this woman was referring to was the other dimension in Rastafarian thinking, which existed alongside prophecy: utopia. It is a feature that we will extensively discuss later, when we examine the nature of historicality in Rastafari thought.

Claudius Henry, Jah Politics, and African Redemption

While Leonard Howell laid down some of the foundational arguments for Rastafari and focused on building a "community of believers," the practices of Claudius Henry expressed other dimensions and complexities of Rastafari.

The story of Claudius Henry is well known, so we will rehearse here only its barest details.[56] Born in 1903 in the parish of Manchester, Henry at an early age claimed to have received visions. When he was twenty-six years old, he was arrested by the police and sent to a mental asylum, but was released after medical officers declared him cured. He then migrated to America, where he resided for thirteen years, becoming a preacher. In 1957 he returned to Jamaica and made contact with the Rastafari movement. Through his contacts with Prince Emmanuel,[57] he was put in touch with sections of the movement in St. Andrew, and particularly with Edna Fisher, who later became his wife and the key organizer for their movement, the African Reform Church.

Henry's testimony at his 1960 treason trial recounts both his beliefs and the chronological development of his movement. He states that when he returned to Jamaica, he did so with the intention of "instructing the black people in particular to go back to Africa and to reform himself."[58] His testimony also confirms that a significant moment in the evolution of his beliefs came when he met Edna Fisher. He claims that when he met her in 1958, she had a prayer circle in her home, which he joined. By that time, Henry states, he had come to believe that Haile Selassie was "earth's returned messiah [and that] his people should accept him."[59] Using Fisher's prayer circle as his base, Henry embarked upon an extensive campaign. Claiming that he had been to Africa, he publicly portrayed an aura of African authencity that gave him an edge over many of the Rastafari leaders at the time. With the thirty-five members of the prayer group, Henry and Fisher began to build a church. By 1959 the congregation had grown to thousands even though, as Henry observes, "He received opposition from some Rastafarians—those who did want to be reformed personally."[60] One of the major points of dispute between Henry and other Rastafarians was his insistence on keeping the Sabbath on Saturday. Another was the fact that Henry's congregation behaved more like traditional Christians, typically engaging in rituals of regular church attendance. The other major Rastafari currents at the time, such as that of Prince Emmanuel, were establishing a utopian community, and the dreadlocks current was cultivating a social-political and religious creed part of which was a distinctive hairstyle as one of its key rituals.[61]

But while Henry might have elaborated new Rastafari rituals, his central organizational and doctrinal claim was his back-to-Africa credo. In October 1959, Henry revealed that there would be "miraculous repatriation." Thousands of Jamaicans left their belongings and gathered for the miraculous event. Such a phenomenon was a regular occurrence in Jamaican history. For example, Alexander Bedward had promised that he and his followers would be taken up to heaven. In the mythology that surrounded Marcus Garvey, the UNIA's shipping company, Black Star Line, had worked its way into a belief that one day a ship would arrive and remove black people from colonial bondage in Jamaica. In the wretched conditions of the colony, such views created hope, gave dignity, and allowed many to live with a sense of themselves as human beings. It also was part of a long tradition in the New World, where slavery was seen as displacement and exile, and could be redeemed only by return to Africa. To return home, to be involved in an exodus, was therefore a consistent feature of black political and intellectual practice in the West. What is unique about Claudius Henry is that he managed to integrate the return to Africa with religious practices and *explicit* political actions against the Jamaican colonial state.

The pamphlet Henry used to mobilize followers for repatriation was titled *Standing in the Gap, with Unquestionable Truth, Pioneering Israel Back Home to Africa.* It spelled out in clear detail how Henry saw himself, and his analysis of Jamaican and colonial politics. Henry viewed himself as "God's appointed and Anointed Prophet."[62] Calling for a meeting on the anniversary of the emancipation of slaves in the British Caribbean colonies, Henry promised that this would be the last such Emancipation Day spent away from Africa. In Africa, Henry declared, "God's Righteous Government of Everlasting Peace on earth" would be created. This "righteous government" was counterposed to "Jamaica self-government or any other self-Government." Henry asked his Jamaican readers:

> Should we sacrifice such a righteous government for a Jamaican self-government . . . shall we sacrifice the continent of Africa for the island of Jamaica? Shall we refuse God's offer for repatriation back home to Africa and a life of everlasting peace and freedom . . . and go back to slavery under these wicked, unrighteous and oppressive rulers of Jamaica . . . they have nothing to offer us! All their sweet promises and what they hope to obtain out of self-government under British colonial rule can only lead us to into destruction and captivity.[63]

By then Henry had developed a cogent analysis of the nature of internal self-government, anticolonial Creole nationalism in Jamaica, and the possibilities of full decolonization. His recognition of the anticolonial political struggles in the island made his ideological view an added feature of Rastafari ideology. This specific concern with Jamaican politics would reappear in the 1960s in the work of Sam Brown and his program of black redemption. At the time that Howell and the early Rastas were developing their symbolic revolt against the colonial order, Jamaica's decolonialziation process was at the stage of internal self-government. The nationalist movement born out of the 1938 worker rebellion had won universal adult suffrage in 1944 and constructed a path to self-government, which was rooted in the political ideas of a Creole nationalism. This form of anticolonial nationalism paid no attention to questions of race or to the place of Africa in the imagination of the Jamaican popular classes. It attempted to build a nation-state in which the hegemonic ideology would be a false multiracialism that operated under the cloak of European norms. Its ideological stance was rooted in late nineteenth-century conceptions of the British Caribbean as populated by "Creole Negroes" who had the capacity to be civilized.[64] What the popularity of the Henry movement signified was that the Creole nationalist movement had been unable to tap into the deepest subjectivities of black Jamaicans.

Henry represented a stream of black redemptive thought that existed in late nineteenth- and twentieth-century Jamaican social life. With its focus on Africa, its explicit vindication of blackness, its Pan-Africanism, and its oftentimes religious expression, this current was seen by the Creole nationalist elites as "backward" and nonmodern. It also was often regarded as atavistic, so much so that Rex Nettleford has argued that Creole nationalism created a Jamaicanism which abhorred black nationalism.[65] In this context the oppositional activities of Henry were warning signs that all was not well with the formal anticolonial movement and the gathering momentum for political independence of the island.

When the miraculous event did not occur, both the native ruling elite and the Colonial Office relaxed, feeling that Henry and his activities would soon disappear; they did not take his creativity into account. The failure of the miraculous event forced Henry to rethink his back-to-Africa strategy. This rethinking led him to an elaboration of an analysis that Jamaica was itself a black country, and therefore should be freed from colonial oppression. In a pamphlet issued in January 1960, Henry elaborated the reasons for this change:

> I have received official communications from Britain through the Jamaican Government advising me not to preach anything to my people regarding repatriation back to Africa. [They say] . . . there is no country in Africa, willing to accept any great amounts of West Indians to settle down. Also they have no reserve funds to sponsor such a Movement. We as Rastafarians . . . are not wanted in Jamaica. . . . Our only hope for world peace and everlasting freedom

is now organizing to reconstruct and to build a new and Righteous Jamaica. A government which will be approved of by Jehovah God, the world's Creator, a Righteous Government.[66]

There are a couple of things we should note here. In the first place, Henry seems to be repeating the establishment arguments against Rastafari's quest to return to Africa. Second, he seems to be saying, at least publicly, that if he and his followers were not allowed to return to Africa, he would organize to remove the Jamaican regime. From this changed perspective Henry developed a three-pronged approach for an overall struggle against British colonialism. In the first prong, Jamaica would be liberated; this was to be followed by struggles against British colonialism in the Caribbean region, using Jamaica as a base; the third prong of the struggle was an armed assault against British colonialism in Africa. All of these struggles were to be carried out by guerrilla movements, and it is clear that at this point Henry was being influenced by the success of the 1959 Cuban Revolution. Such new elaborations would impact upon the doctrine of Rastafari.

With his new political view Henry began to plan, along with Ronald, his son in New York, a strategy for the overthrowing of the Jamaican colonial state and its native political elite. These efforts opened a new chapter in the historical trajectory of the black redemptive movement in Jamaica.

Brian Meeks has painted a detailed picture of the small band of guerrillas led by Ronald Henry.[67] Meeks's portrayal, based on access to important records of the colonial state, indicates what was suspected by many: that the group was ill prepared. Meeks places the rebellion in a black Atlantic radical tradition, but pays little attention to either the organizational layers of the movement or its internal ideology. Using elite archives and the group's publications, we are in a position to construct both the central layers of the organization and its main political ideas. Organizationally the group had three layers. The first was the congregation of the church itself, composed of regular members who, it seems, were not made aware of the plans for guerrilla warfare against the Jamaican colonial state. The second layer was composed of Jamaicans and African-Americans who lived in New York and carried out activities, including robberies, to fund the group. This layer of the group met regularly at 332 Beckman Street in the Bronx, had about fifty members, and called itself First Africa Corps. In a letter to his father, Ronald Henry gives us an idea about some of the plans of the group:

I have started [the] First Africa Corps and doing fine so far with Agard and several other fellows. It is very time consuming and leaves me with no time for school or social activities that I don't mind a bit as long as it is for the cause of our race. The plan is this, to gather a force of about 600 and leave secretly and land on the shore of certain Colony, take the capital and proceed to occupy the place and round up all the Europeans and either kill or ship the hell to their ice box Europe.[68]

The Agard mentioned in Ronald Henry's letter was a New York police officer who was later arrested by the police. The *New York Times* reported that he was arrested for "holdups in this city to finance the operations" of what the newspaper called an "African Nationalist group that plotted revolt in the West Indies."[69] The newspaper report also stated that Agard was "the undercover person responsible for the organization's security" and that the group had secured at least $6000 in holdups to procure weapons.

The third layer of the organization was its Jamaican leadership. Here the organization seems to have been divided into political and military leaders. For example, their letter to Fidel Castro was written and signed by commanders and brigadiers, and Claudius Henry's name was missing from this list. However, the proclamation of the revolt was signed by him along others who were not commanders or brigadiers, with the exception of Claudius Beckford and D. S. Jarrett, both of whom had signed the Castro letter. The level of organization of Henry's group is indicative of a well-worked plan for insurrection, and should tell us that when we examine the politics of the subaltern, it is important to spend time grappling with the ideas of political organization.

On April 7, 1960, the colonial police raided the African Reform Church. The newspaper reports of the raid state that the police found "over 2,500 electrical detonators, 1,800 ordinary detonators, a shotgun, a .32 revolver, about 70 machetes and several sticks of dynamite." But more important, in this period of the cold war, they found a letter addressed to Fidel Castro that was signed by twelve members of Henry's organization, including Edna Fisher. Also found was the proclamation already mentioned. Both documents reveal some of the political ideas which guided Henry at that time.

The letter to Castro was written on a document titled "The Ethiopia Coptic Training Center," and the proclamation was written under the heading, which Henry had proclaimed in October 1959, "Pioneering Israel Back Home to Africa." None of these documents implicated the majority of the African Reform Church congregation, revealing that the leaders of the planned revolt took scrupulous care to distinguish themselves from their church. Armed uprising, they recognized, was not something that all members of the congregation would embrace. Henry's first track of activity, then, was to plan for armed overthrow while continuing to preach regularly in his church.

His other activity was the development of an ideological stance that "secularized" elements of Rastafari. The clearest indication of this is the character of the letter to Castro. The letter begins with an appeal to Castro, asking him to recognize the leader of the group, Reverend Henry, and the organization's twenty thousand members, who were now organizing a "lepers Government." The letter then traces the history of African enslavement in the Caribbean and expresses the desire to return to Africa after four hundred years of colonialism and slavery. It next compares their return to Africa with the government of Castro, which, it states, "gives justice to the poor." Claiming that peaceful efforts at repatriation had failed, the letter declares that its writers have come to the conclusion that they must now "fight a war for what is ours by right," and "assure" Castro "that Jamaica and the rest of the British West Indies will be turned over to you and your government, after this war which [we] are preparing to start for Africa's freedom is completed." The proposed war was part of a larger war for African freedom, which could be realized only when "her scattered children are restored." The letter then confirms that black people in Jamaica support Castro and asks him to grant an audience to their leader, Reverend Henry. It also requests that Castro inform the Soviet leaders of their movements. Finally, the letter asks that any response be sent to Henry's address in New York, 332 Beckman Street. This remarkable document is undated, but what is interesting to note is that Henry left Jamaica in February 1960 for New York, and returned in April of the same year.

At the level of political ideas, the two most important were the clear statement of a wider view of African liberation, which was inclusive of the British colonies, and the view of Fidel Castro. At work here was the argument that colonialism had stolen lands from their original inhabitants, and that part of the work of revolution was to restore such lands to the representatives of the indigenous people. It is a sentiment in black radical Caribbean thought that was embodied in the late eighteenth century when the leader of Haitian independence, Dessalines, renamed the former French colony of San Domingo "Haiti," invoking the memory of the island's first inhabitants.

The "Pioneering Back Home" proclamation repeated some of the arguments of the letter, referring to the history of slavery and describing the organization's desire to return to Africa, if not in peace, "then in war." It announced that the Russian leaders would understand, and that "the Cuban Prime-Minister will be the leader of Jamaica in the very near future, as we do not want Jamaica but to go home." It ended with the declaration "I hereby pledge to defend his government [Castro's] with my 20,000 people, as my soul and God liveth in me, to bring freedom to Africa and everlasting peace to all her scattered slaves those at home and those abroad."[70] The last sentence of the proclamation is the popular paraphrasing of the well-known clarion call of the UNIA, "Africa for Africans, those at Home and abroad."

All this confirms that Henry and his group were participating in a political and discursive practice rooted in the black tradition. But before we address what new ideas Henry brought to this tradition, we will make a short detour and review his consistent reference to his support being around twenty thousand persons. We know that his organization did not have those numbers, so where does the figure spring from? The American state archives reveal that the British and American governments felt that the Rastafari movement numbered around twenty thousand persons. In a set of memoranda between the American consul general, Robert McGregor, and the U.S. State Department, we find the following report:

> One of the avowed Rasta objectives (and perhaps the only commonly held among their various groupings) is to go to Africa. So much is this so that one is led to believe that if the 20,000 hard core were loaded on ships and set down on an African shore, Jamaica would be free of this cancer.[71]

Thus twenty thousand seems to have been a generally accepted figure for the membership of the Rastafari movement, and it is clear that Henry, seeing himself as a representative of this movement, was hoping that at the moment of revolution they would all rally to the cause. The attempted rebellion was not successful. Its early moments were marked by internal strife between those who saw the liberation of Jamaica as a stepping-stone to African liberation and those who did not hold that view. This dispute led to internal executions that obviously had an adverse effect upon the band of guerrillas. The guerrillas were finally captured by colonial state forces, and charged with treason and murder. Four of them were sentenced to hang. Claudius Henry was charged with felony treason and sentenced to prison. Among those hanged by the state were three American citizens (including Henry's son, Ronald) who had joined the revolt.

An episode in the aftermath of their death is a telling one about the Jamaican colonial state's attitude toward the group. The relatives of the three American citizens—Ronald Henry, William Jeter, and Eldred Morgan—requested the return of their remains to America. In a dispatch cable Robert McGregor informed the Department of State that the relatives' petition had been denied by the Jamaican government because, in the words of the colonial governor, "The practice of requiring burial in Jamaica of all executed prisoners in the prison cemetery is a long standing one."[72] McGregor's dispatch continues that the governor felt that "to deviate from long standing practices would make it possible for certain elements to hold demonstrations or cause riots ... delivery of the bodies to other than prison personnel might open the way for unscrupulous persons to give false post mortems with consequent actions injurious to the the government."[73]

We now turn to the question of how far Henry and his group shifted or changed the mainstream doctrines of Rastafari. As was explained before, the Jamaican context of the mid-twentieth century was different from that of the 1930s. Self-government was now on the agenda, and the African decolonziation movement that had begun in Ghana was picking up steam. The Cuban Revolution had inspired nationalist anticolonial movements, and its theory of guerrilla warfare caught the attention of many Third World radicals. In all of this Henry continued to focus on African liberation. His view that to achieve repatriation to Africa, Jamaica had to be liberated by armed struggle was a long way from that of Howell and the early Rastafari. The symbolic counterrevolution had now taken on another dimension, suggesting that it might be a short step from the symbolic world to the domain of practical politics and social revolution. When Henry was released from prison in 1967, he moved his operations to the parish of Clarendon and established a successful community economic venture. However, his influence continued to be important as a progressive, symbolic one. In 1972 the center-left People's National Party (PNP), under the leadership of Michael Manley, sought and received his support. After the 1980 general election in which the anti-imperialist project of the PNP was defeated, Henry gave his support to the small Communist movement in the island.

What are we to make of Henry, and how do his activities suggest an alternative way to understand, in concrete historical contexts, the prophetic stream of the black radical tradition? The answers to this question surround some current issues of postcolonial theory, the nature of subaltern studies, and critical questions about the human sciences. A great deal of postcolonial studies is about the marginality of the *other*. This marginality is a site of subversion from which powerful critiques of colonialism are launched. In grappling with accounts of this critique, Gayatri Spivak asks, "Can the Subaltern Speak?"[74] For Spivak the problematic of the subaltern voice relates to women and the silencing of female voices. However, she makes a general point about subaltern voices and the "permission to narrate." This permission, she argues, is related to an essentialist agenda that "must traffic in a radical textual practice of difference. A deviation from an ideal."[75] From this stance Spivak asks, "How can we touch the consciousness of the people, even as we investigate their politics? With what voice-consciousness can the subaltern speak?"[76] These are questions that must animate anyone attempting to grapple with the nature of human domination and the discourses and political practices which have sought to overturn various forms of domination. In raising the issue, Spivak does not venture any answer that deals with the questions of consciousness and hegemony; instead, she focuses on Derrida's deconstruction strategy and attempts to read a set of Indian texts through this lens. My rendering of the lives and prophetic redemptive activities of Leonard Howell and Claudius Henry indicates that the "subaltern" *does* have a voice. So powerful is this voice that I want to suggest that we need to rethink two things. The first is the space for a theory of hegemony, and the second is how we might approach the question of subaltern history.

Subaltern and Hegemony

Let us begin with the subaltern. Gramsci's "Notes on Italian History" is a methodological essay on the nature of historical research into the activities of the "subaltern classes." Operating from the stance that the state equals both "dictatorship and hegemony,"[77] Gramsci was concerned to map the subalterns' "active or passive affiliation to the dominant political formations, their attempts to press claims of their own and the consequences of these attempts in determining the processes of decomposition, renovation or neo-formation."[78] However, he felt that the subaltern produced formations which were limited and partial. Why was this so? The answer resides in two things: Gramsci's conception about the revolutionary party serving as an external trigger in the creation of counterhegemonic ideas, and the suggestion that subaltern activity in general is incapable of independently elaborating a coherent set of radical political ideas.

Steven Feierman has critiqued this dimension of Gramsci's theory with reference to Africa.[79] James Scott, in his elaboration of "thin" and "thick" versions of hegemony,[80] also has suggested weaknesses in Gramsci's notion of hegemony. I think that the problems of hegemony in the Gramscian frame relate to Gramsci's understanding of the relationship between "philosophy" and the "folk." It is important to note that Gramsci does not follow Marx in making distinctions between intellectual and manual work. For Gramsci there exists a minimum of creative intellectual activity in any physical work. He concedes that the human being "participates in a conception of the world, he has a conscious line of moral conduct, and therefore contributes to sustaining or to modifying a conception of the world."[81] For Gramsci the real conundrum is the degree to which thought is philosophy, common sense, or folk. So although in the Gramscian frame all humans are "philosophers," properly speaking, "philosophy is an intellectual order, which neither religion nor common sense can be."[82] As a consequence, he says, "Religion and common sense cannot constitute an intellectual order, because they cannot be reduced to unity and coherence. . . ."[83] At this point Gramsci is caught within his own discursive practice and a conception of knowledge within a frame of "cognitive hierarchies."[84] In this frame, religion is seen as low-level intellectual activity. At the level of common sense, what Gramsci calls "the active man in the mass," there exist only practical activity and contradictory consciousness, which become critical in understanding a political struggle[85] For Gramsci, political struggle and the role of the party are the catalyst for the transformations in political and social knowledge. Thus, Gramsci's achievement is to recognize the partial agency of social groups who are dominated.

The initial work of the Indian Subaltern Collective follows Gramsci's lead and attempts to create more space for subaltern thought. Ranajit Guha's inaugural statement of the collective regarding the dominant historiography of India states, "What is clearly left out is the politics of the people . . . this was an autonomous domain, for it neither originated in elite politics nor did this existence depend on the latter."[86] In relation to hegemony, Guha developed the notion of "dominance without hegemony."[87] He correctly asserted that while in the bourgeois state, "The moment of persuasion outweighed that of coercion . . . in the colonial state . . . persuasion [was] outweighed by coercion."[88] Thus dominance in the colonial context did not necessarily express itself in hegemony. This is an important modification of the function of hegemony in the colonial context. However, it does not mean that the colonial power did not attempt to construct hegemony by creating and making efforts to implement regulatory subject behavior.

What I think is more accurate to point out is that in many cases, that dimension of the colonial project very quickly fractured. This means that Guha's conception of an "autonomous" politics of the people as a general rule of subaltern political practices is problematic. The radical politics of the people is constructed *in opposition* to elite and bourgeois politics. It ideologically responds to elite politics. Although there is an "autonomous" aspect to this form of politics, it does have a relationship to elite politics even as it distinguishes itself. The sources from which subaltern radical politics draw are oftentimes ones not necessarily represented in the elite conceptual schema of politics. However when we shift our gaze to the Caribbean and Africa in the colonial period, we see that the "politics of the people" revolve around the establishment of a set of counterhegemonic practices which sometimes derive from some of the ideas of the colonial West, such as Christianity, while simultaneously drawing from other belief systems. The marriage of these counterhegemonic practices creates what Sylvia Wynter calls a "cultural signifying system."[89] Such a system operates at a deep level and constructs a counterworld that is "symbolically articulated and organized."[90]

The articulation of this counterworld for the native and the colonized black does not fall neatly within the Gramscian categories of "common sense" and religion as "lower-level thinking." Indeed, as we have attempted to demonstrate in this chapter, the ideas of Howell (to a lesser degree) and of Claudius Henry were elaborate workings of an ideological negative to the Jamaican colonial order. If hegemony is the glue that holds the state and individual together in a citizen/subject relationship, then the creation of counterworld ideologies in a context where the black is a *nothing* requires us to look anew at the way hegemony functions and fractures. It means that we should now examine the *interiority* of the colonized native. Césaire reminds us that in the colonial context it is not only that the black native is not a citizen. He puts it this way: "We are dealing with the only race which is denied even the notion of humanity."[91] One has only to recollect the numerous murderous campaigns of pacification of the colonial enterprise to see the social truth of Césaire's statement.

The consequence of all of this is that the natives' resistance becomes, as we said before, a project of human validation, of creating within their own reality the quotidian new meanings for their lived experiences. So in the end the subaltern *does* speak, has a voice and agency, and is a subject who creates a symbolic order, which sometimes moves beyond symbolic inversion to symbolic *displacement*. This displacement oftentimes emerges as a radical configuration with a line of alternative historical explanation. To fully capture this turn, I now want to address the question of subaltern historicality in the Caribbean.

Making History: Caribbean Historiography and Dread History

In his 1969 commentary on J. J. Thomas's classic text of nineteenth-century Caribbean anticolonialism, *Froudacity*, C. L. R. James notes "that I have long believed that there is something in the West Indian past . . . something in the West Indian historical development, which compels the West Indian intellectual . . . to place us in history."[92] James further states that the reason for this is that "We of the Caribbean are a people more than any other people constructed by history." Now I think that there is a bit of exaggeration here on James's part, since all people are constructed by history. But I think what James means is that the modern Caribbean was born in a unique historical moment in the development of global capitalism. However, what is perhaps more important for our present purposes is James's claim that one of the distinctive features of J. J. Thomas is the fact that he was a better historian than the English Regis professor, Anthony Froude. James opines: "Thomas bases himself on a sense of history which he defines as a controlling law."[93] The Caribbean novelist Wilson Harris, in his seminal essay "History, Fable and Myth," draws our attention to the fact that the view of history as controlling law is a highly problematic one for the Caribbean: ". . . what is bitterly ironic . . . is that the present day historians . . . militant and critical of imperialism as they are have fallen victim, in another sense, to the imperialism they appear to denounce."[94] For Harris the issue is not history as such but the *nature* of the historical categories that Caribbean intellectuals, radical or otherwise, have deployed in grappling with Caribbean society. The poet Derek Walcott has argued that "The Caribbean sensibility is not marinated in the past. It is not exhausted. It is new. But it is its complexity, not its historically explained simplicities, which is new."[95] Edouard Glissant, the Antillean poet and cultural critic argues that, "one of the most disturbing consequences of colonization could well be this notion of a single History." He further makes the point that for the Caribbean, "the repossession of the meaning of our history begins with the awareness of the real discontinuity that we no longer passively live through."[96] The centrality of history to the Caribbean experience and the ways in which the novelists of the region have sought to use and explore it is ably explicated in Nana Wilson-Tagoe's *Historical Thought and Literary Representation in West Indian Literature* (1998). Paget Henry, in *Caliban's Reason,* has made an effort to dissect the Caribbean quarrels over history and in doing so has classified the quarrels as a tension between "poeticism and historicism."

While this classification is a provocative one, it is limited. Thus I want to draw attention to another current in the Afro-Caribbean intellectual tradition, that does not fall neatly within either of these two streams. In doing so, I am reviewing the Afro-Caribbean intellectual tradition and, I hope, pointing out its rich complexities. What I explore here is another set of archives, which are normally closed to Caribbean scholarship. The Caribbean poet and historian Kamau Brathwaite calls these archives the "inner plantation."[97] Brathwaite makes the point that the "inner plantation" is concerned with "cores and kernels; resistant local forms; roots, stumps, survival rhythms; growing points." How does all of this relate to the issues that surround radical Caribbean historiography, the nature of historicality and Rastafari thought?

Historiography and Caribbean Society

There are of course different currents within Caribbean historiography, and Barry Higman's *Writing West Indian Histories* (1999) and his edited volume, *General History of the Caribbean: Methodology and Historiography of the Caribbean* (1999) give us good snapshot of these. However, arguably the defining work on English-speaking Caribbean historiography is that of Elsa Goveia. At the level of historical discipline and knowledge, this extraordinary scholar refocused the study of history in the Caribbean. In 1956 Goveia argued that "The meaning of Caribbean history should be sought not in the narrative of events but in a wider understanding of the thoughts, habits and institutions of a whole society."[98] Goveia's work raised the question of the nature of the Caribbean historical enterprise, historical interpretation (how did it happen?), and causation (evidence). Her project was to demonstrate that until the nineteenth century, a significant number of the writers of Caribbean history "worked on the assumption that one man was different in kind, and not merely in degree, from others and that this difference was a matter of race, not of individuals."[99] As a consequence, she argues, "The historians of these regions have not hesitated to generalize, and have sometimes generalized extremely rashly from principles by no means based upon the finds of historical empiricism. Cultural and racial differences have been interpreted in terms of superiority and inferiority."[100] I take Goveia's "historical empiricism" to mean the concrete specificities of the region, seen through the view that the black Caribbean person was a human being, and therefore any history of Caribbean society should begin there. In this regard she remakes the point that W. E. B. Du Bois made in his *Black Reconstruction*. However, there was an additional point about "historical empiricism," and that was the gaze of the historian and how he or she understood social change. For Goveia, a study of history supplied what she called "the principle of change."[101] And for history to understand this principle required a wider field of historical writing than the political narrative.

It is fair to say that while there continues to be the practice of different forms of history in the Caribbean, some of the general questions initially posed by Goveia about assumptions of historical writings and the purposes of history have not been vigorously debated. Of course any debates about history and its meanings today have to take into account the questions of the narrative, representation, and historical discourse. In a recent publication on some of these questions, the issue was posed that in the general epistemological problems of Caribbean history, "The history of resistance becomes a complement to the history of power . . . there is no history of slavery told by those who suffered from it."[102] Now while this is a legitimate question, it still has been posed without regard to the ways in which the narratives of slavery are recounted in the Caribbean.

Recognizing this while grappling with questions of political thought in the region, I asked: What would happen if we were to shift our archives? Instead of focusing on standard forms of historical production, what would happen if we were to study the interpretations of the Caribbean that have originated from the "inner plantation" and ask whether there are historical questions posed in *this* archive? Second, if there are historical questions, do they represent a current of philosophy of history within the Caribbean? This is a different question than the one Wilson Harris posed when he queried whether or not there was a philosophy of history "which may be buried in the arts of the imagination."[103] The conclusion of this journey led me to the notion of *Dread history* as both *poetics* and *philosophy of history*. Dread has many meanings in the idiom of Rastafari. It can mean the description of an authentic Rastafarian, used as a form of greeting or as word suggesting great difficulty and trouble. We know of course that for Soren Kierkegaard, dread was about forms of anxieties that consumed "all definite ends and discovers all their deceptions."[104] However what happens in what I am calling *Dread history* is the development of a historical gaze that seizes upon the so-called black experience, boldly reconfigures its meanings and shatters the silences in mainstream historical knowledge. It is also a heterological form of historical practice that destabilizes the division between thought and being, because as Joseph Owen puts it, in Rastafari, dread is also about the confrontation with the historically denied black self-hood.

Let me start with what *Dread history* is not. It is not a history of Rastafari, nor a version of history that reproduces only Rastafari ideas.[105] Dread history is not concerned to make distinctions between poeticism and standard historical narrative or historicism. It is not preoccupied with events per se, but rather with the *meaning* of events. Its preoccupation with the past is a preoccupation with the questions of the present and the specific contours of oppression in the Caribbean. As such, it does not operate in the structure of what Walter Benjamin has called "homogeneous, empty time."[106] So what are its features?

Dread History's Meaning

First, Dread history is an attempt both to grapple with the lived experiences of the Afro-Caribbean masses and to link these experiences to quests for emancipation and philosophies of hope. Second, Dread history attempts to excavate from the practices and ideas of the subaltern resistance movements in the Caribbean a worldview in which hope is rooted in a conception of the bourgeois colonial world turned upside down and in radical desire. Third and most obviously, Dread history draws from elements of the Rastafari worldview, to which it has a semantic relationship. Fourth, Dread History collapses standard historical time to understand patterns of oppression and speaks to the silences in the dominant productions of historical knowledge. Fifth, Dread history is redemptive and utopian. Sixth, Dread history speaks in what Kamau Brathwaite has called "the Jamaican Nation language" and in forms of syllabic intelligence. Finally, Dread history is a profound radical ontological claim at two levels. The first level is what Heidegger calls the "whoness"—the claim of *who am I*. The second level is the claim about historical knowledge—the conditions under which we construct the past, and how narrative and collective memory function.

At this point one might well ask if Dread history is the form of history enunciated by Rastafari. My answer to this would be both "yes" and "no." "Yes," in the sense that it draws from some of the ideas of Rastafari worldview, and "no," in the sense that the Rastafari worldview is not totally reducible to a historical one.

Dread history is a general stance, a view of history, that I suggest is rooted in critical dimensions of the Jamaican subalterns' worldview. It is from within this perspective that native rebellious forms emerge in politics, music, or culture. From the religious practices of Alexander Bedward to the contemporary lyrics of Bounty Killer, there is a remembering, a particular form of historicality, that can be discerned. Paul Ricoeur, in defining historicality, argues that human actions produce meanings, and these meanings are organized into time zones and passages. The nature of this organization is shaped by the weight of the past and its function in the present.[107] Michel-Rolph Trouillot makes the point that "Human beings participate in history both as actors and narrators."[108] What happens in Dread history is that the emplotments which reconfigure human action establish new meanings and these meanings conflate poeticism with historicism.

We should recollect here that conceptions of poeticism originated in the Western tradition from Aristotle's *Poetics*. One key point about its genealogy is the way in which Aristotle develops the concept of *mimesis* as representation. Aristotle notes that there exist continuities between lower forms of human activity and poetry. Poetics is, then, not only *techne* but mimetic representation that is directed at making a plot. Aristotle remarks, "It is clear then . . . that the poet should be a maker of plot . . . in that he is a poet by virtue of his imitation and he imitates action."[109] Oftentimes in Dread history, in forms that resemble the poetic there are no imitative representations of the past. Common historical knowledge production is often seen as surrounding what R. G. Collingwood calls "events which have finished happening, and conditions no longer in existence."[110]

Dread history emplots a narrative that carries the meanings of past events forward into the present. The clearest examples of this are the ways in which the memory of slavery is narrated in Rastafari thought. Dread history deals with the narration of traumatic events. While historical writings and thinking draw distinctions between absence and loss, Dread history does not. Dominick La Capra observes that when one blurs the distinction or "conflate[s], absence and loss may itself bear striking witness to the impact of trauma and the post-traumatic, which create a state of disorientation, agitation or even confusion."[111] In Dread history, because there is the trauma of slavery and the double loss of Africa and the victims of slavery, the conflation of absence and loss does not lead to agitation. Instead, it leads to a different representative quality about historical knowledge. In this quality of representation, there is no image of the past; rather, there is an *experience* of the past, therefore making the past not a foreign country. This obviously is far different from the practices of standard historical evidence gathered under positivist research models.

If Paget Henry is right—and I think that to a degree, he is—that there is a form of historicism called "Providential," represented by Edward Bldyen, David Walker, and others, then Rastafari, by suggesting that "almighty god is a living man" and that humans share in that divinity, collapses the realms of the temporal and the spiritual. In this frame, oppression is man-made, not God-decided or -fated. Obviously these positions can be interpreted in many ways, and different houses of Rastafari do. But Dread history places oppression firmly in the social systems of the earth and their historical evolution. It is the narrative of that historical evolution which makes Dread history a novel form of historical knowledge. Let us briefly examine how this works.

In the early Rastafari worldview, the nature of colonial and racial oppression was narrated through two sources: a biblical exegesis and the refutation of the Western historical claims about colonial rule and racial slavery. In terms of biblical exegesis, Rastafari claims that Christianity originated in Africa and then spread to other lands. The empire of Babylon (today the generic name for Western civilization and the security forces of the Jamaican state) has always been a place of evil, its history marked by the struggle for world power. Babylon was succeeded by a series of empires: Persian, Greek, Roman, British, and today American. This form of historical discourse is not atypical of the many groups whose conceptions were profoundly shaped by Ethiopianism. What is different about Rasta historical discourse is the character of time in historical narratives. In recounting the origins of colonialism, Rastafari begins with the expeditions of Columbus. From this point on, however, all forms of colonial oppression are collapsed into a Babylonian system full of pirates and "downpressors." So, for example, John Hawkins, Cecil Rhodes, and David Livingston are lumped together in the service of Queen Elizabeth I. This of course is not chronologically accurate, since these figures operated in different centuries. However, I think the purpose of this form of collapsed historical discourse is to suggest that the larger project of British colonialism was centuries long, and that while Hawkins was a sixteenth-century pirate, Rhodes and Livingstone were nineteenth-century ones. From this perspective, English colonialism involved both the slave trade and the imperialist partition of Africa. There was no rupture between what is oftentimes seen as two distinct economic and political phases.

Such a form of historical discourse focuses not on events but on larger meanings, and the rearrangement of time is not due to historical ignorance. Paul Ricoeur makes the point that "Time becomes human to the extent that it is articulated through a narrative mode, and narrative attains its full meaning when it becomes a condition of temporal existence."[112] What Dread history does through this form of historical discourse is to point to patterns of continuous oppression and seize "hold of a memory of history, as moments of danger"[113] in order to communicate present forms of oppression. It is able to do this because, to cite Walter Benjamin again, "The tradition of the oppressed teaches us that the state of emergency in which we live is not the exception but the rule."[114] Central to Dread history, then, are memory and a complex set of political imaginaries.

The recent experiences of the Truth and Reconcilation Commission (TRC) in South Africa have opened up a wave of examinations of the linkages, the differences, and the role of memory. Wole Soyinka makes the point that there exists in situations of injustice the "burden of memory." In the discussion of historical discourses there exists the notion of collective memory as something that remains in the past of the lived reality of groups, and the constructions they make of that past. The past is not fiction; what is at stake is its interpretation, its representation, and thus the production of historical knowledge. Of course central to memory is the imaginary. In this context, Dread history develops a complex set of political imaginaries about Africa, its place in the world as the home not only of humankind but also of the African diaspora. The West then becomes a place of barbarism, and Africa the utopia of a land far away—the *Satta massagana*.[115]

One does not have to hold on to this mythic invention of Africa, except to point to the relationship between the Caribbean and Africa, and the seminal importance of Africa to Caribbean radical political and social consciousness. I would also point out that the Rastafari political imaginary of Africa is very different from the "civilizing mission" of many New World blacks who wanted to modernize and Christianize the African continent. At the level of memory and identity, the historical memory of Rastafari creates new meanings of continental African traditions. So, for example, the emergence and development of the Nyabingi in Rastafari discourse, which was translated in the early Rastafari lexicon as "death to the white oppressors" and then, in the postindependence period, became "death to the white and black oppressors," originates from a popular perception of the Nyabingi healing group, originally women but later also men, in the Great Lakes area of Uganda, Rwanda, and Burundi. These healers organized consistent anticolonial resistance to the British, and many of them were eventually sent to mental asylums.[116] The Rastafari adaptation of the rhetoric of Nyabingi was not tied to knowledge of its social organization since, as we know, Rastafari was/is highly patriarchal.[117] So it seems that the appropriation of Nyabingi was only in keeping with the Rastafari project of centering Africa in the worldview of the Afro-Jamaican.

I now turn to the dimension of Dread history as utopian and redemptive. For Dread history, redemption is the time of the *now*. There is no transition from one stage to the next, and black emancipation is not a distant dream. What is important is how this view of history shapes a different gaze on political philosophy and political modernity. Today much of liberal political philosophy emphasizes questions of justice and fairness rooted in schemes of contract theory abstracted from contexts of political economy. Indeed, if one examines the recent outpourings of mainstream political philosophy from John Rawls to Charles Taylor to Ronald Dworkin, one sees the political angst about these issues. The gaze of Dread history is in another direction: How can humans be free? It is freedom and redemptive justice that Dread history seeks by exploring utopia. As such, Dread history restores to politics the question of possibilities. The political imaginary here is one "where oppression shall be scattered" and songs of freedom will be sung. Ernest Bloch makes the point that the relationship of utopia to the everyday world is that "Concrete imagination and the imagery of its mediated anticipations are fermenting in the process of the real itself and are depicted in the concrete forward dream; anticipating elements are a component of reality itself."[118] Utopian thinking is not simply "dreams of a better life"; it is, as Ruth Levitas points out, "the expression of hope, but that hope is to be understood . . . as a directing act of a cognitive kind."[119] Within this frame Dread history is not so much the utopia of "educated hope" where a world is in the process of becoming. It is, rather, "radical desire," where the utopia can be constructed now and with great force of will. Dread history is a history of redemptive hope, and thus utopian because it expresses this radical desire. So how does Dread history work, and what does it mean for historical writing?

In the first place, it means opening a different set of archives and then understanding the categories that emerge from them.[120] Second, it understands that there is a politics of the people—a politics from below. A central part of this politics is the creation of symbolic orders understood not in some millenarian fashion of prepolitical logic, but on its own terms. In this regard the act of writing Dread history as different from a Rastafarian historical view is one that calls for the historical writer to combine historical imagination (the act of writing history) with what the anthropologist Clifford Geertz has called "thick description."[121] The combination of these two things would perhaps open new archives, and while allowing the historian to fully understand that the subject of history is the human subject and to perform what Ricoeur calls a " subjectivity of reflection,"[122] it might be possible to create a form of "critical realism" about the present questions we ask of the past. In this context history becomes both a reflection and a description of "social configurations" that make political and economic forms possible, while remaining a study of how, in the words of Roger Chartier, "social actors make sense of their practices and discourses." Dread history does not ignore elite archives but subjects them to rigorous critique, knowing that these archives themselves carry a story of knowledge assumptions about events and human action.

In many ways there are some similarities between the practices of a "history from below" and Dread history. Where they part company is that Dread history opens new categories and does not attempt to explain radical action from below solely in the terms of the elite political and historical languages of the times. It instead begins from the interiority of the oppressed and their " hidden texts," working outward to grapple with the meanings and practices of human domination. It operates from a stance that the oppressed class is itself a repository of historical knowledge having a unique experience with history. This fact is even more acute in the cases of racial slavery and colonialism.

Conclusion

In remapping the Caribbean intellectual tradition and the larger Africana intellectual tradition, it is important for us to shift our gaze, to grapple with the formulations that emerge from the subaltern. In doing this, I point to a different set of possible archives and then ask what the study of these means for the Afro-Caribbean intellectual tradition. This kind of question is well within the tradition of the historical thought raised by the heretic segment of the Africana radical intellectual tradition, particularly the works of Walter Rodney, W. E. B. Du Bois, and C. L. R. James. However, in the redemptive prophetic stream the questions of history are posed and discussed differently. The prophetic gaze is different from that of the heretic. The heretics utilize categories that, while plotting an alternative genealogy, do not necessarily step outside the recognized episteme. They sometimes frame the historical questions within the assumptions of Western modernity even when they expand and reorder these categories. Recalling Aimé Césaire's adaptation of Shakespeare's play *The Tempest,* we remember that in Caliban's confrontation with Prospero, he says that he does not want to be called Caliban any longer. It is, he says, a name "given me by your hatred, and every time it's spoken it's an insult."[123] One central feature of the black radical intellectual tradition is the struggle to name. Within the prophetic redemptive stream this struggle is acute. By understanding the narratives of this stream on its own terms and its philosophy of history, we open another space for the Africana radical intellectual tradition and a radical politics of knowledge.

CHAPTER **7**

Get Up, Stand Up
The Redemptive Poetics of Bob Marley

Mi see myself as a revolutionary . . . who nah tek no bribe.
Fight it single-handed with Music.
—Bob Marley, *Catch a Fire* (video)

I man know sey is my work to go out in a Babylon to do the work I do
—Bob Marley

Revelation reveals the truth . . .
—Bob Marley (*Revolution*, 1974)

Introduction

The figure of Robert Nesta Marley is iconic. T-shirts, videos, the entire paraphernalia of international commodification and communication, including the Walt Disney theme park of freedom, seem to work overtime to make the Rastaman who "chanted down Babylon" into a fangless musician, a symbol of exotic difference, trapped and captured in an illusionary rainbow world of dreamers. Whenever I listen to, think of, or teach about Marley, two impulses take hold of me. The first is that of Caribbean pride, that a figure from "region" could have such a high international profile. The second is recognition of the ways in which hegemonic ideology operates, how it is able to rework the most radical ideas and practices of individuals into a mélange of difference, and then claim ownership. This process, which Joy James has called "depoliticizing representations,"[1] can also be seen in the dominant representation of Martin Luther King, Jr. King's life, thought, and praxis fold into the "I have a dream" speech, and he becomes the dreamer who adorns a U.S. postage stamp. In the case of Bob Marley's

"One Love," a Rastafarian phrase meaning unity and respect becomes the theme song of the former British empire to greet the new millennium.

In both these processes radicalism is expunged. Erased is the radical King who in his last years attempted to put together a coalition of labor, the poor, and African-Americans in an effort to fight against what he called the triple evils: "the problem of racism, the problem of economic exploitation and the problem of war."[2] Marley is no longer the defiant Rasta rebel from the Jamaican ghetto of Trench Town, railing against the "the Babylon system . . . as vampire, sucking the blood of the sufferer,"[3] but the light-skinned Jamaican Rastafarian who in transcending racial boundaries and countries also moves beyond race, and therefore belongs no longer to the black radical tradition out of which he sprang.[4] Common to both King and Marley was a universalism, a commitment to social change, and the fact that both were prophetic voices whose visions of a new world were rooted in struggles against racial domination and oppression. It is the irony of ironies that in death the "Buffalo soldier" has been co-opted by the ideological processes of capitalism, and that the man who, the night before he was murdered, saw the coming of the Lord in the masses of the people of the world rising up for freedom, has a public holiday declared for him while thousands of young black men continue to live in America's prisons.

In this essay I want to resituate Marley, to suggest that he, like King, belonged to a prophetic black radical tradition. Furthermore, I hope to demonstrate that Marley *saw* himself as part of this tradition. Marley represented one segment of the voice of Rastafari. His lyrical and musical weapons were used in an effort to describe events while signaling hope for the oppressed. The revolution he sang and spoke about was a form of *symbolic insurgency*, a way to replace the old ideas about racial oppression and exploitation in general and to promote a radical desire for a new life. Such an analysis of Marley does not ignore the way in which black popular culture is commodified, becomes deformed and incorporated. Rather, it agrees with Stuart Hall that while commodification occurs, we should

> see in the figures and the repertoires on which popular culture draws . . . [that] black popular culture has enabled the surfacing, inside the mixed and contradictory modes even of some mainstream popular culture, of elements of a discourse that is different—other forms of life, other traditions of representation.[5]

Marley understood this process of commodification in the ways he referred to the producer Chris Blackwell as his "translator." He consistently navigated the music business, trying not to get trapped in its glitz and glamour, since for him the justification for the entire enterprise was the use of his artistic gifts as a medium of prophetic social criticism. Thus we get two competing contemporary representations of Marley. The first is his in-corporation into hegemonic modes of representation symbolized by the prominent billboard with his picture in Times Square in New York City, and the second is the way he is appropriated by people who are marginal-ized by their own societies. This latter mode of representation is demon-strated by the many instances of his music being played and sung with hope in the *musseques, favelas, bidonvilles,* and inner cities of the world.

Adebayo Ojo writes about this kind of representation and appropria-tion in Nigeria: "It is fascinating to see so many ardent militant fans prance away to Marley's tunes, mumbling substitute phrases for his lyrics . . . many fans are only sustained by [a] knowledge of Bob Marley's . . . uncom-promising stand for equal rights and justice."[6] It is Marley's prophetic call for the oppressed to "Get Up, Stand Up" that has made him such a popular radical icon for many today. If, as Raymond Williams argues, hegemony is not static but constantly shifts its internal arguments and symbols while renewing and re-creating itself, then inside the contestation within the do-main of the popular, the successful integration of Marley was crucial.[7] The "depoliticized representation" of Marley, then, is of a successful singer and cultural icon, not a prophetic social critic, since hegemony selects, bends, and reshapes figures who contest it. Thus one secondary purpose of this chapter is to attempt to untangle some of those bends done on Marley.

The life and career of Bob Marley are very well documented,[8] so I will not spend a great deal of time recounting them. What I think is important in Marley's intellectual and artistic life, which in turn shaped his music and ideas, was the influence of Rastafari, in particular the teachings of Mor-timer Planno. Planno is a major figure in Rastafari history who first came to Jamaican public attention when, in the wake of the aborted Henry rebel-lion and the rise of state repression against the Rastafarian movement, he suggested to members of the regional university academic community (University of the West Indies) that a study of the Rastafari movement was required.[9] This study, conducted by Rex Nettleford and Roy Augier, both historians, and M. G. Smith, an anthropologist, became the famous *Rasta-fari Report.*

One consequence of the discussions that surrounded the report was a 1961 mission to Africa on which Planno, Filmore Alvaranga, and Douglas Mack represented the Rastafarian movement. Planno again came to public attention in 1966 when Emperor Haile Selassie arrived in Jamaica on an official state visit. Amid the tumultuous welcome that destabilized normal official state protocol, Planno went inside the plane and then returned to the tarmac, announcing: "[The] Emperor has instructed me to tell you be calm. Step back and let the Emperor land." An imposing figure with a mel-lifluous bass voice, Planno had by the 1960s become a figure of enormous prestige among the Rastafari movement in the western end of Jamaica's capital city, Kingston. His Rasta "camp" was known for all-night "reasoning sessions,"[10] and he himself was open to academics and curiosity seekers. Along with Sam Brown, who was more politically inclined, and Ras Daniel Hartman, the visual artist from western Kingston, Planno was part of a boiling cauldron of black redemptive ideas during the 1960s.[11] Amid the grinding poverty, the "political tribalism", the dung heap on which many inhabitants scrounged for food, and the May Pen cemetery, which was called "Must Pen," since sooner or latter one had to be buried there, these Rastafarians stood majestically guarding the *black male being*. It was in this context that Marley came in contact with Rastafari.

The Early Reasonings

In 1968, Marley began to spend a great deal of time with Planno, attending different Rastafari Nyabingi nights. In the end the relationship with Planno became a central one in his life, with Planno also becoming his manager when Marley began his relationship with the African-American signer Johnny Nash. There are different segments of the Rastafarian movement, and Planno at the time belonged to the Divine Theocratic Temple of Rastafari. This group was different from, for example, Sam Brown's Rastafari Movement Association. Brown, a very able poet who had backed out of the 1961 mission to Africa, claiming that the delegation was composed of a "bunch of trip seeks,"[12] had by this time shifted his position from that of immediate repatriation to the enunciation of a position which would allow for direct radical political involvement in Jamaica. In one of the central documents of Rastafari, *The Foundation of the Rastafarian Movement*, Brown now argued that "Members of the Rastafarian Movement are an inseparable part of the Black people of Jamaica, and as such we cannot and do not proclaim any higher aims than the legitimate aims and aspirations of the Black people of Jamaica."[13]

The political result of this shift was that Jamaica was now seen as an African outpost which needed to be liberated. This Rastafarian current that proclaimed radical liberation for Jamaica became very important in radical political circles in the late 1960s and 1970s. During this period this radical current was represented by the Rastafari Movement Association, formed by Ras Desilva and Ras Historian, who for many years published the journal *Rasta Voice*. Both individuals were central in the post-Rodney period in Jamaican radical politics, and became closely aligned with the Abeng movement.[14] In the eastern end of Kingston, Ras Negus, who was an important ally of Walter Rodney, was representative of the current.[15]

At this time Planno was more representative of the more theologically inclined current in the Rastafari movement. His interpretation of the doctrine stressed not only the divinity of Selassie but also the fact that Rasta-fari was a cultural-religious practice rather than an explicitly political one. This did not mean that he was closed to radical black nationalist political currents. He, too, had "reasonings" with Walter Rodney, and wrote a poem to commemorate the anniversary of the Walter Rodney riots. Rupert Lewis speaks about the influence of Planno in a interview with Robin Small: "The chief thing why people listened to him in the past, you know, is that Planno wasn't really talking for himself but was talking on behalf of a whole generation."[16]

Marley therefore became a Rastafarian at a time when the movement was aggressively attempting to find a space for itself in Jamaican society. All wings of the movement had a critique of Jamaican society and its polity. All currents believed in the divinity of Selassie, and all saw themselves as captives in "Babylon." To this bubbling cauldron we should add that Marley was a restless spirit drawn to the different transgressive modes of conduct practiced by many urban unemployed male youths of west Kingston, since the 1960s was also the era of the "Rude Bwoy." This era has been canonized in the popular Jamaican imagination with Marley and the Wailers' invocation to the "Rude Bwoys" to "Simmer Down," Desmond Dekker's "Rude Boy," and Prince Buster's minor hit "Judge Dread."[17]

But who were the "Rude Bwoys," and what did they represent? The Ja-maican social and music critic Garth White, in a remarkable article, writes: "Rude Bwoy is that person, native, who is totally disenchanted with the ruling system; who generally descended from the 'African' elements in the lower class and who is now armed with ratchets, other cutting instruments and with increasing frequency nowadays, with guns and explosives."[18] White further argues that Rudie culture items, such as shoes, hats, music, and stripped bicycles, as well as the dance forms that accompanied this mode of urban male youth practice, were ones which took into account "the suffering of the people of his own color and his own class."[19] The "Rude Bwoy" was a defiant figure. His cultural trappings, and his facial and body language, spoke menacingly to the dominant order. He was rude be-cause he was an outlaw and consciously transgressed the boundaries of the ways in which the Jamaican citizen was supposed to be a subject in the early postindependence period.[20]

Pierre Bourdieu makes the point that some of the ways that subjects are formed are through the "seemingly most insignificant details of *dress, bear-ing,* physical and verbal manners."[21] The "Rude Bwoys," with their dress code and verbal and physical manners, attempted to carve out a cultural space for themselves. The "screw face" was a mark of defiance. Many com-mentators on the early Wailers have made reference to their location in this west Kingston milieu. However, what I wish to suggest is that the cultural and political manners of the "Rude Bwoy" had a profound influence on Marley that is sometimes understated.[22] The Wailers' music of the 1960s not only reflects the "Rude Bwoy" ethos; the group was an integral part of its cultural self-fashioning. There were therefore two urban sources that shaped Marley's musical intelligence—the theology of one segment of Rastafari and the defiant manners and cultural practices of "Rude Bwoy." Both these practices were profoundly transgressive in early postindependence society. Of the two, Rastafari, along with its countersymbolic doctrine, seemed to Marley to represent the answer to his queries, as it did for many other bright and sensitive youths during the same period. Over time Rastafari would become dominant, but many of the cultural gestures associated with "Rude Bwoys" never left Marley.

Within the black redemptive current, Marley's music draws on proverbs, biblical wordplay, double meanings, particular sections of the Bible, and the language of Rastafari. But most of all, Marley believed that truths had been revealed to him. Like many other prophets before him, he had to make these truths known globally while rallying people to rebel. He sings, in "Chanting Down Babylon":

> Music you're the key
> Talk to whom, please talk to me
> Bring the voice of the Rastaman
> Communicating to everyone . . .
> Come, we go chant down Babylon one more time . . .[23]

In taking this path of using words, music, and culture to chant down an oppressive system, Marley was walking a road previously traveled by other Rastafarians who were musicians. Perhaps the most important of these earlier figures was Count Ossie, the *burru* drummer whose drumming and musical arrangements shaped popular Jamaican music.[24] Count Ossie affirmed this use of words and culture as a weapon against oppression when he stated in an interview, "We were fighting colonialism and oppression but not with gun but wordically, culturally."[25] In a set of lyrics that celebrates the inhabitants of Trench Town in western Kingston, Marley offers a similar perspective when he sings:

> Up a cane river to wash my dread
> Upon a rock I rest my head
> There I vision through the seas of oppression
> Don't make my life a prison
> We come from Trench Town . . .
> Can we free our people with music[26]

After posing the question and appealing to history in the same song, Marley answers in the affirmative: "Lord, we free the people with music; we free the people with music, sweet music."[27]

Having briefly pointed out some of the central influences that shaped Marley, we now turn to three things. First is a broader understanding of the relationship of his music and lyrics to the black redemptive tradition in which we have located him. Second, we want to further explore the nature of Marley's practice of symbolic insurgency. Finally, we want to examine why his prophetic social criticism still resonates in the contemporary world.

Music, Ideas, and Culture

Within the Western intellectual tradition the work of Kant continues to frame some of the philosophical debates about music. Kant's claim that music communicates by sensations, while poetry does so by means of concepts, obviously does not take into account many modern forms of music.[28] Ernst Bloch, in his seminal text *The Spirit of Utopia*, attempts to correct this, and makes the point that within much of Western thinking, "Music becomes far too much a mere revenant, related all too historically to the past, instead of being illuminated from the direction of the future."[29] Although Bloch does not tackle the issues of music as "high art" and music as "low art," the point he makes is generally a useful one.

In thinking about the complexities of black popular music, some issues arise. In the first place, one has to dispense with the "high" and "low" distinctions. As an art form, black popular music in the New World functions in ways that Samuel A. Floyd, Jr., has called "cultural memory."[30] Second, given the nature of slavery and colonialism, black popular music came to represent a black public sphere.[31] In social theory, the "public sphere" has come to mean, in the words of Jürgen Habermas, "the domain of our social life in which such a thing as public opinion can be formed . . . a portion of the public sphere is constituted in every conversation in which private persons come together to form a public."[32] However, we know that colonial society was an authoritarian state and society, so that the "public sphere" did not operate for the black slaves or the colonial natives. One consequence of this was that alternative spaces were created, ones that, as James Scott has pointed out, exist outside of the official stage.[33] The matter becomes more complicated when the main communicative modes in a society are oral, storytelling, dance, and music. Erna Brodber and Edward Greene, in a study of Jamaican music, analyzed twenty-three of the most popular songs between 1963 and 1978. Their analysis convincingly demonstrated that these songs were engaged in different forms of communication:

What emerges from our analysis of the form and mood of these top 23 songs is that in the two earlier periods . . . the lecture and the announcement were the popular forms of communication. In the latter two periods . . . no one form predominates but there is a tendency towards reflection and particularly for the period 1973–76, a tendency to communicate in a mood of reasoning.[34]

Popular music in Jamaica became a "public sphere" because for many musicians "the act of making music was enmeshed in community life."[35] This means that Jamaican popular music is not only a form of "cultural memory," but a *social* one as well. Brodber and Greene make the point that "The appeal of music and of words set to music is indeed universal, but its function is more central in communities which depend primarily on the human body for the transmission of messages from person to person and from generation to generation."[36] As a site of the "public sphere," Jamaican popular music could not be ignored by the major political parties, and increasingly popular music became a political weapon to be used in election campaigns.[37]

So how did popular Jamaican music begin? Any history of Jamaican music begins from the fact of plantation racial slavery. Garth White convincingly argues that "the traditional" forms of Jamaican music, which were developed through "the grunts of pain, lamenting wails, the notes of a thumb piano or stick or drum, scores of feet stomping, repeated song choruses, rhythmic clapping, sailors' ditties, hymns and marches blowing in the winds of the Atlantic,"[38] formed the basis for Jamaican music. He makes the point that the traditional forms of Jamaican music are the foundations of much of contemporary popular Jamaican music: "the percussive approach . . . the centrality of drums . . . the use of improvisation . . . and the call and response."[39] One cannot say precisely when "traditional" Jamaican music began; the view that argues about a series of smooth linear changes which eventually climax into contemporary dance hall is misleading, since the changes were subtle and drew from myriad rich musical sources, some indigenous to the island and others external to it.

What we can be clear on is that there were two popular Jamaican musical traditions. One tradition drew heavily from Afro-religious Jamaican practices and their musical forms. These practices included *kumina, pocomania,* and what has been called "revival" religions. Bilby states: "Many Revivalists used a combination of two or three drums—one or more "side drums" played with sticks . . . and a bass drum played with a padded beater."[40] Paying special attention to *kumina* drumming, Bilby argues that the emergence of Rastafarian drumming is linked to the historic move made by Leonard Howell in the 1930s to integrate "Congo based drumming, songs, and ritual language of the local *Kumina* religion into his vision of Ethiopian divinity."[41] Thus Rastafari music drew from the existing popular religious sources, and would provide both the musical and the ideological link between the Afro-Jamaican religious music and what one might call the "secular" popular. The "secular" popular tradition was called *mento*. Bilby's account of *mento* describes it thus:

> ... born of a creolizing process that blended elements of a variety of European social-dance musics with African-derived stylistic features ... this Creole social-dance music, originally more European-sounding, eventually acquired a new rhythmic feel, due to the African-derived aesthetic preferences of the musicians who played it.[42]

Many musicians who played this form of music over time became influenced by other external sources, including the other Caribbean islands and the R&B of black America, particularly music that came out of New Orleans and jazz. By the time of the start of the Jamaican recording industry, *mento* was being eclipsed by other musical forms.[43] Therefore, the musical foundations of contemporary Jamaican popular music reside in the musical crosscurrents we have described, fused together by the inner-city inhabitants of the island's capital city.

Given this history, Jamaican popular music did not just entertain; it moved one's dancing feet, it sought to communicate, and oftentimes it became a chant against oppression. In other words, the music functioned, in the words of Count Ossie, as a cultural weapon. Given the present international popularity of reggae, writers on the subject oftentimes silence or elide this cultural practice as a form of politics. With its musically hypnotic offbeat and danceability, reggae becomes an exotic tropical sound to ease the burden of the technologically advanced West. It is one way in which Cartesian anxieties can be momentarily dispelled. Thankfully, not all commentators or fans of reggae view the music in this way. For others, Jamaican music and lyrics can be read as forms of representation, as telling a different set of narratives about Jamaican society. However, it also seems to me that because in that society music functions as a social memory, then as *practice* it performs a communicative role. Thus the sites of its early recorded reproduction, the ubiquitous "sound system dances," become zones/spaces of enclosed rebellion, where every man leaps and shouts, the DJ communes with his audience, and to the sounds of reverb echo, the dancers cross over to a "land far, far away," until the state forces rudely crush the enclosed space of community, rupturing it with the "uniforms of brutality." Adding this communicative dimension to Jamaican popular music, along with understanding the ideological role of Rastafari in the lyrical and rhythmical developments of the music, allows us to better grasp

Marley's role as prophetic social critic, the rich sources of his lyrics, and the often conversational style of many of his songs.

Prophecy and Marley Texts

Marley's verbal texts are creations of the wordplay of Rastafari, the Creolized use of proverbs, and the everyday speech acts of the ordinary Jamaican, as well as biblical language. Carolyn Cooper, in an important text on Jamaican culture, sees Marley's lyrics as part of the struggle of self-validation that many Jamaican poets engaged in, particularly the popular poet and dramatist Louise Bennett.[44] Cooper writes that "Marley's skilful verbal play—his use of biblical allusion, Rastafarian symbolism . . . is evidence of a highly charged literary sensibility."[45] This literary sensibility facilitates Marley's lyrics as a complex configuration of poetry, chants, and speeches. The use of Jamaican proverbs means that Marley is able to engage in conversation both with his audience and within the structure of the song itself. Listen to the some of the lines from " Coming in from the Cold":

> Well you, it's you, it's you
> It's you I am talking to now
> Why do you look so sad and forsaken
> When one door is closed
> Don't you know another is opened.[46]

At the start of the song Marley had announced to his audience that he was coming in from the cold. Then, in the middle of the song, he asked whether one would make a system get on top of one's head or kill your brother man, and the I-Threes Chorus replied, "No No No." There are various interpretations of this song, ranging from Marley's announcement of his return to Jamaica after a period of self-imposed exile to a general response of someone who had fallen upon bad times, and now those times were over. But at this point our focus is not the possible meanings of the lyrics but how they are constructed, how the use of a typical Jamaican proverb signals the possibility of hope in situations where despair seems to be the order of the day. It is a strategy of songwriting that is rooted in the rich soil of local knowledge. Swami Anand Prahlad, in a pathbreaking work which examines proverbs in Jamaican music, notes that in general the use of proverbs in reggae music evokes the study of proverbs at the level of social meaning. He also makes the point that proliferation of the social use of proverbs in reggae lyrics means that there is a clear reggae discourse.[47] Kwame Dawes writes about the pervasive influence of reggae, arguing that its emergence marks a "pivotal and defining historical moment in the evolution of the West Indian aesthetic."[48]

Though both points are well taken, it would seem that one has to make a clear distinction between the discourse of Rastafari, and how it shaped one form of lyrics and music and the other forms of this genre of music. In popular parlance this is the distinction between "roots reggae," "lovers rock," and dance music. This would suggest, therefore, that only one segment of reggae discourse is *profoundly shaped* by Rastafari. In a very obvious sense, Marley's lyrics are representative of that aspect of Jamaican popular culture which challenges the episteme of the colonial and neocolonial order, and engages in symbolic warfare against this order. Thus one not only dances to Marley, but one has to *listen* to Marley, since he is both singing and engaging in social criticism. This consistent engagement in social criticism, making "truth bust out of man like a river,"[49] points to Marley's different function in comparison to many seminal musicians or figures in black popular culture—or in black music, for that matter.

Greg Tate, in a brilliant snapshot of Miles Davis, makes the point that Davis was a "certain heroic master narrative of Black male artistry . . . the power of Miles Davis was that he always seemed to be waving back from the other side of black culture's transcendable horizon, from the post liberated side of black potentiality."[50] On the other hand, Marley, representing black potentiality, was engaged in a struggle that would rally the oppressed, here and now, onto Zion Train. In other words, Marley functioned explicitly as prophet. It is this practice of prophecy rooted within the discursive traditions of the black radical tradition that gives Marley his power. So it is the nature of Marley's practice of prophecy to which we now turn.

Prophecy and Memory Text

We have seen in chapter 6 how prophecy functions within the framework of black religious practices and that within black politicoreligious practices the theme of redemption looms large. For the prophet to declare redemption, he has to be a social critic, and the character of this criticism should be organic, rooted in the discursive practices of the culture in which he operates. Under these conditions the prophet then invokes a tradition. In the case of Marley, we know that this tradition is Rastafari. But, as is often the case, outstanding prophets bring something new to the tradition. Marley functioned as prophet while adding nothing new doctrinally to Rastafari, but his mode of interpretation offered him an audience that took him out of a specific geographical site, Jamaica. He recognized this, stating in a 1973 interview that he would go wherever Jah sent him: to London, America, or Australia.[51] In doing this, Marley did not shape his verbal text to suit a new audience. This, I want to suggest, is a unique function in the ways of prophecy, which is conventionally circumscribed by local knowledge. The question we must then answer is: What was it about Marley's practice that allowed this to happen?

V. Y. Mudimbe makes the point in a study on the narrative about the origins of the Luba empire that this myth of origins is a "memory text in which the Luba genealogy actualizes itself as both reality and project . . . strictly speaking it is not history. On the other hand it cannot be reduced to a purely mythical legend."[52] The "memory text," Mudimbe argues, "presents itself as a political rationale in three operations: It duplicates a real human space . . . integrates a nowhere into a mythified past and . . . correlates actual customs, socioeconomic transformations . . . discursive practices, and displacements demanded by historical changes."[53] How did this "memory text" function in the verbal texts of Marley? We already know that central to Rastafari doctrine is the notion of Dread history, and that one kind of difference between this form of history and conventional narratives of history is time. Rastafari conflates linear time. History functions as a marker of the present. The internal markers of Marley's "memory text" are slavery, displacement, black survival, redemption, celebration of ordinary people, and praise for Jah. These markers coalesce in the themes that frame his last three concept albums: *Survival, Uprising,* and *Confrontation.*[54] In Marley's musical texts, the past is ever present; it is not a distant moment that has *shaped* the present, but it *is* the present, as he proclaims in "Buffalo Soldier":

> I mean it, when I analyze the stench
> To me it makes a lot of sense
> How the dreadlock Rasta was the Buffalo Soldier
> And he was taken from Africa, brought to America
> Fighting on arrival, fighting for Survival[55]

It is clear that for Marley, mainstream history is understood as stench. But the word also conveys an immediate meaning of the material conditions in which the Jamaican poor live, and Marley was deeply aware of this, as he notes in the 1973 interview: "Dem divide in classes . . . as those some [of us] have four foot . . . this is wickedness."[56] In this context it makes sense that the Rastaman had to be *like* a Buffalo soldier. The imagery of the Buffalo soldier was taken from the segregated black units in the U.S. Army used to crush the Native American population, who called them "Buffalo soldiers." Marley switches the character of this fight in the contemporary period, suggesting that the Buffalo soldier was someone who fought for survival. In this regard he used a cultural memory to re-create an image of black resistance. So in the remainder of the text of the song, the Buffalo solider is transformed into a dreadlock Rasta man, "trodding through San Juan, in the arms of America, trodding thru Jamaica. . . ."[57] All this defiant reordering is part of the way "memory text" operates, but more important, it is at the core of the symbolic insurgency that Marley engages in. It is to this insurgency and its relationship to his praxis of prophetic criticism that I will now discuss.

Symbolic Insurgency and Prophecy

Sylvia Wynter argues that within the framework of the symbolic, the central "strategy of the politics of black culture is the counter invention of the self."[58] Attached to this counterinvention, Wynter tells us, is an ultimate "revolutionary demand, the demand for happiness now."[59] However, this demand for immediate happiness can be fulfilled only in the symbolic counterworld. Wynter tells us:

> . . . the power of the black counter culture lies in its symbolic negativity, thus its politics is a politics that can never be realized except in that symbolic world—Zion—in which all structures of power having been overturned, the autonomous, separate concept of politics—will have been made obsolescent and meaningless.[60]

I want to suggest that to achieve this "symbolic negativity," Marley engages in practices of *symbolic insurgency*. The nature of this insurgency resides in two things. First are the ways in which Marley uses words in his texts, and second is the reordering of questions of history of the black diaspora and the emphasis he places upon mental slavery. We know that a central aspect of domination is what Pierre Bourdieu calls the "formation and reformation of mental structures."[61] The crucial orders for this process are of course knowledge production and the creation of a symbolic universe. Symbolic power, Bourdieu suggests, is "a power of constructing reality."[62] To practice *symbolic insurgency* means that an individual is engaged in consistent efforts to rearrange the ways in which mainstream reality is both constructed and explained. This of course breaks the pattern of social integration and shatters the legitimacy of the dominant order. *Symbolic insurgency* does not have to lead to the overthrow of an oppressive system, but it creates everyday spaces of hope. Its primary preoccupation is with creating and contesting the old order at the level of ideas and the self. It punctures the self-image of the old order, critiquing its moral bankruptcy while seeking to profoundly influence people. In Marley's case it is a call for people to sing "redemption songs," to emancipate oneself from mental slavery.

Second, we should note that in the Jewish tradition, Michael Walzer has pointed out, prophecy, because of its rootedness in local particularism, is not utopian.[63] In the black tradition this is not so. What makes Marley an outstanding prophetic critic is that he was able to weave together some of the doctrinal tenets of Rastafari, join them to the local knowledge embodied in proverbs, and then present them in a powerful critique of the system, producing a Zion train that would leave Babylon oppression behind. Within the Africana tradition of prophecy we can distinguish the feature of *mantic* (a possession and declaration of knowledge) and concern for the wider "moral community at a social and political level."[64] On all these accounts Marley qualifies as prophet. What was distinctive about his practice is what is distinctive about Rastafari, its capacity to overturn core elements of the dominant symbolic order. Of course Marley took the teachings of Rastafari to the world and was centrally responsible for making reggae an international phenomenon. But the overarching motivation for his work was, as he said, doing the business of "my fathers work." In Marley's practice, popular culture became a site for ideological struggle. Marley as prophet practiced *symbolic insurgency* in a struggle for the minds of the oppressed, rallying them to Zion in the chants against Babylon. His last three albums are ample evidence of this.

From all reports it seems that sometime in 1978, Marley decided that he needed to do a trilogy. The names of the albums were chosen: *Black Survival, Uprising,* and *Confrontation.* Given Rastafari attention to the meaning of words, we can be assured that the names of the albums had profound significance. One possible meaning is that at this moment of history, black people had been able to survive, but that continued black survival meant first an uprising and then confrontation. These three titles are also moments of struggle for the dethroning of the hegemonic symbolic order of Babylon. The *Confrontation* album cover is interesting in this regard, since it has Marley on a white horse, dressed in white tunic and gold shirt with a green breastplate, barefooted, his riding blanket red and gold with a faint touch of green on the inside, dreadlocks flying while he is about to slay a dragon. He is dressed in the manner of an Ethiopian, but he is about to slay a dragon. So a cover that at first blush would make the Western mind, and those of us trained in its tradition, think about English mythology and St. George is not quite accurate. On the other side of the album cover is an Ethiopian illustration featuring the famous nineteenth century battle of Adowa. Taken together, this album jacket indicates a line of continuity between Marley's work and that of defeating the colonial attempt to conquer Ethiopia. What is happening here in this strange symbolic portrait is what has been called "symbolic inversion."[65]

At another level, when we think about these album covers and their possible meanings, we should also see that they resemble historic moments in concrete revolutionary praxis. The oppressed survive, and then rise up to confront their oppressors. In Marley's case the first moment, survival, depends upon the last moment in a historical cycle. Given all of this, I therefore suggest that these three concept albums are a piece of *one* musical movement, both symbolically and as musical verbal text. However, I will limit my present analysis to some of the songs on one of the albums—*Survival.*

In the Beginning—Black Survival

Against the backdrop of the flags of independent African nations and blazoned in white, the word *survival* is written inside the plan of a slave ship that wraps around the album cover. The liner notes tell us about the slave ship: "This plan of a slave ship shows the stowage for the dreaded crossing of the Atlantic. The bounded slaves were packed like so many non-human commodities."[66] The center spread of the album jacket has a wide photograph of members of the Wailers cooking outside in a tenement yard with an epigraph from Marcus Garvey: "A people without the knowledge of their past history, origin and culture is like a tree without roots." What is interesting about this photograph is that the fire for the cooking is being stoked by a long stick taken from a tree and that two men are sitting around the fire with small sticks or branches in their hands. The message from this visual production is clear: fire, roots, and branches—all central images in the Rastafari symbolic order—are critical to various ways in which black people have survived. There is also another possible reading of this album cover: that it is a realist depiction of the many "boats" in Jamaica, where men cook once a day, so that different people in the tenement yard are able to eat. Whatever interpretation one puts on this photograph, it is clear that Marley and Neville Garrick, the talented visual artist, were putting together an unusual album.[67]

The album opens with the recording mike catching Marley instructing, "A little more drums"; then there is a drum roll lick accompanied with a high-pitched guitar that draws our attention to the opening announcement of the album—that there is "so much trouble in the world." The ability to see that there is "so much trouble in the world" is possible because this is Jah's world and there is a prophet who has knowledge of the trouble. What is the nature of this trouble? For Marley it has the following dimensions: the fact that men are sailing on ego trips, using spaceships that take them away from the realities of the earth. And as they do this, they have no care for the ordinary person—"No care for you. No care for me." And who are these persons who do not care? They are the current rulers of the world with their plans for conquering space while humans on earth suffer. In the opening lines of this song Marley is drawing the stark contrast between the use of wealth and the condition of many people on earth.

From these opening lines Marley engages in something that is common in all his verbal texts: he weaves a story that moves from point to counterpoint, at each stage speaking to different actors in the drama of the song. At one moment he is addressing the powerful, and the next he is speaking in the personage of the oppressed. So the verbal text says, "You think you have found the solution, but it is just another illusion"; this is followed by a warning to the world's rulers: "Do not leave the cornerstone standing there behind." Why? Because "We the street people talking, we the people struggling." Because of this struggle of the street people, the rulers and the powerful are sitting on a "time bomb" that will soon explode, since in Jamaican folk wisdom and the law of gravity, "What goes up is coming down." This song, which opens the album, calls our attention to trouble in the world and is a warning to the rulers and powerful that their time is up and redemptive judgment is nigh. Then, with an offbeat organ chord accompanied by a militant stand-up bass, Marley changes from his warning mood to one of rebellious defiance, and to the militant verbal text "Zimbabwe."

This song, written in Ethiopia, became one of the anthems of the national liberation guerrillas in Zimbabwe. Horace Campbell gives us a flavor of the night that Marley played in Zimbabwe in 1980:

> After 15 minutes of the supposed two minutes, the Wailers sang "Africans a liberate Zimbabwe." In one section of the stadium the whole gathering stood and joined in chanting this song of freedom, saying that they did not want to be fooled by mercenaries. It was an experience filled with emotion, and Bob Marley responded with the slogans of Pan-African Unity which were an essential . . . part of his outlook as Rastafari.[68]

In listening to a recording of the entire concert, what emerges is a Bob Marley whose stage presence seems to be organically linked with the audience's responses to him. Therefore, both in performance and in recording, "Zimbabwe" leaves the realm of symbolic African struggles and becomes an integral part of revolutionary struggles all over the world. In other words, the national liberation struggle in Zimbabwe of that period becomes the canvas on which all struggles to free colonial Africa, as well as other oppressed people, are played out. The verbal text begins with the statement "Every Man gotta right to decide his own destiny." This statement of self-determination can be read at two levels. The first is the level of the fight against colonialism—political freedom and decolonization. But at the second level the statement is about the nature of human existence and the nature of autonomy. This autonomy is a complex one, because it can be achieved only "arms in arms with arms." This is one of Marley's most complex lines in the song, and shows his ability to weave stories with the use of words that, when shifted in position, invoke different meanings—so arms become arms of human collectivity as well as weaponry. It is a brilliant play on words.

Marley then turns his attention to the concrete struggle of Zimbabwe and Africa. He announces, "We will fight this little struggle 'cause that the only way we can overcome our little trouble." Here Marley's Jamaican roots are clear. In Jamaican "nation-language"[69] the word "little," pronounced "likl," is used in different ways. It can be used in front of the words "more" or "most" to mean two different things. "Likl more" means "in a little while." On the other hand, "likl most" means "almost." However, a "likl" trouble can be a major problem, but by describing it as small, the Jamaican nation-language reorders the significance of the difficulty.[70] So for Marley the overcoming of the colonial relationship and the fight for self-determination was a small but important matter that was secondary to the real issue: "To overcome the little trouble soon we will find out who is the real revolutionary."

It seems that this "little trouble" has two dimensions. In the first there is the general colonial problem, and in the second there is the internal conflict between the colonized peoples. Coming from Jamaica, where he had seen the devastating effects of manufactured intraclass violence, Marley was alert to its consequences in Zimbabwe. He also was aware of the history of the colonial practice, which would rule by creating a native elite or transforming the new political elite into its ally. With this in mind, Marley appeals in the song for the revolutionaries not to allow themselves to be divided. This is then followed by the proclamation, "And I don't want my people to be tricked by mercenaries." The song then moves to merge Africans and "natty dread," indicating that Marley thought blacks in the Caribbean were exiled Africans and, since Rastafari recognized this fact, then they, too, had claims to being called Africans. The three lines of the final verse indicate this: "Natty trash it up in Zimbabwe Africans a liberate Zimbabwe I and I a liberate Zimbabwe." The song ends the way it began, with the explicit political statement "Every Man gotta right to decide his own destiny." It was a clarion call for African liberation, but it was also a call for that revolution to be pure. There is, in addition, a certain universalism as the song speaks to the deepest emotional structures of all those who are oppressed. The song is rooted in the Jamaican and Zimbabwean experiences, but it resonated with people engaged in political and social struggles where questions about social division, revolutionaries who have other political agendas, and the nature of community that explodes in moments of revolution are posed.

The final song I wish to pay some attention to on the *Survival* album is "Babylon System." Slowing down the music, this track is the only one on the album that is musically constructed in a Rastafari Nyabingi format. All the instruments surround the bass drum, and the repeater drum fills the spaces between lyrics as the organ and I-Threes chorus carry us along in this prophetic meditation. In a cool but militant voice, Marley begins by announcing, "We refuse to be what you wanted us to be, we are what we are that's the way its going to be." Several things are remarkable about these lines. Not only are they an eloquent testimony of resistance, but they begin a song whose lyrical construction continuously shifts. The next lines, which continue to speak to the oppressor group, make one of the most profound points in radical politics. Marley asserts that the typical solution of education as a means of social mobility and equal opportunity is a false one, since "you can't educate for no equal opportunity, talking about my freedom people, freedom and liberty." By juxtaposing education to freedom, Marley is intimating that freedom is a higher value. Why should this be so? We find the answer in the third verse, where Marley sings to the oppressed people, claiming knowledge about the system:

> Babylon System is the vampire
> Sucking the children Day by Day
> Babylon System is the vampire
> Sucking the Blood of the Sufferers
> Building Church and University
> Deceiving the People Continually
> Me say Them Graduating Thieves
> And Murderers look out now
> Sucking the Blood of the Sufferers.

It is clear from the above that the problem is that education as presently constructed, along the with the teachings of mainstream Christianity, produces individuals who are morally unfit. Therefore both churches and universities are involved in a massive deception. As a consequence, education cannot be a substitute for freedom. The system of oppression is metaphorically described as a vampire that sucks blood. It is therefore evil, with no redeeming features.

In the fourth verse Marley enunciates his prophetic calling by chanting, "tell the children the truth." This truth is that the oppressed ". . . 've been trodding on the winepress much too long," and therefore should now "Rebel." This call for rebellion continues to the last verse, in which Marley paints a historical picture of the nature of black oppression:

> From the very day we left the shores
> Of our Father's land
> We've been trampled on.
> Oh Now, Now we know everything we got to rebel.

For Marley the time has come when full knowledge is revealed about the history and present condition of people of African descent. Thus there are no more reasons for remaining quiescent. Marley's call for rebellion is a general one. He does not state the nature of the rebellion. What he is clear on is that resistance must now turn to rebellion and freedom. It is not in the nature of prophetic criticism to always be specific or have a defined political program of change. Therefore one should not expect this from Marley. What Marley does is to call the system to order, to create an alternative mental universe, and to rally people toward this new possibility.

Some Conclusions

In the end there is no mystery about Marley's international appeal. In a time of pessimism, when radical thought seems to be on the retreat and skepticism abounds, finding, in one element of the popular, defiance and hope that can also give joy is rare. Mario Vargas Llosa, in a commentary on Marley and Rastafari, notes their "bid against moral disintegration and human injustice."[71] In a world where both these things are the order of the day, it should be no surprise that Marley's appeal a decade after his death still resonates. In the end, whenever I think of Marley, I cannot help recalling my arrival in Mexico City in the mid-1980s, seating myself in cab with a driver who spoke only Spanish and who, after I finally communicated my destination, wondered if I was a Jamaican. Receiving an affirmative answer, he stopped the car, searched under the seat for a set of tapes, placed one in the cassette player of the car, and proclaimed with joy on his face, "Jah! Jah lives!" He was not a Rastafarian, and did not seem to have profound understanding of the doctrine, but somehow he had heard the voice of prophetic criticism, and it was that which he was celebrating. Surely the time has come for us to chant down Babylon one more time.

Closing Chant

We are now at the end. Prophets, heretics, history, politics, revolution, radical political thought, freedom, redemptive utopias, equality, symbolic life, counterworld orders—all these swirl and collide within the black radical intellectual tradition. They are the workings of humans as we labor to interpret our existence and to invest it with meanings. That the governing orders of language, of words, of history and human possibilities pay little attention to the swirl and the collision is a mark of how far we still are from grappling with all the different labors that human beings have constructed. If this text has been able to open another door, demonstrate another angle of vision, then it will have been a very modest contribution to chanting down Babylon, and of some assistance in framing the questions that human beings have perennially asked themselves, and continue to ask today: Who are we? What shall we do? How should we live together?

Oftentimes how we answer these questions are framed by our knowledge of the social world, its history as well as, obviously, by the material interests of our lives. However, this means that there is no radical political thought without an accompanying radical politics of knowledge that is able to open up the categories in which we have previously thought about ourselves as humans. Radical thought today also means understanding what is the nature of the human that has been constructed in the last five hundred years or so. What the tradition of black radicalism has attempted to do is to put that issue on the table.

Perhaps the last word should be left to the African writer Ayi Kwei Armah. At the end of the novel *The Beautyful Ones Are Not Yet Born*, a character who remains nameless throughout the book watches a scene of corruption. As the driver and the passenger bus leave the scene of corruption, our character notices an "inscription carefully lettered to form an oval shape":

THE BEAUTYFUL ONES
ARE NOT YET BORN

That may well be so as the drums of human freedom recede, sounding now ever so faintly, replaced with the bellicose drums of empire. In the tradition that this book has sought to elucidate, the deepest concern has always been the *human*. It is something from which we might want to learn.

Notes

Opening Chant

1. See Immanuel Wallerstein, *The End of the World as We Know It* (Minneapolis: University of Minnesota Press, 1999), for a discussion of this point.
2. See Lewis R. Gordon, *Existentia Africana* (New York: Routledge, 2000), 22–40, for an extended discussion on this habit.
3. For an extensive review of Skinner's methodologies, see James Tully, ed., *Meaning and Context: Quentin Skinner and His Critics* (Princeton, N.J.: Princeton University Press, 1988).
4. Ibid., 66.
5. Joseph Femia, "An Historicist Critique of 'Revisionist' Methods for Studying the History of Ideas," in ibid., 165.
6. Michel Foucault, *The Archaeology of Knowledge* (London: Routledge, 1992), 155.
7. Robert Young's, *White Mythologies: Writing History and the West* (London: Routledge, 1990), discusses very well the way in which many European critics are still implicated in a philosophical anthropology of European normativity.
8. See *Washington Post*, August 8, 2000, for a news story of ongoing investigations into U.S. government interventions in the Congo and the murder of Lumumba.
9. See Neal Ascherson, *The King Incorporated: Leopold the Second and the Congo* (London: Granta, 1999); and Adam Hochschild, *King Leopold's Ghost* (New York: Houghton Mifflin, 1999).
10. For a discussion of "colonial governmentality," see David Scott, *Refashioning Futures: Criticism After Postcoloniality* (Princeton, N.J.: Princeton University Press, 1999), chap. 1.
11. Charles Mills makes the point that there is a racialized polity in modernity that located Africans in a global racial order. See his *Racial Contract* (Ithaca, N.Y.: Cornell University Press, 1997) for a discussion of this.
12. Antonio Gramsci, *Selections from Prison Notebooks* (New York: International Publishers, 1971), 9.
13. Cornel West, *Keeping Faith* (New York: Routledge, 1993), 72–73.
14. For a critique of this dimension of West's thought, see Lewis Gordon, "The Unacknowledged Fourth Tradition: An Essay on Nihilism, Decadence, and the Black Intellectual Tradition in the Existential Pragmatic Thought of Cornel West," in George Yancy, ed., *Cornell West: A Critical Reader* (Oxford: Blackwell, 2001).

15. For a discussion of the usefulness and limits of Gramsci's notions of intellectuals in an African context, see Steven Feierman, *Peasant Intellectuals: Anthropology and History in Tanzania* (Madison: University of Wisconsin Press, 1990), chap. 1.
16. Edward Said, *Representations of the Intellectual* (New York: Vintage, 1996), xvii.
17. Ibid., 109.
18. Ibid., 44.
19. Ibid.
20. Four volumes that express these debates are John Michael, *Anxious Intellects* (Durham, N.C.: Duke University Press, 2000); Leon Fink, Stephen T. Leonard, and Donald M. Reid, *Intellectuals and Public Life* (Ithaca, N.Y.: Cornell University Press, 1996); Jeremy Jennings and Anthony Kemp-Welch, eds., *Intellectuals in Politics* (London: Routledge, 1997); and, most recently, Helen Small, ed., *The Public Intellectual* (Oxford: Blackwell, 2002).
21. Karl Mannheim, *Ideology and Utopia* (London: Routledge, 1966), 10.
22. Russell Jacoby, *The Last Intellectuals: American Culture in the Age of Academe* (New York: Basic Books, 1987).
23. Ibid., 235.
24. Michael Walzer, *The Company of Critics* (New York: Basic Books, 2002), 9.
25. Julien Benda, *The Treason of Intellectuals* (New York: Norton, 1963), 43.
26. Ibid., 44.
27. Isaiah Berlin, *The Power of Ideas* (Princeton, N.J.: Princeton University Press, 2000), 103.
28. Ibid., 105.
29. Perhaps one of the best descriptions of this process and its complexities is provided by the Kenyan writer Ngugi wa Thiong'o in *Decolonising the Mind: The Politics of Language in African Literature* (London: James Currey, 1986).
30. Jürgen Habermas, *The New Conservatism: Cultural Criticism and the Historians' Debate* (Cambridge, Mass.: Harvard University Press, 1989), 89.
31. Cedric Robinson, *Black Marxism* (Chapel Hill: University of North Carolina Press, 2000), 181.
32. W. E. B. Du Bois, *The Souls of Black Folks* (New York: Dodd and Mead, 1979), 189.
33. C. L. R. James, *Beyond a Boundary* (London: Serpent's Tail, 1994), 4.
34. Ibid., 32.
35. Frantz Fanon, *Black Skin, White Masks* (New York: Grove Press, 1967), 17–18.
36. Thiong'o, *Decolonising the Mind* (London: Heinemann, 1986), 23.
37. In January 2000, there was a conference on African languages held in Asmara, Ethiopia. The conference declared that "The vitality and quality of African languages must be recognized as the basis for the future empowerment of African peoples." For a discussion of this conference, see Ngugi wa Thiong'o, "The Politics of Self-Reliance," in David A. McDonald and Eunice Njeri Sahle, eds., *The Legacies of Julius Nyerere: Influences on Development Discourse and Practice in Africa* (Trenton, N.J.: Africa World Press, 2002).
38. My understanding of heresy during this period of European history draws heavily on Deborah Root, "Speaking Christian: Orthodoxy and Difference in Sixteenth Century Spain," *Representations* 23 (Summer 1998): 18–134. Thanks to Professor Sylvia Wynter for drawing it to my attention.
39. Pierre Bourdieu, *Outline of a Theory of Practice* (Cambridge: Cambridge University Press, 1995), 164.
40. Ibid., 165.
41. Shamoon Zamir, *DarkVoices* (Chicago: University of Chicago Press, 1995), 106.
42. All the quotations are taken from the Norton Critical Edition of this text. W. E. B. Du Bois, *The Souls of Black Folks*, Henry Louis Gates, Jr., and Terri Hume Oliver, eds. (New York: W. W. Norton, 1999).

43. Ibid., 10.

44. Ibid., 11.

45. Ibid.

46. W. E. B. Du Bois, *Dusk of Dawn* (New York: Schocken Books, 1968), 3.

47. C. L. R. James, *Beyond a Boundary* (London: Hutchinson, 1963) (unpaginated in text).

48. George Lamming, *Pleasures of Exiles* (London: Allison & Busby, 1984), 98.

49. Ibid., 118–119.

50. Roberto Retamar, *Caliban and Other Essays* (Minneapolis: University of Minnesota Press, 1997), 6.

51. Aimé Césaire, *A Tempest,* Richard Miller, trans. (New York: Ubu Repertory Theater Publications, 1993).

52. Ibid., 11.

53. Ibid.

54. Ibid., 15.

55. Gramsci, *Prison Notebooks,* 9.

56. Michel Foucault, *Madness and Civilization* (New York: Vintage, 1988), x.

57. Megan Vaughan, *Curing their Ills: Colonial Power and African Illness* (Stanford, Calif.: Stanford University Press, 1991), 101.

58. Ibid.

59. See Robert Edgar and Hilary Sapire, *African Apocalypse* (Athens: Ohio University Press, 2000), for the story of the life and importance of Nontetha Nkwenkwe. To date there are no biographies of either Bedward or Howell.

60. Much of my understanding of this dimension of the black intellectual tradition emerges from my discussions with Geri Augusto, whose work on indigenous knowledge systems in South Africa opens new ways to think about epistemological categories and their relationship to political ideas about freedom in the discursive practices of the black tradition.

61. For a discussion of this point, see David M. Anderson and Douglas H. Johnson, *Revealing Prophets* (London: James Currey, 1995). For a discussion of prophecy in South Africa, see John Comaroff and Jean Comaroff, *Of Revelation and Revolution,* 2 vols. (Chicago: University of Chicago Press, 1991 & 1997).

62. Michael Walzer, *Interpretation and Social Criticism* (Cambridge, Mass.: Harvard University Press, 1987), 75.

63. See Eric Hobsbawm, *Primitive Rebels* (Manchester, U.K.: Manchester University Press, 1978). C. L. R. James's *A History of Negro Revolt* (1938) used this categorical quality of the "primitive" and prepolitical. This category and its relationship to political modernity and radicalism haunts black radicalism.

64. Walter Benjamin, *Illuminations: Essays and Reflections* (New York: Schocken Books, 1988), 261.

65. See J. L. Austin, *How to Do Things with Words* (Cambridge, Mass.: Harvard University Press, 1975), 99–100.

66. See Sylvia Wynter's unpublished essay "From Myalism to Bob Marley" (1977) for a brilliant discussion of how the countersymbolic world is created.

67. This phrase is Lewis Gordon's.

68. John Dunn, *Western Political Theory in the Face of the Future* (Cambridge: Cambridge University Press, 1993), 137. By "Western political theory" Dunn means the canon of political texts that for some time have constituted the main staple for courses in political thought and theory.

69. Fanon, *Black Skin, White Masks,* 232.

70. Immanuel Wallerstein, "A Left Politics for the 21st Century? Or, Theory and Praxis Once Again," *New Political Science* 22, no. 2 (June 2000): 143–159.

71. Michael Hardt and Antonio Negri, *Empire* (Cambridge, Mass.: Harvard University Press, 2000), xi.
72. This silence is even starker in Antonio Negri, *Insurgencies, Constituent Power and the Modern State* (Minneapolis: University of Minnesota Press, 1999).
73. Langston Hughes, poem "To You."

Chapter 1
The Political Thought of Quobna Cugoano

1. Arna Bontemps, ed., *Great Slave Narratives* (Boston: Beacon Press, 1969).
2. For a discussion of how autobiographical forms limit black writers and thinkers to experience, see Lewis Gordon, *Existentia Africana* (New York: Routledge, 2000), chap. 4.
3. "Vindicationism" is the term of St. Clare Drake. He makes the point that the process of writing black history which validates the humanity of people of African descent can be called "vindicationism." See his *The Redemption of Africa and Black Religion* (Chicago: Third World Press, 1977). However, while "vindicationism" establishes humanness, it often does so on the terms of the dominant conceptions of the society. In the case of the slave narratives, because in early modernity writing was a sign of reason, many saw the written slave narratives as a sign that the slaves, too, had the capacity to be part of the human species. It is one reason why the frontispiece of many narratives proclaimed that the slave wrote the text. In this instance there was the need for double authenticity. First, the content of the text was accurate because it was written by someone who experienced slavery. This authenticity was required in the propaganda struggles against slavery because such descriptions were necessary to show how inhumane slavery was. Second, by writing, the slave-author had arrived at the status where he or she could be considered human. The operation of these two processes can be called "literary vindicationism."
4. See C. Peter Ripley, ed., *The Black Abolitionist Papers*, vols. i–iv (Chapel Hill: University of North Carolina Press, 1985–1991), for the documents of the period. A reading of these volumes will reveal the dimensions of the international nature of the black abolitionist movement of the time and its independent political import in nineteenth-century world politics. This is a story waiting to be written.
5. Henry Louis Gates, Jr., *The Signifying Monkey* (Oxford: Oxford University Press, 1988), 128.
6. Ibid.
7. For a discussion of this, see Paul Ricoeur, "Heidegger and the Question of the Subject," in his *The Conflict of Interpretations* (Evanston, Ill.: Northwestern University Press, 1974), 223–235.
8. Henry Louis Gates, Jr., and William L. Andrews, *Pioneers of the Black Atlantic: Five Slave Narratives from the Enlightenment 1772–1815.* (Washington, D.C.: Civitas Counterpoint, 1998), vii.
9. Dena Goodman, *Criticism in Action* (Ithaca, N.Y.: Cornell University Press, 1989), 4.
10. Ibid., 3.
11. See Christopher Hill, *The World Turned Upside Down* (London:Penguin, 1991), and his *The English Bible and the Seventeenth-Century Revolution* (London: Penguin, 1994), for a discussion of this point.
12. There is a noticeable phenomenon in late eighteenth-century and early nineteenth-century Western radicalism that is not often discussed in the standard his-

torical accounts of radicalism. This silence is about the ways in which many radicals of the period wove religious discourse into their political thought. Thus this was not just a feature of slaves' radical political discourse. Later, on English plebeian radicalism in the nineteenth century, much of it influenced by Thomas Paine's writings, developed a critique of bourgeois society that drew from both religious and secular sources. The most important individual here of course is Thomas Spencer. While English plebeian radicalism and black radical thought of this period drew from some of the same sources, they drew on different parts of the Bible.

13. Michel Foucault, "The Political Technology of Individuals," in Luther Martin, Huck Gutman, and Patrick Hutton, eds., *Technologies of the Self* (Amherst: University of Massachusetts Press, 1998), 149.

14. For a discussion of the "Chain of Being" and its influence on racial thinking, see Winthrop D. Jordan, *White over Black: American Attitudes Toward the Negro, 1550–1812* (Chapel Hill: University of North Carolina Press, 1969), chap. 13.

15. Cited in P. J. Marshall and Glyndwr Williams, *The Great Map of Mankind* (Cambridge: Cambridge University Press, 1982), 1.

16. Some theories of the origins of human society located Asia as site of the origin of humankind, then argued that each race had a turn at being a dominant civilization. For example, Voltaire in his "Essay on the Manners and Spirit of Nations" makes the point of Asia being civilized and then becoming partly uncivilized. However, Africans were excluded from this paradigm, and it was concluded that Africa was never civilized. This view of the historical development of humanity continued well into the nineteenth century and can be found in the writings of Hegel, particularly his lectures on the philosophy of world history.

17. See Marshall and Williams, *Great Map of Mankind,* for a discussion of this, especially 56–57.

18. See for a discussion of the features of the system of western ancient slavery, Moses I. Finley, *Ancient Slavery and Modern Ideology,* Brent D. Shaw, ed. (Princeton, NJ: Markus Wiener Publishers, 1998).

19. John Locke, *Two Treatises of Government,* Peter Laslett, ed. (Cambridge: Cambridge University Press, 1988), 283–285. (Emphasis in the original.)

20. Isaiah Berlin, *Four Essays on Liberty* (Oxford: Oxford University Press, 1969), 121.

21. See Charles Mills, *The Racial Contract* (Ithaca, N.Y.: Cornell University Press, 1997), for a excellent discussion of how this social contract was really a racialized one that operated in the interest of whites.

22. The central figures who explicate this tradition are J. G. A. Pocock, *The Machiavellian Moment: Florentine Political Thought and the Atlantic Republican Tradition* (Princeton, N.J.: Princeton University Press, 1975), and Quentin Skinner, *Liberty Before Liberalism* (Cambridge: Cambridge University Press, 1998). For a recent attempt to develop the ideas of civic republicanism in the modern political context see, Philip Pettit, *Republicanism: A Theory of Freedom and Government* (Oxford: Oxford University Press, 1997).

23. For an early discussion of the Correspondence Clubs, see E. P. Thompson, *Making of the English Working Class* (New York: Vintage, 1966). For a first-class discussion of the plebeian radicalism of the period, see Peter Linebaugh and Marcus Rediker, *The Many Headed Hydra* (Boston: Beacon Press, 2000). Robert Wedderburn's writings are available in Ian McCalman, ed., *The Horrors of Slavery and Other Writings by Robert Wedderburn* (Kingston, Jamaica: Ian Randle Press, 1997).

24. Rogers Smith, *Civic Ideals* (New Haven, Conn.: Yale University Press, 1997), 165.

25. Cited in Robert H. Webking, *The American Revolution and the Politics of Liberty* (Baton Rouge: Louisiana State University Press, 1989), 116. (Emphasis added.)

26. For a discussion of political propaganda and anticolonial newspapers of the period that confirms this position, see Patricia Bradley, *Slavery, Propaganda and the American Revolution* (Jackson: University Press of Mississippi, 1998).

27. Thomas Paine, "African Slavery in America," in Michael Foot and Isaac Kramnick, eds., *The Thomas Paine Reader* (London: Penguin, 1987), 53.

28. Montesquieu, *The Spirit of the Laws*, Anne Cohler, Basia Miller, and Harold Stone, eds. (Cambridge: Cambridge University Press, 1989).

29. Cited in Marshall and Williams, *Great Map of Mankind*, 248.

30. Ibid.

31. For a discussion of Mary Wollstonecraft's attitudes to slavery and African people, see Moira Ferguson, *Colonialism and Gender Relations:From Mary Wollstonecraft to Jamaica Kincaid* (New York: Columbia University Press, 1993).

32. Extract of review in Angelo Costanzo, ed., *The Interesting Narrative of the Life of Olaudah Equiano* (Peterborough Ontario: Broadview Press, 2001), 262.

33. This is the text I will use. The version cited throughout this essay is the one edited and introduced by Vincent Carretta, *Thoughts and Sentiments on the Evil of Slavery* (London: Penguin, 1999).

34. Gates, *Signifying Monkey*, 147.

35. *Thoughts and Sentiments*, xx.

36. June Ward, "The Master's Tools: Abolitionist Arguments of Equiano and Cugoano," in Tommy Lott, ed., *Subjection and Bondage* (New York: Rowman and Littlefield, 1998), 80.

37. *Thoughts and Sentiments*, 11.

38. Ibid.

39. Ibid., 15.

40. David Brion Davis, *The Problem of Slavery in Western Culture* (Oxford: Oxford University Press, 1966) and *The Problem of Slavery in the Age of Revolution 1770–1823* (Ithaca, N.Y.: Cornell University Press, 1975).

41. Davis, *The Problem of Slavery in Western Culture*, 355.

42. *Thoughts and Sentiments*, 17.

43. Ibid., 4.

44. I think that such a declaration was his way of saying that he was a radical.

45. Paine, "African Slavery in America," 52. (Emphasis in original.)

46. *Thoughts and Sentiments*, 11.

47. Thomas Paine, *The Rights of Man*, in *The Thomas Paine Reader*, 216. (Emphasis in original.)

48. *Thoughts and Sentiments*, 51.

49. Ibid., 20.

50. For a reader that attempts to include the major Western writings on the subject, see Amelie Oksenberg Rorty, *The Many Faces of Evil: Historical Perspectives* (New York: Routledge, 2001). For a sustained philosophical discussion on evil, see also Richard J. Bernstein, *Radical Evil: A Philosophical Interrogation* (Cambridge: Polity Press, 2002).

51. Cited in Dana R. Villa, *Politics, Philosophy, Terror: Essays on the Thought of Hannah Arendt* (Princeton, N.J.: Princeton University Press, 1999), 32.

52. Hannah Arendt, *Origins of Totalitarianism* (New York: Harcourt Brace Jovanovich, 1968), 447.

53. Lotte Kohler and Hans Saner, eds., *Hannah Arendt/Karl Jaspers: Correspondence 1926–1969* (New York: Harcourt Brace Jovanovich, 1992), 69.

54. See Orlando Patterson, *Slavery and Social Death: A Comparative Study* (Cambridge, Mass.: Harvard University Press, 1982).

55. *Thoughts and Sentiments*, 36.

56. Ibid., 23.

57. Ibid., 26.
58. Ibid.
59. Ibid., 27.
60. Ibid., 30.
61. Ibid., 41.
62. Ibid., 51.
63. *Thomas Paine Reader,* 217.
64. Ibid., 218.
65. *Thoughts and Sentiments,* 43.
66. Ibid., 51.
67. Ibid., 45.
68. Ibid., 72.
69. For a discussion of Locke, property rights, and the conquest of the New World, see James Tully, *An Approach to Political Philosophy: Locke in Contexts* (Cambridge: Cambridge University Press, 1993), chaps. 2–5.
70. *Thoughts and Sentiments,* 65.
71. Cugoano worked among the free black poor in London. For a brief discussion of this and the organization, see James Walvin, *An African Life: The Life and Times of Olaudah Equiano, 1745–1797* (London: Continuum, 1998), chap. 10. Walvin and others have argued that there was a small free black community, of which Cugoano was a part. This community was critical in the early stages of the abolitionist movement.
72. *Thoughts and Sentiments,* 19.
73. Denis Diderot, *Political Writings* (Cambridge: Cambridge University Press, 1992), 186.
74. Locke, *Two Treatises.*
75. *Thoughts and Sentiments,* 11.
76. Ibid., 71. (Emphasis added.)
77. Cited in Anthony Pagden, *Peoples and Empires* (New York: Modern Library, 2001), 92.
78. See John Stuart Mill, *On Liberty* (London: Penguin, 1974), for a clear enunciation of this point.
79. Cited in *Peoples and Empires,* 103.
80. Keith A. Sandiford, *Measuring the Moment: Strategies of Protest in Eighteenth-Century Afro-English Writing* (London: Associated University Presses, 1988), 104. This text attempts to detail some of the intellectual influences that shaped Cugoano's thinking. However, it does not deal with the issues of the political languages of the period and sees Cugoano's work as primarily that of an abolitionist rather than of a political thinker who was primarily concerned with racial slavery and colonialism.
81. See Lewis R. Gordon, *Bad Faith and Anti-Black Racism* (Atlantic Highland, N.J.: Humanities Press, 1995), for a sustained elaboration of the workings of anti-black racism.
82. Henri Gregoire, *An Enquiry Concerning the Intellectual and Moral Faculties and Literature of Negroes,* D. B. Warren, trans. (College Park, Md.: McGrath, 1967), 192.

Chapter 2
The Radical Praxis of Ida B. Wells-Barnett

1. For a substantial discussion on the racial state, see David Theo Goldberg, *The Racial State* (Oxford: Blackwell, 2002).
2. Billie Holiday, "Strange Fruit."

3. Hazel V. Carby, *Reconstructing Womanhood: The Emergence of the African-American Novelist* (Oxford: Oxford University Press, 1987), 108.

4. Richard J. Bernstein, *Praxis and Action* (Philadelphia: University of Pennsylvania Press, 1971), xiv.

5. Alfreda M. Duster, ed., *Crusade for Justice: The Autobiography of Ida B. Wells* (Chicago: University of Chicago Press, 1970), 10.

6. Herbert Aptheker, ed., *A Documentary History of the Negro People in the United States*, vol. 2. (New York: Citadel Press, 1992), 546. (Emphasis added.)

7. For a discussion of this ideology, see Kevin K. Gaines, *Uplifting the Race* (Chapel Hill: University of North Carolina Press, 1996), particularly the introduction.

8. Another author is Paula Giddings, *When and Where I Enter: The Impact of Black Women on Race and Sex in America* (New York: Bantam Books, 1984).

9. Hazel Carby, "On the Threshold of Woman's Era": Lynching, Empire, and Sexuality in Black Feminist Theory," in Henry Louis Gates, Jr., ed., *"Race," Writing and Difference* (Chicago: University of Chicago Press, 1986), 302.

10. Ibid., 311.

11. Charles Lemert and Esme Bhan, eds., *The Voice of Anna Julia Cooper* (Lanham, Md.: Rowman and Littlefield, 1998), 63. (Emphasis in original.)

12. Ibid., 62. (Emphasis in original.)

13. Ibid., 61.

14. For a discussion of this, see Demetrius Eudell, *Political Languages of Emancipation in the British Caribbean and the U.S. South* (Chapel Hill: University of North Carolina Press, 2002); and Thomas Holt's seminal work on postemancipation Jamaican society, *The Problem of Freedom: Race, Labour, and Politics in Jamaica, 1832–1938* (Kingston, Jamaica: Ian Randle, 1992).

15. Gaines, *Uplifting the Race*, 2.

16. Jacqueline Jones Royster, ed., *Southern Horrors and Other Writings: The Anti-Lynching Campaign of Ida B. Wells, 1892–1900* (Boston: Bedford Books, 1997), 50.

17. For a discussion of this point and the relationship between the two sets of ideas, see Richard Hofstadter, *Social Darwinism in American Thought* (Boston: Beacon Press, 1992). For a more recent survey, see Mike Hawkins, *Social Darwinism in European and American Thought, 1860–1945* (Cambridge: Cambridge University Press, 1997).

18. Hawkins, *Social Darwinism*, 5.

19. Cited in Lee D. Baker, *From Savage to Negro: Anthropology and the Construction of Race, 1896–1954* (Berkeley: University of California Press, 1998), 16.

20. Cited in Philip Dray, *At the Hands of Persons Unknown: The Lynching of Black America* (New York: Random House, 2002), 99.

21. Ibid., 100.

22. Ibid.

23. Cited in Hawkins, *Social Darwinism*, 58.

24. Walter White, *Rope and Faggot* (Notre Dame, Ind.: University of Notre Dame Press, 2001), chap. 6.

25. See Hofstadter, *Social Darwinism*, 178–180, for a discussion of Strong's importance.

26. Ibid., 178.

27. Ibid.

28. Cited in Anders Stephanson, *Manifest Destiny—American Expansion and the Empire of Right* (New York: Hill and Wang, 1995) 80.

29. Cited in Lawrence Goodwyn, "Populist Dreams and Negro Rights: East Texas as a Case Study," *American Historical Review* (December 1971): 1435–1456.

30. Two very important recent studies are Dray, *At the Hands of Persons Unknown*, and James H. Madison, *A Lynching in the Heartland* (New York: Palgrave, 2001). For a extraordinary pictorial documentary on lynching, see James Allen, ed., *Without Sanctuary: Lynching Photography in America* (Santa Fe, N.M.: Twin Palms, 2000).
31. These figures are taken from Madison, *A Lynching*, chap. 2.
32. Wells states that in that period, over ten thousand blacks were killed. The congressional report of 1872 suggested that in Louisiana, over two thousand African Americans were killed in the years immediately after the end of the Civil War.
33. Royster, *Southern Horrors*.
34. Cited in Dray, *At the Hands of Persons Unknown*, 14.
35. Cited in ibid., 101.
36. W. J. Cash, *The Mind of the South*, (New York: Vintage Books, 1991), 116.
37. Ibid.
38. "Mob Law in Arkansas," *New York Times* February 23, 1892, 4.
39. Frantz Fanon, *Black Skin, White Masks* (New York: Grove Press, 1967), 157.
40. Ibid., 161–163.
41. The history of lynching began in the late 1700s as a way to deal with the counter-revolutionaries after the Revolutionary War. Charles Lynch, a justice of the peace, developed an informal court in which those found guilty were whipped. In the early nineteenth century the group called the Regulators continued this practice of informal courts; by the middle of the century this practice became more developed and began to be used against slaves. By the late nineteenth century the practice had become a public ritual of murder of the black population. For a good survey of the different periods of lynching, see Dray, *At the Hands of Persons Unknown*, chap. 2.
42. For a discussion of these forms of torture and punishment, see Alexander Butchart, *The Anatomy of Power: European Constructions of the African Body* (London: Zed Press, 1998).
43. Gail Bederman, *Manliness and Civilization: A Cultural History of Gender and Race in the United States, 1880–1917* (Chicago: University of Chicago Press, 1995), 52.
44. Cited in Herbert Shapiro, *White Violence and Black Response* (Amherst: University of Massachusetts Press, 1988), 48.
45. Ibid., 49.
46. Ibid., 51.
47. Philip S. Foner, ed., *Frederick Douglass: Selected Speeches and Writings*, abridged and adapted by Yuval Taylor (Chicago: Lawrence Hill Books, 1999), 751.
48. Ibid., 755.
49. Ibid.
50. Duster, *Crusade for Justice*, 64.
51. W. E. B. Du Bois, *Dusk of Dawn* (New York: Schocken Books, 1968), 67.
52. Ida B. Wells, *A Red Record: Lynchings in the United States*, in Royster, *Southern Horrors*, 79.
53. Ibid., 127.
54. Ibid.
55. Angela Y. Davis, *Women, Race & Class* (New York: Random House, 1981), 175.
56. Raymond Williams, *Keywords: A Vocabulary of Culture and Society* (New York: Oxford University Press, 1983), 58.
57. The nineteenth-century dominance of Europe led to the development of what can only be called "world's fairs." Given the growing importance of America in the late nineteenth century, it was decided to hold such an event on American

soil. These fairs are important as a window into the mind of the time—how human beings, science, industry, colonies, and so on were classified. Given the hegemonic episteme of the time, African Americans initially were not invited to participate in the American-hosted event.

58. Ida B. Wells, "The Reason Why," in Trudier Harris, ed., *Selected Works of Ida B. Wells-Barnett* (New York: Oxford University Press, 1991), 74.

59. Ibid., 85.

60. Ibid., 75.

61. Cash, *Mind of the South,* 86.

62. Ibid., 116.

63. Royster, *Southern Horrors,* 55.

64. Ibid., 54–55.

65. Ibid., 53.

66. For a good discussion of the controversy and the reaction of different segments of the reform movement in America to it, see Patricia A. Schechter, *Ida B. Wells Barnett and American Reform, 1880–1930* (Chapel Hill: University of North Carolina Press, 2001), 110–112.

67. Dray, *At the Hands of Persons Unknown,* 106.

68. For an excellent description of the black women's club movement and its importance, see Deborah Gray White, *Too Heavy a Load: Black Women in Defense of Themselves, 1894–1994* (New York: W. W. Norton, 1999).

69. For this description, see Linda O. McMurry, *To Keep the Waters Troubled: The Life of Ida B. Wells* (New York: Oxford University Press, 1998), chap. 13.

70. Cited in ibid., 251.

71. Ula Y. Taylor, " 'Negro Women Are Great Thinkers as Well as Doers': Amy Jacques-Garvey and Community Feminism in the United States, 1924–1927," *Journal of Women's History* 12, no. 2 (Summer 2000): 104–126.

72. Ibid., 105.

73. For a discussion of this, see Oyeronke Oyewumi, *The Invention of Women: Making an African Sense of Western Gender Discourses* (Minneapolis: University of Minnesota Press, 1997).

74. The best biography of Sojourner Truth is Nell Irvin Painter, *Sojourner Truth: A Life, A Symbol* (New York: W. W. Norton, 1996). For readings on Harper, see Frances Smith Foster, "Frances Ellen Watkins Harper (1825–1911)," in Darlene Clark Hine, ed., *Black Women in America: An Historical Encyclopedia* (New York: Carlson, 1993).

75. Elizabeth Cady Stanton, "Address to the New York State Legislature," in Miriam Schneir, ed., *Feminism: The Essential Historical Writings* (New York: Vintage Books, 1992), 119.

76. Ibid.

77. Foner, *Frederick Douglass,* 600.

78. Cited in Painter, *Sojourner Truth,* 225.

79. Schneir, *Feminism,* 78.

80. Ibid.

81. Joy James, *Representations of Black Feminist Politics* (New York: Palgrave, 2002), 55. In her other writings on Wells, James focuses on Wells's relationship to Du Bois and how in some instances she overturned the notion of the "talented tenth." See Joy James, *Transcending the Talented Tenth* (New York: Routledge, 1997), and "The Profeminist Politics of W. E. B. Du Bois with Respects to Anna Julia Cooper and Ida B. Wells Barnett," in Bernard W. Bell, Emily R. Grosholz, and James B. Stewart, eds., *W. E. B. Du Bois on Race and Culture* (New York: Routledge, 1996).

82. Patricia Hill Collins, "Introduction," in Ida B. Wells-Barnett, *On Lynchings* (New York: Humanity Books, 2002), 9.

Chapter 3
C. L. R. James and W. E. B. Du Bois

1. See for example, Homi K. Bhabha, *The Location of Culture* (New York: Routledge, 1994), 39.
2. For a discussion of this, see Michael Walzer, *Interpretation and Social Criticism* (Cambridge, Mass.: Harvard University Press, 1993), 42.
3. Reinhart Koselleck, *The Practice of Conceptual History: Timing History, Spacing Concepts* (Stanford, Calif.: Stanford University Press, 2002), 65.
4. For a discussion of the American Civil War and Reconstruction as a site of memory contestation, see David W. Blight, *Race and Reunion* (Amherst: University of Massachusetts Press, 2001). For discussions on the Haitian Revolution, see Michel-Rolph Trouillot, *Silencing the Past: Power and the Production of History* (Boston: Beacon Press, 1995), chap. 2.
5. Cited in Jeremy Jennings and Anthony Kemp-Welch, eds., *Intellectuals in Politics* (London: Routledge, 1997), 9.
6. For a revealing discussion of James's early life, see C. L. R. James, *Beyond a Boundary* (London: Hutchinson, 1963).
7. For the importance of this text to international Trotskyism, see Anthony Bogues, *Caliban's Freedom: The Early Political Thought of CLR James* (London: Pluto, 1997), chap. 3.
8. For a discussion of James's early writings in Trinidad, see Reinhard Sander, *West Indian Literature of the 1930's* (Westport, Conn.: Greenwood Press, 1988).
9. C. L. R. James, "The Old World and the New," in his *At the Rendezvous of Victory* (London: Allison & Busby, 1984), 211.
10. These lectures have been published in *Small Axe: A Journal of Criticism* (Kingston, Jamaica) no. 8 (December 2000): 65–112.
11. C. L. R. James, "Lectures on *The Black Jacobins*," in ibid., 67.
12. There is still an engrossing debate about history and its relationship to literary production. For some readings on this debate, see Roger Chartier, *On the Edge of the Cliff: History, Language and Practices* (Baltimore: Johns Hopkins University Press, 1997); Hayden White, *The Content of the Form: Narrative Discourse and Historical Representation* (Baltimore: Johns Hopkins University Press, 1987); F. R. Ankersmit, *Historical Representation* (Stanford, Calif.: Stanford University Press, 2001).
13. C. L. R. James, *The Black Jacobins* (New York: Vintage, 1989), xi. This is the edition I will use in this essay.
14. James, "Lectures on *The Black Jacobins*," 71.
15. Ibid., 85.
16. W. E. B. Du Bois, *Dusk of Dawn* (New York: Schocken Books, 1968), vii–viii.
17. Ibid., 20.
18. Ibid., 30.
19. Ibid., 27. (Emphasis added.)
20. See Lewis R. Gordon, *Existentia Africana* (New York: Routledge, 2000), chap. 5, for an excellent review of the philosophical significance of Du Bois's early sociological work. Another assessment of Du Bois's sociological contributions can be found in "Sociology Hesitant: Thinking with W. E. B. Du Bois," a special issue of *boundary 2*, Ronald A. T. Judy, ed., 27, no. 3 (Fall 2000).

21. Du Bois, *Dusk of Dawn*, 67.

22. See John Dewey, Liberalism *and Social Action* (New York: Prometheus Books, 2000), for a discussion of this renascent liberalism and it relationship to social criticism and activism. Du Bois and Dewey worked together for a brief moment in 1929 in the short-lived League of Independent Political Action.

23. Du Bois, *Dusk of Dawn*, 288.

24. David W. Blight, *Beyond the Battlefield: Race, Memory, and the American Civil War* (Amherst: University of Massachusetts Press, 2002), 230.

25. Cited in David Levering Lewis, *W. E. B. Du Bois: The Fight for Equality and the American Century, 1919–1963* (New York: Henry Holt, Company, 2000).

26. Eric J. Hobsbawm 's magisterial four volumes stand as the exemplar of radical historical narratives about the world over the last two hundred years. The volumes, all published by Vintage Books, are *The Age of Revolution, The Age of Capital, The Age of Empire,* and *The Age of Extremes.* What is interesting to note about this work is its silences. However, for our purposes, in the *Age of Revolution* Hobsbawm argues that the "French Revolution . . . remains *the* revolution of its time." He then goes on to describe the rise of the Jacobins and asserts that their actions in the revolution "helped to create the first independent revolutionary leader of stature in Toussaint-Louverture." After this reference the Haitian Revolution is consigned to historical oblivion. What I am suggesting here is that no serious examination of the "Age of Revolution" can occur without any study of the meaning of the Haitian Revolution for that period, since it successfully overthrew one of the foundations of the modern world—racial slavery.

27. James, *The Black Jacobins,* 85–86.

28. Ibid., 243.

29. C. L. R. James, "Revolution and the Negro," in Scott Mclemee and Paul Le Blanc, eds. *C. L. R. James and Revolutionary Marxism: Selected Writings of C. L. R. James 1939–1949* (N.J.: Humanities Press, 1994), 77. (Emphasis added.)

30. It is interesting to note something that is not often talked about with reference to James. In two interviews done in 1980 and 1981, and published in Paul Buhle, ed., *C. L. R. James: His Life and Work* (London: Allison & Busby, 1986), James makes the point about *The Black Jacobins* that since he had returned to the Caribbean, "A great deal of my time has been spent in seeing how much I failed to understand when I was young and my whole life was toward European literature, European sociology. Now I'm beginning to see and it is helping me to write" (167). One can only speculate what it would have meant if he had to rewrite *The Black Jacobins* from this frame.

31. For a discussion of this point about James, see Paget Henry, *Caliban's Reason* (New York: Routledge, 2000), 48.

32. James, *The Black Jacobins,* 88.

33. Ibid., 246.

34. For discussions of some of these views, see Carolyn Fick, *The Making of Haiti: The Saint Domingue Revolution from Below* (Knoxville: University of Tennessee Press, 1990). See also the various articles by John K. Thorton, in particular his "African Soldiers in the Haitian Revolution," *Journal of Caribbean History* 25, nos. 1 and 2 (1991) 58–80. There are of course major disputes about this. See in particular the work of David Geggus; his *Slave Resistance Studies and Saint Domingue Slave Revolt: Some Preliminary Considerations,* Latin American and Caribbean Center Miami, Florida Occasional Paper, 4th ser. (Winter 1993) is a good example of the main arguments in this dispute.

35. For a description of and discussion about *Lwa* in Haitian religious practices, see Donald Cosentino, ed., *Sacred Arts of Haitian Vodou* (Los Angles: University of California Press, 1995).

36. For an excellent discussion of this and the importance of Haitian vodou as "a project of thought," see Joan Dayan, *Haiti, History and the Gods* (Berkeley: University of California Press, 1998).

37. James, "Revolution and the Negro," 77. Where there was no historical neglect, the revolution was seen as a manifestation of the bourgeois-democratic revolution of the period. For this discussion, see Eugene D. Genovese, *From Rebellion to Revolution: Afro-American Slave Revolts in the Making of the Modern World* (Baton Rouge: Louisiana State University Press, 1979), chap. 3.

38. W. E. B. Du Bois, *Black Reconstruction in America 1860–1880* (New York: Atheneum, 1969), 5. This is the edition I will use for this essay.

39. Ibid., 30.

40. Karl Marx, *Capital,* vol. 1 (London: Penguin 1976), 53.

41. Michael Sandel, *Democracy's Discontent* (Cambridge, Mass.: Harvard University Press, 1996). For a discussion about the ideology of free labor during the Reconstruction period, see Heather Cox Richardson, *The Death of Reconstruction: Race, Labor and Politics in the Post Civil-War North, 1865–1901* (Cambridge, Mass.: Harvard University Press, 2001).

42. These discussions can be found in the political discourse of Southern black representatives, particularly after the 1870s and before black political equality was destroyed.

43. Du Bois, *Black Reconstruction,* 9. (Emphasis added.)

44. Ibid., 67.

45. James Allen, *Reconstruction: The Battle for Democracy* (New York: International Publishers, 1937), 11.

46. William Gorman, "W. E. B. Du Bois and His Work," *Fourth International* 11, no. 3 (May–June 1950) 80–86. Gorman was a close associate of James in the Johnson-Forest Tendency. Gorman was a political name; his real name was George Rawick, and he went on to write histories of slave life in America. I want to thank Jim Murray of the C. L. R. James Institute for a copy of this paper.

47. James, "Lectures on *The Black Jacobins,*" 85.

48. James, *The Black Jacobins,* xi.

49. Du Bois, *Black Reconstruction,* 122–123.

50. Ibid., 122.

51. Ibid., 125.

52. W. E. B. Du Bois, *Darkwater Voices from Within the Veil* (New York: Schocken Books, 1969), 30.

53. "The Present Outlook for the Dark Races of Mankind," *Church Review* 17 (1900). Cited in John Carlos Rowe, *Literary Culture and U.S. Imperialism* (Oxford: Oxford University Press, 2000) 203.

54. Cited in Mike Hawkins, *Social Darwinism in European and American Thought, 1860–1945* (Cambridge: Cambridge University Press, 1997), 205.

55. Du Bois, *Black Reconstruction,* 383.

56. See Kent Worcester, *C. L. R. James: A Political Biography* (Albany: State University of New York Press, 1996), for a review of James's political life.

57. Published as C. L. R. James, *Notes on Dialectics* (London: Allison & Busby, 1980).

58. Transcript of talk by C. L. R. James at Tougaloo College, May 9, 1972. Thanks to Jim Murray of the C. L. R. James Institute for sending me a copy.

59. W. E, B. Du Bois, *The Souls of Black Folks* (New York: Dodd, Mead, 1979), 3.

60. Pierre Bourdieu, *Outline of a Theory of Practice* (Cambridge: Cambridge University Press, 1995), 171.

61. This section owes much to Z. Bauman's discussion of intellectuals in his *Legislators and Interpreters* (Stanford, Calif.: Stanford University Press, 1987).

62. Etienne Balibar, *Masses, Ideas and Politics* (London: Verso, 1994), 200.

63. Walzer, *Interpretation and Social Criticism*, 42.
64. See Steven Lukes, "Liberty and Equality: Must they Conflict?," in David Held, ed., *Political Theory Today* (Stanford, Calif.: Stanford University Press, 1996), chap. 2.
65. Michel de Certeau, *The Writing of History* (New York: Columbia University Press, 1988).
66. Du Bois, *Black Reconstruction*, 1.
67. Cited in Arnold Rampersad, *The Art and Imagination of W. E. B. Du Bois* (New York: Schocken Books, 1990), 315–316.

Chapter 4
Julius Nyerere

1. C. L. R. James, *A History of Negro Revolt*, 3rd ed. (London: Race Today Publications, 1985), 85. The revised edition was first published by Drum and Spear Press, in Washington, D.C. (1969). This edition includes a new section, "Always Out of Africa," as the result of a request by the Center for Black Education, in association with Drum and Spear Press, for James to update the book. It is important to note that critical individuals in this organization became some of the central organizers of the Sixth Pan-African Congress, held in Tanzania in 1974. The politics of Tanzania and the political meanings of *Ujamaa* and *Arusha* obviously were important to elements of the radical black movement in the United States.
2. It is fair to say that African philosophy is now an established field of study. For a brief introduction to this field, see Barry Hallen, *A Short History of African Philosophy* (Bloomington: Indiana University Press, 2002). In political thought and theory, African political thought is neglected. At the present moment there is no history of African political thought in English. However, a recent volume has been published that attempts to examine thematically some dimensions of African political thought: Teodros Kiros, ed., *Explorations in African Political Thought* (New York: Routledge, 2001).
3. Julius Nyerere, interview with Ikaweba Bunting, *New Internationalist Magazine* no. 309 (January–February 1999): www.dantford-hmp/archives/.
4. For example, in the August 2002 issue of *Political Theory* (30, no. 4), one of the most important journals of political theory in the English language, there is a robust debate titled "What Is Political Theory?" Many of the writers argue about the most important events of the twentieth century that shape such a debate in the early twenty-first century. The writers recognize the fall of communism, the significance of Nazism and Stalinism, and the rise of feminism and environmentalism. There is no reference whatsoever to the collapse of empires and the anticolonial movement. It is as if such a movement and event did not occur.
5. For an example of the now typical political studies of African societies as failed states, see I. William Zartman, *Collapsed States: The Disintegration and Restoration of Legitimate Authority* (London: Lynne Rienner, 1995). However, two more recent texts have staked out a different position for the political studies of Africa: Mahmood Mamdani, *Citizen and Subject: Contemporary Africa and the Legacy of Late Colonialism* (Princeton, N.J.: Princeton University Press, 1996), and Achille Mbembe, *On the Postcolony* (Berkeley: University of California Press, 2001).
6. The invention of Africa as the place of darkness and hopelessness is still very prevalent in Western thought and practices, as is evident from a review of the reportage by the major Western newspapers. For a discussion on this, see *New African* no. 397 (July/August 2000). In the academy, discussion on Africa often centers on the issues of Africa as diseased. Therefore, many of the arguments are

framed by pathologies or the notion that Africa is either culturally or geographi-
cally bounded. The clearest expression of this can be seen in some of the essays in
Lawrence E. Harrison and Samuel P. Huntington, eds., *Culture Matters: How Values Shape Human Progress* (New York: Basic Books, 2000). This complex continent of over fifty nations is still lumped together as one political and social space
without any distinctions. The political, philosophical, and social arguments
about the nature of Africa in the West also continue to be driven by theories of
modernization.

7. This is a 1974 political statement made by Nyerere in the Sudan. It summarizes
    much of his political thinking at the time, but I would also suggest that it was in
    part a response to the Tanzanian and African critics of his earlier political
    thought. To my mind it is a tactical document of thought and discourse, and is
    very reflective of extensive Third World debates at the time.

8. As late as 1996, one prominent political theorist could write a text on the history
    of political theory without any reference to African political thought. See John
    Dunn, *The History of Political Theory and Other Essays* (Cambridge: Cambridge
    University Press, 1996). It is also interesting to note that publication of the vari-
    ous companions to political thought or political philosophy, while gesturing to-
    ward feminism, ignore anticolonial thought. When the discussion of anticolonial
    thought *is* conducted, it is now typically done under the rubric of "postcolonial-
    ism." See, e.g., Robert J. C. Young, *Postcolonialism: An Historical Introduction*
    (Oxford: Blackwell, 2001).

9. Robert July, *An African Voice: The Role of Humanities in African Independence*
    (Durham, N.C.: Duke University Press, 1987), 231.

10. Terence Ranger, "The Invention of Tradition in Colonial Africa," in Eric Hobs-
    bawm and Terence Ranger, eds. *The Invention of Tradition* (Cambridge: Cam-
    bridge University Press, 1983), 247–248. Another important discussion of
    modernity and tradition in African thought can be found in Kwame Gyekye, *Tra-
    dition and Modernity: Philosophical Reflections on the African Experience* (Oxford:
    Oxford University Press, 1997). For a discussion of the debate about tradition
    and modernity in African philosophy, see D. A. Masolo, *African Philosophy in
    Search of Identity* (Bloomington: Indiana University Press, 1995).

11. For a brilliant and succinct discussion of this point and the nature of history, see
    Michel-Rolph Trouillot, *Silencing the Past: Power and the Production of History*
    (Boston: Beacon Press, 1995).

12. Bruce Fetter, ed., *Colonial Rule in Africa: Readings from Primary Sources* (Madi-
    son: University of Wisconsin Press, 1979), 131.

13. William Kymlicka, *Multicultural Citizens: A Liberal Theory of Minority Rights*
    (Oxford: Clarendon Press, 1995), 2.

14. James Tully, "Political Philosophy as a Critical Activity," *Political Theory* 30, no. 4
    (August 2002): 536.

15. The term "command state" is taken from Mbembe's *On the Postcolony.*

16. V. Y. Mudimbe, *The Invention of Africa: Gnosis, Philosophy, and the Order of
    Knowledge* (Bloomington: Indiana University Press, 1988), 2.

17. See, as an early instance of this, Christopher Clapham, "The Context of African
    Political Thought," *Journal of Modern African Studies* 8, no. 1 (1970). 1–13.

18. This lecture is in Leo Strauss, *What Is Political Philosophy?* (Chicago: University
    of Chicago Press, 1988).

19. Peter Laslett's article is in Peter Laslett, ed., *Philosophy, Politics and Society,* 1st
    edition (Oxford: Blackwell, 1956). For Isaiah Berlin's see "Does Political Theory
    Still Exist?" in Berlin's *The Proper Study of Mankind* (New York: Farrar, Straus and
    Giroux, 1998), 59–90.

20. Strauss, *What Is Political Philosophy?,* 12.

21. See Skinner's essay, "Meaning and Understanding," in James Tully, ed., *Meaning and Context: Quentin Skinner and His Critics* (Princeton, N.J.: Princeton University Press, 1988), 47.
22. The definition typically used here is ideology as a lower form of reasoning and knowledge, more akin to opinion. Of course all of this is mixed up with the debate about ideology in social and political theory.
23. It is useful here to note that the concept of ideology and political life and studies is a much contested one. For a discussion of this, and the possible relationship between ideology and political theory, see Michael Freeden, *Ideologies and Political Theory* (New York: Oxford University Press, 1986).
24. One result of this view of African political thought as ideology is J. Ayo Langley's wonderful documentary text, *Ideologies of Liberation in Black Africa, 1856–1970* (London: Rex Collings, 1979). This is a important text for students of African intellectual history, and nothing else like it exists in English. Although Langley attempts to critique the view that Africa has no intellectual history worth speaking of, in the end he proceeds to document African political thought and theory in specific categories of political ideology. Langley defines political ideology as concerned "with stating what *ought* to be." He is very aware of the problem that this creates, and in his essay that introduces the volume, he comments, "That is not always possible, of course, to make neat distinctions between philosophical and ideological writing, nor indeed between ideological and sociological writing" (8).
25. Hannah Arendt, *Between Past and Future* (New York: Penguin, 1977), 115.
26. An important article in this regard is Adriana Cavarero, "Politicizing Theory," *Political Theory* 30, no. 4 (August 2002): 506–532. One should also observe here that although some political theorists were aware of this problem, it was never addressed directly. For an attempt to understand politics as practice, see Isaiah Berlin, "Political Judgment," in his *Studies in Ideas and Their History: The Sense of Reality* (New York: Farrar, Straus and Giroux, 1998).
27. Walter Rodney, "Tanzanian Ujamaa and Scientific Socialism," *Africa Review*. 1, no 4 (1971): 61–76.
28. For a discussion of this, see Louis Lindsay, *The Myth of Independence*, Working Paper no. 6. (Kingston, Jamaica: ISER Publications, 1975).
29. The evidence for this is abundant. In doing the research for this essay, I came across numerous pamphlets, collected readers, radio transcripts, newspaper articles, and commentaries about *Ujamaa* and the *Arusha Declaration*. Much of this discussion took place in KiSwahili, and therefore I was unable to learn from the documents the texture and feel of many of these debates. However, the volume of the output and what was available in English strongly suggest to me that there was intense public debate about these ideas, and that *Ujamaa* and *Arusha* were part of a wider public political discourse. The range of the debate also suggests that there existed what can safely be called a Dar-es-Salaam school of thought. This would include both the University of Dar-es-Salaam and the public debates. One condition that led to these debates was the fact that for many years Tanzania housed the headquarters, and rear-base camps, of all the major African liberation movements in its capital city, something upon which few commentators on Africa reflect. Horace Campbell alludes to this Dar-es-Salaam school of thought in a brief article. See Horace Campbell, "The Impact of Walter Rodney and Progressive Scholars on the Dar-es-Salaam School," *Social and Economic Studies* (Institute of Social and Economic Research, University of the West Indies) 40, no. 2 (June 1991), 99–135.
30. A good selection of these can be found in the following volumes of his selected writings: *Freedom and Unity* (London: Oxford University Press, 1966); *Uhuru na*

Ujamaa: Freedom and Socialism. A Selection from Writings and Speeches, 1965–1967 (Dar-es-Salaam: Oxford University Press, 1968); *Freedom and Development, Uhuru na Maendeleo: A Selection from Writings and Speeches, 1968–1973* (Dar-es-Salaam: Oxford University Press, 1974).

31. Langley, in *Ideologies of Liberation in Black Africa*, lists Nyerere's political thought under two headings. The first is "race, nationalism and Pan-Africanism." The second is that of socialism. Gyekye, in *Tradition and Modernity*, discusses Nyerere in the chapter "The Socialist Interlude." However, Gyekye goes on to argue that there is a large dose of humanism in Nyerere's thought.

32. Julius Nyerere, "Ujamaa—The Basis of African Socialism," in his *Freedom and Unity*, 162.

33. Ibid.

34. Ibid.

35. Ibid., 162–163.

36. Ibid., 163.

37. Ibid., 164.

38. Ibid., 166.

39. Ibid.

40. Ibid., 170.

41. Ibid., 164–165.

42. Ibid., 324–325.

43. Nyerere remained, since his baptism at twelve, a Roman Catholic.

44. Nyerere, *Freedom and Unity*, 2.

45. Rodney, "Tanzanian Ujamaa and Scientific Socialism." The copy in my possession is a photocopy of a version published and passed around to radical groups in the Caribbean in the mid-1970s. It is not dated, so I refer readers to the journal article.

46. Ibid.

47. For the sharpest internal critiques of *Ujamaa* in English, see *The Silent Class Struggle* (Dar-es-Salaam: Tanzanian Publishing House, 1974). The articles in this volume represent part of the intense political debate at the time. Some of them first appeared in the journal *Cheche,* the publication of the party's youth league and the university students organized in a group called the African Revolutionary Front. The title of the volume was taken from the one of the articles written by Issa G. Shivji, a graduate law student at the time. In Tanzanian radical political culture, the document was of seminal importance. For another important critique, see Michaela von Freyhold, *Ujamaa Villages in Tanzania* (New York: Monthly Review Press, 1979). For a favorable view of *Ujamaa,* see Stefan Hedlund and Mats Lundahl, *Ideology as a Determinant of Economic Systems: Nyerere and Ujamaa in Tanzania,* Research Report no. 84 (Uppsala: Scandinavian Institute of African Studies, 1999).

48. For a critique of the planned villagization process, see James C. Scott, *Seeing like a State* (New Haven, Conn.: Yale University Press, 1998), chap. 7.

49. Mbembe, *On the PostColony,* 34.

50. Nyerere, *Freedom and Unity,* 7–8.

51. Julius Nyerere, "Socialism and Rural Development," in ibid., 339.

52. Ibid., 339–340.

53. Kwame Nkrumah, *Consciencism: Philosophy and Ideology of Decolonization* (New York: Monthly Review Press, 1970) 78–79.

54. Ibid., 106.

55. Ibid., 70.

56. Kwame Nkrumah, *Class Struggle in Africa* (London: Panaf Books, 1970), 10.

57. Julius Nyerere, *The Rational Choice—Capitalism or Socialism* (Tunapuna, Trinidad: New Beginning Movement, 1974), 3.
58. Amilcar Cabral, "The Weapon of Theory," in his *Revolution in Guinea: An African People's Struggle* (London: Stage One, 1971), 83.
59. Ibid., 77. (Emphasis in original.)
60. For a discussion of this, see William G. Martin and Michael O. West, *Out of One, Many Africas: Reconstructing the Study and Meaning of Africa* (Urbana: University of Illinois Press, 1999).
61. Mamdani, *Citizen and Subject.*
62. Ibid., 3.
63. Léopold Senghor, "Nationhood: Report on the Doctrine and Program of the Party of African Federation," in Okwui Enwezor, ed., *The Short Century: Independence and Liberation Movements in Africa, 1945–1994.* (New York: Prestel, 2002).
64. Issa G. Shivji, *Class Struggles in Tanzania* (London: Heinemann, 1976), 79.
65. *New Internationalist* no. 309 (January–February 1999).
66. A comparative comment may be useful here. In Jamaica, the People's National Party (PNP), under the political leadership of Michael Manley, was profoundly influenced by the *Arusha Declaration.* However, in spite of intense attempts to develop a party leadership code that would deal with the problem of a similar rising social group, such a code was not passed in the 1970s. In the 1980s the discussion was again started, but the matter has never been settled. There are many reasons for this; one of them is a radical view of politics that was noticeably absent from the PNP leadership political discussion particularly in the 1980s. In the TANU there was a political/philosophical basis that formed around human equality which facilitated the passage of the document.
67. Julius Nyerere, "The Arusha Declaration," in his *Freedom and Socialism,* 234.
68. For a discussion of these theories, see Ankie M. M. Hoogvelt, *The Third World in Global Development* (London: Macmillan, 1982).
69. Nyerere, *Freedom and Socialism,* 239.
70. Ibid., 243.
71. Perhaps one important influence here on Nyerere's political thought was the Chinese example, where the peasant population was given revolutionary agency. It is one area of his thought that needs exploring.
72. A. K. L. J. Mlimuka and P. J. A. M. Kabudi, "The State and the Party," in Issa G. Shivji, ed., *The State and the Working People in Tanzania* (Dakar: CODESRIA, 1986), 70–71.
73. Andre de La Rue, "Ujamaa on the March," in Lionel Cliffe and John S. Saul, eds., *Socialism in Tanzania: An Interdisciplinary Reader,* Vol. 2, *Policies* (Dar-es-Salaam: East African Publishing House, 1973), 42.
74. Walter Rodney, "Some Implications of the Question of Disengagement from Imperialism," in *The Silent Class Struggle,* 64–65.
75. For a good summary of these debates, see Will Kymlicka, *Contemporary Political Philosophy* (Oxford: Oxford University Press, 1990).
76. See extract of *Nicomachean Ethics* in Louis P. Pojman and Robert Westmoreland, eds., *Equality: Selected Readings* (Oxford: Oxford University Press, 1997), 17–25.
77. Kymlicka, *Contemporary Political Philosophy,* 52–53.
78. Thomas Nagel, *Equality and Partiality* (Oxford: Oxford University Press, 1991), 63.
79. Ibid., 4.
80. The divide between equality and liberty has been the cause of great debate in Western political theory. For a brief summary of this debate, see Steven Lukes, "Equality and Liberty, Must they Conflict," in David Held, ed., *Political Theory Today* (Stanford, Calif.: Stanford University Press, 1991).

81. For a multidisciplinary approach to this question of personhood in the West and Africa, see Michael Carrithers, Steven Collins, and Steven Lukes, *The Category of the Person: Anthropology, Philosophy, History* (Cambridge: Cambridge University Press, 1999).
82. Julius Nyerere, "The Purpose Is Man," in his *Freedom and Socialism*, 316.
83. A. W. Singham and Shirley Hune, *Non-Alignment in the Age of Alignments* (London: Zed Press, 1986), 22.
84. It is intriguing to read the present antiglobalization debates and to see how they neglect to locate the movement's demands in the 1970s demands of the Third World countries. Again there is a way in which ideas that originate in the Third World do not seem to have any legitimacy unless they gain currency in so-called First World settings. For a discussion on some of these debates, see James H. Mittelman, *The Globalization Syndrome: Transformation and Resistance* (Princeton, N.J.: Princeton University Press, 2000). For a discussion about international distributive justice, see Onora O'Neill, "Transnational Justice," in David Held, ed., *Political Theory Today* (Stanford, Calif.: Stanford University Press, 1991).
85. Fetter, *Colonial Rule in Africa*, 34. (Emphasis added.)
86. Ibid., 36.
87. Aimé Césaire, *Discourse on Colonialism* (New York: Monthly Review Press, 1972), 37.
88. Frantz Fanon, *The Wretched of the Earth* (New York: Grove Press, 1963), 313.
89. For an extensive discussion of Wynter's thought, see David Scott, interview with Sylvia Wynter, *Small Axe* no 8 (September 2000): 119–207; and Paget Henry, *Caliban's Reason* (New York: Routledge, 2000), ch. 5.
90. Karl Marx, *Collected Works* vol. 3, 154.
91. One very important American current, which called itself Marxist-humanist, was founded by Raya Dunayevskaya. For a discussion on the ideas of this current, see Raya Dunayevskaya, *Marxism and Freedom* (New York: Columbia University Press, 1988).
92. Césaire, *Discourse on Colonialism*, 86.
93. Ibid., 37.
94. Julius Nyerere, "Freedom and Development," in Andrew Coulson, ed., *African Socialism in Practice: The Tanzanian Experience* (Nottingham, U.K.: Spokesman, 1982), 27–28.
95. David Scott *Small Axe* no 8 (September 2000), 119–207.
96. For a brief but illuminating discussion on this point, see Suzanne Césaire, "Leo Frobenius and the Problem of Civilization," in Michael Richardson, ed., *Refusal of the Shadow: Surrealism and the Caribbean* (London: Verso, 1996), 82–87.
97. Frantz Fanon, *Black Skin, White Masks* (New York: Grove Press, 1967).
98. African humanism of course has many currents, and some of them begin and end with the common definition of humanism, the concern with man in the European sense. For this current in Africa, see Kenneth D. Kaunda, *A Humanist in Africa* (London: Longmans, 1966).
99. Benjamin Mkirya, cited in Viktoria Stoger-Eising, "European Influences in Nyerere's Social and Political Thought," *Africa* 70, no. 1 (2000) 118–134. This article gives an excellent account of the social and cultural anthropological studies of the Zanaki group. My arguments closely follow this summary.
100. Ibid., 120–121.
101. Ibid., 121.
102. Ibid.
103. Ibid., 123.
104. Cited ibid.

105. For a discussion of precolonial African societies, see, for example, Elizabeth Isichei, *A History of African Societies to 1870* (Cambridge: Cambridge University Press, 1997). I have not paid any attention in this essay to the democratic practice of Nyerere, which is a mixed one. For an assessment of this dimension of his political practice, see David A. McDonald and Eunice Njeri Sahle, eds., *The Legacies of Julius Nyerere: Influences on Development Discourse and Practice in Africa* (Trenton, N.J.: Africa World Press, 2002).

106. Daniel R. Smith, *The Influence of the Fabian Colonial Bureau on the Independence Movement in Tanganyika,* Africa series, no. 44 (Athens: Ohio University Press, 1985), 4.

107. Ibid., 56.

108. In her book on Nyerere, Shirley Graham-Du Bois tells of his relationships to the group of individuals who were around the West African secretariat formed after the Fifth Pan-African Congress. See Shirley Graham-Du Bois, *Julius K. Nyerere, Teacher of Africa* (New York: Julian Messner, 1975). For a insightful personal account of Nyerere's years in Scotland, see John Hatch, *Two African Statesmen* (Chicago: Henry Regnery, 1976), chap. 2.

Chapter 5
Walter Rodney

1. For a discussion about the meaning of the "new man" in Cuban politics in the late 1960s, see Bertram Silverman, ed., *Man and Socialism in Cuba: The Great Debate* (New York: Atheneum, 1973).

2. *Walter Rodney Speaks: The Making of an African Intellectual* (Trenton, N.J.: Africa World Press, 1990), 102.

3. Rupert Lewis, *Walter Rodney's Intellectual and Political Thought* (Kingston, Jamaica: The Press University of the West Indies, 1998), xvii.

4. There are many texts that currently engage in this debate. See, for example, Bart Moore-Gilbert, *PostColonial Theory: Contexts, Practices, Politics* (London: Verso, 2000); Gayatri Spivak, *A Critique of PostColonial Reason* (Cambridge, Mass.: Harvard University Press, 1999). For a recent set of critiques of postcolonalist theory, see Crystal Bartolovich and Neil Lazarus, eds., *Marxism, Modernity and Post Colonial Studies* (Cambridge: Cambridge University Press, 2002).

5. David Scott, *Refashioning Futures: Criticism and Postcoloniality* (Princeton, N.J.: Princeton University Press, 1999), 13.

6. Ibid., 14.

7. The phrase is from my *Small Axe* colleague Nadi Edwards.

8. For discussion on the Caribbean intellectual tradition, see Denis Benn, *The Growth and Development of Political Ideas in the Caribbean, 1772–1983* (Kingston, Jamaica: Institute of Social and Economic Studies, 1987). Of course there is Gordon Lewis's magisterial work on the subject, *Main Currents in Caribbean Thought* (Kingston, Jamaica: Heinemann Educational Books, 1983).

9. Cited in Ian Munro and Reinhard Sander, *Kas-Kas Interviews with Three Caribbean Writers in Texas* (Austin: African and Afro-American Institute, University of Texas, 1972), 25.

10. Cited in Ken Post, *Arise Ye Starvelings* (The Hague: Martinus Nijhoff, 1978), 217.

11. Ibid., 131.

12. See Diane Austin, "History and Symbols in Ideology: A Jamaican Example," *Man* 14, no 3. (September 1979): 497–514.

13. Velma Pollard, *Dread Talk: The language of Rastafari* (Kingston, Jamaica: Canoe Press, 1994), 33.

14. For discussion about Jamaican nation-Language, see Edward Kamau Brathwaite, *History of the Voice: The Development of Nation-Language in Anglophone Caribbean Poetry* (London: New Beacon Books, 1984).

15. F. G. Cassidy and R. B. Le Page, eds., *Dictionary of Jamaican English* (Cambridge: Cambridge University Press, 1967), 211.

16. His ban was never completely lifted formally by any Jamaican government, although at the insistence of a group of students, youth, and journalists, he was allowed to enter Jamaica in 1976 to attend the first regional cultural festival, under the strict condition that he did not engage in any public speaking.

17. The term is that of Richard Hart, a leading Marxist in the Jamaican anticolonial movement. For a reflective interview with Hart, see *Small Axe* no. 3 (March 1998): 65–114. Hart is also the author of the seminal two-volume study on the Jamaican slave revolt, *Slaves Who Abolished Slavery* (Kingston, Jamaica: ISER, 1982–1985).

18. Carl Stone, *Class, Race and Political Behaviour in Urban Jamaica* (Kingston, Jamaica: ISER, 1973), 112.

19. *Walter Rodney Speaks*, 28.

20. Ibid.

21. Ras Negus, in *Abeng* leaflet no. 1 (Kingston, n.d.). See Lewis, *Walter Rodney's Intellectual and Political Thought*, chap. 5 for a description of Ras Negus. For many radical middle-class high school students in the late 1960s and early 1970s, Ras Negus's yard in the eastern part of the Kingston was the place where we got our first dose of revolutionary black nationalist thought framed within the categories and language of Rastafari.

22. Walter Rodney, *Groundings with My Brothers* (London: Bogle L'Overture, 1971), 12.

23. Ibid., 67–68.

24. Ibid., 68.

25. Ibid., 56.

26. Ibid., 51.

27. Ibid., 62.

28. Ibid.

29. Mike Marqusee, *Redemption Song* (London: Verso, 2000), 191.

30. Rodney, *Groundings with My Brothers*, 63.

31. Ibid. (Emphasis in the original.)

32. Amilcar Cabral, *Return to the Source* (Conakry, Guinea: PAIGC, 1973), 43.

33. Rupert Lewis, "Learning to Blow the Abeng: A Critical Look at Anti-establishment Movements of the 1960's and 1970's," *Small Axe* Kingston, Jamaica: no. 1 (1977): 5–17.

34. Colin Prescod, "Guyana's Socialism: An Interview with Walter Rodney," *Race and Class* 18 (Autumn 1976): no. 2, 111–28.

35. Frantz Fanon, *The Wretched of the Earth* (New York: Grove Press, 1963), 40.

36. The two most famous of these black radicals who were deeply involved in the anticolonial movement, and were at the same time important Communist figures before they broke with the Marxist parties and the international Communist movements, were George Padmore and Aimé Césaire. For an account of Padmore's political life and career, see James Hooker, *Black Revolutionary: George Padmore's Path from Communism to Pan-Africanism* (London: Pall Mall Press, 1967). For Padmore's definition of Pan-Africanism and its differences from Marxism, see George Padmore, *Pan-Africanism and Communism* (New York: Anchor Books, 1972). Padmore however is a much neglected figure. For Césaire's account of why he resigned from the French Communist Party in 1956, see Aimé Césaire, *Letter to Maurice Thorez* (Paris: Présence Africaine, 1957).

37. Walter Rodney, "Pan-Africanism and Neo-Colonialism in Africa," *Black Liberator* 2, no 3 (June 1974/January 1975): 256–66.
38. Ibid.
39. Walter Rodney, *Marxism in Africa,* undated and unpaginated pamphlet in author's possession.
40. Ibid.
41. Ibid.
42. Ibid
43. Ibid
44. Ibid.
45. *Walter Rodney Speaks,* 82.
46. Ibid.
47. Ibid., 84.
48. Ibid., 100.
49. Ibid., 102.
50. Ibid., 103.
51. This is a very important point, and one I think Rodney wrestled with. In a recent conversation with Andaiye, a leading Guyanese political figure, she responded to my query about how the political program of the WPA (Working People Alliance) was written and the debates surrounding the program by suggesting that Rodney was more focused on what one could call political organizational work, leaving the programmatic work to others. I found this strange, but then, thinking about Rodney's political thought, realized that his preoccupation with the concrete and praxis would lead him to the position that any serious Caribbean revolutionary theory could emerge only from a successful Caribbean revolution. His political objective was to help make that revolution.
52. *Race and Class,* 127.
53. Ibid.
54. Ibid., 105.
55. E. P. Thompson, *The Poverty of Theory and Other Essays* (London: Merlin Press, 1978), 356.
56. C. L. R. James, "Rodney and the Question of Power," in Edward A. Alpers and Pierre-Michel Fontaine, eds., *Walter Rodney, Revolutionary and Scholar: A Tribute* (Los Angeles: Center for Afro-American Studies and African Studies Center, University of California, 1982), 134. (Emphasis in original.)
57. Walter Rodney, "Problems of Third World Development," *Ufahamu* 3, no. 2 (Fall 1972): 27–47.
58. Ibid.
59. Ibid., 34.
60. Walter Rodney, "Some Aspects of the Political Economy of the Caribbean," unpublished text of a speech in author's possession.
61. Walter Rodney, "Contemporary Political Trends in the English-Speaking Caribbean," *Black Scholar* (September 1975), 15–21.
62. Ibid.
63. R. Ulyanovsky, *Socialism and the Newly Independent Nations* (Moscow: Progress Publishers, 1975), 56.
64. Rodney, "Contemporary Political Trends in the English-Speaking Caribbean."
65. Lewis, *Walter Rodney's Intellectual and Political Thought,* 21.
66. Ibid., 232.
67. For a discussion of Caribbean political leadership styles, see Anton Allahar, ed., *Caribbean Charisma: Reflections on Leadership, Legitimacy and Populist Politics* Kingston, Jamaica: Ian Randle, 2001).

68. Hill, a formidable historian, is the editor of the massive project of the Garvey papers. A close associate of James for many years, he is currently the literary executor of James's work. He currently teaches in the history department at UCLA. For an extensive description and discussion of his radical political activity and his scholarship, see David Scott, "The Archaeology of Black Memory: An Interview with Robert A. Hill," *Small Axe* no. 5 (March 1999): 80–150.
69. Letter from James to Robert Hill, March 16, 1981, in library of Oilfield Workers Trade Union, San Fernando, Trinidad. Thanks to the OWTU, which invited me to deliver the annual C. L. R. James lecture in 2000, thus allowing me the opportunity to work in the library and discover the letter.
70. *Trinidad Express,* August 21, 1979.
71. James, "Rodney and the Question of Power," 138.
72. Ibid., 139.
73. Lewis, *Walter Rodney's Intellectual and Political Thought,* 241–243.
74. James, "Rodney and the Question of Power," 139.
75. Walter Rodney, *Sign of the Times* (London: WPA Support Group, n.d.).
76. Fanon, *Wretched of the Earth,* 224.
77. George Lamming, "Foreword," in Walter Rodney, *A History of the Guyanese Working People, 1881–1905* (Baltimore: John Hopkins University Press, 1981), xix.
78. *Walter Rodney Speaks,* 111.
79. Ibid.
80. Ibid., 113–114.
81. Walter Rodney, *How Europe Underdeveloped Africa* (Washington, D.C.: Howard University Press, 1982), viii.
82. See, in particular, Trevor Campbell, "The Making of an Organic Intellectual—Walter Rodney, 1942–1980," *Latin American Perspectives* 8, no 1 (1981): 49–63.
83. It is oftentimes forgotten that Fanon also wrote *Towards the African Revolution,* a collection of many of his editorials for the Algerian national liberation movement newspaper, *El Moudjahid,* which was published after his death. This collection includes two remarkable pieces titled "The West Indian and Africans" and "This Africa to Come." See Frantz Fanon, *Towards the African Revolution* (New York: Grove Press, 1967).
84. Fanon, *The Wretched of the Earth,* 37.
85. For a discussion of Fanon's revolutionary violence, see Lewis Gordon's, "Fanon's Tragic Revolutionary Violence," in Lewis R. Gordon, T. Denean Sharpley-Whiting, and Renee T. White, eds., *Fanon: A Critical Reader* (Oxford: Blackwell, 1996).
86. Reported in Lewis, *Walter Rodney's Intellectual and Political Thought,* 243.
87. Theda Skocpol, *Social Revolutions in the Modern World* (Cambridge: Cambridge University Press, 1994), 5.
88. Ngugi wa Thiong'o, *The First Walter Rodney Memorial Lecture* (London: Bogle L'Overture, n.d.).
89. There is a very interesting review by the Caribbean historian and poet Kamau Brathwaite of Rodney's *How Europe Underdeveloped Africa,* in which Brathwaite calls for Rodney to pay more attention to the dialect. What I have been arguing here is that it is this tension between the dialect and the dialectic which accounts for Rodney's rich political thought and practice. For Brathwaite's review, see Edward Kamau Brathwaite, "Dialect and Dialectic," *African Studies Association of the West Indies Bulletin* no. 6 (December 1973), 89–99. I have obviously appropriated Brathwaite's phrase and used it as an overarching theme in this chapter.

Chapter 6
Rastafari

1. Umberto Eco, *Kant and the Platypus: Essays on Language and Cognition*, trans. Alastair McEwen (New York: Harcourt, 1999), 9.
2. Frantz Fanon, *Black Skin, White Masks* (New York: Grove Press, 1967), 210.
3. Cited in G. Shepperson, "Ethiopianism: Past and Present." In C. G. Baeta, ed., *Christianity in Tropical Africa* (Oxford: Oxford University Press, 1968), 250. (Emphasis added.)
4. John Comaroff and Jean Comaroff, *Of Revelation and Revolution: The Dialectics of Modernity on a South African Frontier* (Chicago: University of Chicago Press, 1997), 101.
5. For a view on the nature of Ethiopianism in the black Atlantic world, see St. Clair Drake, *The Redemption of Africa and Black Religion* (Chicago: Third World Press, 1977). A more recent view that examines the politics of Ethiopianism in South Africa and the America is George M. Fredrickson, *Black Liberation: A Comparative History of Black Ideologies in the United States and South Africa* (Oxford: Oxford University Press, 1995), chap. 2.
6. Bengt Sundkler, *Bantu Prophets in South Africa* (Oxford: Oxford University Press, 1961), 56.
7. Ken Post, "Ethiopianism in Jamaica, 1930–38," in Christopher Allen and R. W. Johnson, eds., *African Perspectives* (Cambridge: Cambridge University Press, 1970), 187.
8. Drake, *The Redemption of Africa and Black Religion*, 11.
9. Eddie S. Glaude, Jr., *Exodus! Religion, Race and Nation in early Nineteenth-Century Black America* (Chicago: University of Chicago Press, 2000), 4–5.
10. See Geri Augusto's work on collaboration and conflict across knowledge cultures in South Africa, "Knowing Differently, Innovating Together? A Study of Transepistemic Relations in a South African Biotechnology Project" Ph.D. diss., George Washington Uinversity, 2003), for an insightful discussion on the nature of knowledge and the practices of indigenous therapeutic systems.
11. Michael Walzer, *Interpretation and Social Criticism* (Cambridge, Mass.: Harvard University Press, 1987), 75.
12. Gerhardus C. Oosthuizen, *The Healer-Prophet in Afro-Christian Churches* (Leiden, New York: E. J. Brill, 1992), 15.
13. Ibid.
14. Robert R. Edgar and Hilary Sapire, *African Apocalypse* (Johannesburg: Witwatersrand University Press, 2000).
15. See A. B. Davidson, " African Resistance and Rebellion Against the Imposition of Colonial Rule," in T. O. Ranger, ed., *Emerging Themes of African History* (Dar es Salaam: East Africa Publishing House, 1965).
16. See W. F. Elkins, *Street Preachers, Faith Healers and Herb Doctors in Jamaica, 1890–1925* (New York: Revisionist Press, 1977), chap. 2, for an extensive discussion on Bedward.
17. Robert Hill, "Dread History: Leonard P. Howell and Millenarian Visions in Early Rastafari Religion in Jamaica," *Epoche: Journal of the History of Religions* 8 (1981): 38.
18. Michel Foucault, *The Order of Things* (New York: Vintage, 1973), xx.
19. See Lord William Hailey, *An African Survey: A Study of Problems Arising in Africa South of the Sahara* (London: Oxford University Press, 1938), for how tutelage was to be organized and how good government, meaning the modern institutions of the West, were to be implanted and developed in the British colonies.

20. Hill, "Dread History," 38.

21. Ken Post, "The Bible as Ideology: Ethiopianism in Jamaica, 1930–38," in Christopher Allen and R. W. Johnson, eds., *African Perspectives* (Cambridge: Cambridge University Press, 1970), 191.

22. This section closely follows Robert Hill's examination of Howell's life in "Dread History."

23. Ibid., 38.

24. *Daily Gleaner,* December 16, 1933, 1.

25. John Chilembwe was a prophet who in January 1915 led an insurgency against the British colonial power in what was then called Nysaland (now Malawi). He was the leader of the Province Industrial Mission and part of the black independent church movement. He appealed across ethnic lines, to the Nguni, Senga, and Tumbuku, attempting to put together a movement that would overthrow the colonial power. Sir Robert Lyall-Grant was therefore keenly aware of the role of prophets in the British colonies.

26. *Daily Gleaner,* March 14, 1934, 21.

27. Ibid.

28. Ibid.

29. Ibid.

30. Cited in Robert A. Hill, *Dread History: Leonard P. Howell and the Millenarian Visions in the Early Rastafarian Religion* (Kingston and Chicago: Research Associates/School Times Publications and Miguel Lorne, 2001), 35. This is the book version of the Hill's article.

31. *Daily Gleaner,* March 16, 1934, 16.

32. *Daily Gleaner,* March 15, 1934, 20.

33. Ibid.

34. Ibid.

35. Ibid.

36. For an excellent description of the relationship of radical postcolonial politics in Jamaica and the Rastafari movement, see Rupert Lewis, *Walter Rodney: Intellectual and Political Thought* (Kingston, Jamaica: University of the West Indies Press, 1998), chap. 5.

37. Nathaniel Samuel Murrell, William David Spencer, and Adrian Anthony McFarlane, eds., *Chanting Down Babylon* (Kingston, Jamaica: Ian Randle, 1998). *The Promised Key,* with commentary by William David Spencer, is in chap. 21 of this reader.

38. Ras Sekou Sankara Tafari, "Foreword," in Robert Athlyi Rogers, *The Holy Piby: The Blackman's Bible* (Chicago and Kingston, Jamaica: Research Associates/School Times Publications and Headstart Printing and Publishing, 2000), 17.

39. Rupert Lewis, "Marcus Garvey and the Early Rastafarians," in Murrell et al., *Chanting Down Babylon,* chap. 8.

40. *The Holy Piby,* 55.

41. *Chanting Down Babylon,* 364.

42. Ibid.

43. Ibid., 367.

44. See Paget Henry, *Caliban's Reason* (New York: Routledge, 2000), chap. 8.

45. Murrell et al., *Chanting Down Babylon,* 372.

46. Ibid.

47. Here the text was influenced by *Royal Parchment Scroll of Black Supremacy.*

48. Murrell et al., *Chanting Down Babylon,* 376.

49. Ibid.

50. Ibid., 380.

51. Ibid.
52. Ibid., 383.
53. Ken Post, *Arise Ye Starvelings* (Hayne: Martinus Nijhoff, 1978), chap. 6.
54. Barry Chevannes, *Rastafari: Roots and Ideology* (Kingston, Jamaica: University of the West Indies Press, 1995), 122.
55. *Jamaica Times,* July 19, 1941, 4.
56. For an account of Henry's life, see, Barry Chevannes, "Repairer of the Breach: Reverend Claudius Henry and Jamaican Society," in Frances Henry, ed., *Ethnicity in the Americas* (The Hague: Mouton, 1976).
57. Prince Emmanuel is a major figure in the history of the Rastafari movement in Jamaica. See Chevannes, *Rastafari: Roots and Ideology,* 172–188, for a description of this figure and the section of the movement he leads, the Bobos.
58. *Daily Gleaner,* October 25, 1960, 9.
59. Ibid.
60. Ibid.
61. See Chevannes, *Rastafari: Roots and Ideology,* chap. 5, for a discussion of the emergence of the dreadlocks current.
62. *Daily Gleaner,* October 11, 1960, 3.
63. Ibid.
64. For a discussion of this, see Anthony Bogues, "Nationalism and Jamaican Political Thought," in Glen Richards and Kathleen E. A. Monteith, eds., *Jamaica in Slavery and Freedom: History, Heritage and Culture* (Kingston, Jamaica: University of the West Indies Press, 2002).
65. Rex Nettleford, *Identity, Race and Protest in Jamaica* (New York: William Morrow, 1972), chap. 2.
66. Claudius Henry, *Standing in the Gap, with Unquestionable Truth, Repairing the Breach to Fall the Nations.* (Kingston). January 15, 1960.
67. Brian Meeks, *Narratives of Resistance* (Kingston, Jamaica: University of the West Indies Press, 2000), chap. 1.
68. Cited in ibid., 29.
69. *New York Times,* July 27, 1960, 4.
70. All citations from the letter and proclamation are taken from their reproduction in *Daily Gleaner,* October 13, 1960, 1, 3.
71. Classified General Records, 1956–1962, Records of the Foreign Service Posts of Department of State, Record Group 84 (Washington, D.C.: National Archives).
72. Ibid.
73. Ibid.
74. Gayatri Spivak, "Can the Subaltern Speak?," in Cary Nelson and Lawrence Grossberg, eds., *Marxism and the Interpretation of Culture* (Chicago: University of Illinois Press, 1988), 271–316.
75. Ibid., 285.
76. Ibid.
77. Cited in Joseph V. Femia, *Gramsci's Political Thought* (Oxford: Clarendon Press, 1987), 28.
78. Antonio Gramsci, *Selections from Prison Notebooks* (New York: International Publishers, 1987), 52.
79. See Steven Feierman, *Peasant Intellectuals: Anthropology and History in Tanzania* (Madison: University of Wisconsin Press, 1990).
80. John Scott, *Domination and the Arts of Resistance* (New Haven, Conn.: Yale University Press, 1990).
81. Gramsci, *Selections from Prison Notebooks,* 52.
82. Ibid., 324.

83. Ibid., 326.

84. Augusto uses this phrase in her "Knowing Differently, Innovating Together?"

85. Gramsci, *Prison Notebooks,* 333.

86. Ranajit Guha and Gayatri Spivak, *Selected Subaltern Studies* (Oxford: Oxford University Press, 1982), 40.

87. See Ranajit Guha, *Dominance Without Hegemony* (Cambridge, Mass.: Harvard University Press, 1997).

88. Ibid., xii.

89. Sylvia Wynter, "We Know Where We Are From': The Politics of Black Culture from Myal to Marley," unpublished paper (November 1977).

90. Ibid.

91. Aimé Césaire, *Discourse on Colonialism* (New York: Monthly Review Press, 2000), 94.

92. C. L. R. James, "The West Indian Intellectual," in J. J. Thomas, *Froudacity* (London: New Beacon, 1969), 45.

93. Ibid., 32.

94. Wilson Harris, *History, Fable and Myth in the Caribbean and Guianas* (Wellesley, Mass.: Calaloux Publications, 1995), 22.

95. Derek Walcott, "The Muse of History," in his *What the Twilight Says* (New York: Farrar, Straus and Giroux, 1998), 54.

96. Edouard Glissant, *Caribbean Discourse: Selected Essays* (Charlottesville: University Press of Virginia, 1989), 92.

97. Kamau Brathwaite, "Caribbean Man in Space and Time," *Savcou* 11/12 (Kingston 1973) 1–11.

98. Elsa Goveia, *Historiography of the British West Indies* (Washington, D.C.: Howard University Press, 1980), 177. This volume was originally published in Mexico City by Instituto Panamericano de Geografía Historia (1956).

99. Ibid., 170.

100. Ibid., 171.

101. Ibid., 177.

102. Thomas Bremer and Ulrich Fleishmann, eds., *History and Histories in the Caribbean* (Madrid: Iberoamericana, 2001), 8.

103. Harris, *History, Fable and Myth in the Caribbean and Guianas,* 18.

104. Soren Kierkegaard, *The Concept of Anxiety,* (Princeton, New Jersey: Princeton University Press, 1980) 55.

105. The term "Dread history" was first used by Robert Hill to introduce his pathbreaking essay on Leonard Howell in "Dread History: Leonard P. Howell and Early Millennian Visions in Early Rastafarian Religion in Jamaica." David Scott in 1998 suggested Dread history as a poetic form of subaltern thought in Jamaica. I wish to use to term in a more general way to describe a series of historical questions that are raised by subaltern thought in Jamaica. A first iteration of this was elaborated in *Small Axe* no. 8 (September 2000).

106. Walter Benjamin, "Theses on Philosophy of History," in his *Illuminations* (New York: Schocken Books, 1968), 261.

107. Paul Ricoeur, *Time and Narrative* (Chicago: University of Chicago Press, 1983), 65.

108. Michel-Rolph Trouillot, *Silencing the Past* (Boston: Beacon Press, 1995), 2.

109. Cited in Ricoeur, *Time and Narrative,* 41.

110. R. G. Collingwood, *The Idea of History* (Oxford: Oxford University Press, 1994), 223.

111. Dominick La Capra, *Writing History, Writing Trauma* (Baltimore: Johns Hopkins University Press, 2001), 46.

112. Ricoeur, *Time and Narrative*, 52.

113. Benjamin, "Theses on the Philosophy of History," 255.

114. Ibid., 257.

115. This is the title of one of the most utopian reggae songs sung by the group The Abyssinians.

116. See Elizabeth Hopkins, "The Nyabingi Cult of Southwestern Uganda," in Robert Rotberg and Ali Mazrui, eds., *Protest and Power in Black Africa* (New York: Oxford University Press, 1970), for a discussion of this grouping.

117. For a sharp critique of Rastafari patriarchy, see Obiagele Lake, *Rastafari Women: Subordination in the Midst of Liberation Theology* (Durham, N.C.: Carolina Academic Press, 1998).

118. Ernest Bloch, *The Principle of Hope* (Cambridge, Mass.: MIT Press, 1986), 197.

119. Ruth Levitas, "Educated Hope: Ernst Bloch and Abstract and Concrete Utopia," in Jamie Owen Daniel and Tom Moylan, eds., *Not Yet: Reconsidering Ernst Bloch* (London: Verso, 1997), 66.

120. One brilliant example of how the opening of new archives gives different sets of historical representation can be seen in Joan Dayan's *Haiti, History and the Gods* (Berkeley: University of California Press, 1998).

121. For a discussion of this and its complexities, see Clifford Geertz, *The Interpretation of Cultures* (New York: Basic Books, 1973), chap. 1.

122. Paul Ricoeur, *History and Truth* Evanston, Ill.: Northwestern University Press, 1965), 22.

123. Aimé Césaire, *A Tempest* (New York: Ubu Repertory Theater Publications, 1999).

Chapter 7
Get Up, Stand Up

1. Joy James, *Representations of Black Feminist Politics* (New York: Palgrave, 2002), chap. 6.

2. Martin Luther King, Jr., "Where Do We Go from Here," in his *I Have a Dream: Writings and Speeches That Changed the World*, James Washington, ed. (New York: Harpers, 1992), 177.

3. Bob Marley, "Babylon System," from the CD *Survival* (Tuff Gong: Island Records, 1979).

4. See in particular the arguments developed by Gregory Stephens *On Racial Frontiers* (Cambridge: Cambridge University Press, 1999), chap. 4.

5. Stuart Hall, "What Is this 'Black' in Black Popular Culture," in *Black Popular Culture*, a project by Michele Wallace, Gina Dent, ed., Seattle, Wash.: Bay Press, 1992), 27.

6. Adebayo Ojo, *Bob Marley: Songs of African Redemption* (Lagos: Malthouse Press, 2000), xi.

7. Raymond Williams develops these arguments in his *Problems in Materialism and Culture* (London: Verso, 1980).

8. Besides the two biographies of Marley, *Catch a Fire* by Timony White and *Bob Marley* by Stephen Davis, there are numerous books and articles on Marley and his music; only the Beatles have a comparable record of secondary literature. Marley also has a few lines in the college text *History of Western Music* (New York: Harper Perennial, 1991), in which he is correctly credited with bringing reggae music to a world audience.

9. The importance of Planno can be seen in Barry Chevannes, *Rastafari: Roots and Ideology* (Kingston, Jamaica: University of the West Indies Press, 1995), chap. 9. In the late 1990s the faculty of social sciences at the University of the West Indies,

Mona Campus, gave Planno a fellowship as a "folk philosopher." To read Planno's more recent writings, see Mortimer Planno, *The Earth Most Strangest Man: The Rastafarian*, www.Rism.org/Planno/mp61.html.

10. Velma Pollard, *Dread Talk: The Language of Rastafari* (Kingston, Jamaica: Canoe Press, 1994), lists "reason" as a category number 1 word in which known items bear new meanings. She states that in Rasta discourse "reason" means to talk, to discuss. I want to suggest that it means more. It is a form of discussing and talking in which individuals come to a deeper understanding of a subject. As is typical with words, context becomes important—to "reason" informally with someone on a one-on-one basis can be different from going to a Rasta "camp" for a reasoning. The latter entails forms of discussion of a philosophical or theological bent. At the same time one cannot help but notice how reason, that crucial index and practice of difference constructed under the colonial episteme, has been transformed in this instance.

11. For a sound recording of some of Sam Brown's ideas, listen to Teacher Ras Sam Brown, *History Past and Present* (Washington, D.C.: Ras Records, 1996).

12. Frank Jan van Dijk, "Jahmaica: Rastafari and Jamaican Society" (Ph.D. diss., 1993), 152.

13. Ibid., 162.

14. One of the stories waiting to be told of this period of Jamaican political history is of these men and their involvement in the labor movement of the 1970s and radical politics. The Independent Trade Union Action Council, formed in this period by Chris Lawrence, was an umbrella organization of the unions that had developed independently from the political unionism of Jamaican mainstream politics. Ras Desilva was a leading member of this council. When I last spoke to him in 1999, he had turned his attention to working for the unity of the Rastafari movement.

15. See Rupert Lewis, *Walter Rodney: Intellectual and Political Thought* (Kingston, Jamaica: University of the West Indies Press, 1998), chap. 5 for a discussion of Ras Negus and his relationship to Rodney.

16. Ibid., 101.

17. For a very fine description of the music of this period, see Lloyd Bradley, *Bass Culture* (London: Viking, 2000), chap. 9. A confirmation of how the "Rude Bwoy" is represented in the Jamaican popular culture can be noted in the most recent CD of Bounty Killer, *Ghetto Dictionary*. Here the artist critiques inner-city male youth who claim to be "rude bwoy" but behave in antisocial ways to the inhabitants of the inner city. In particular, listen to Bounty Killer, "Petty Thief," on *Ghetto Dictionary: The Mystery* (New York: VP Records, 2002).

18. Garth White, "Rudie, Oh Rudie!" in *Caribbean Quarterly* 13 (September 1967): 39–44.

19. Ibid.

20. For a discussion on subject formation in colonial Jamaica, see Catherine Hall, *Civilising Subjects* (Chicago: University of Chicago Press, 2002); for the postcolonial period, see Anthony Bogues, "Politics, Nation and Post Colony," *Small Axe* no. 11 (March 2002): 1–30.

21. Pierre Bourdieu, *Outline of a Theory of Practice* (Cambridge: Cambridge University Press, 1977), 94. (Emphasis added.)

22. The evidence of this can be gleaned both from the ways that Marley related to the persons who embodied "Rude Bwoy" manifestations in the 1970s and from his role in the organization of the first peace treaty between the warring inner-city political factions in the mid-1970s.

23. Bob Marley, "Chant Down Babylon," on *Confrontation* (Tuff Gong: Island Records, 1983), CD.

238 • Notes

24. It is now agreed that the 1961 record *O Carolina* by the Folkes Brothers and produced by Prince Buster, with drumming by Count Ossie, is a watershed in Jamaican musical and social history. It marked the first time that a record was produced with pronounced Rastafari rhythms. Count Ossie went on to develop the
band called The Mystic Revelation of Rastafari. Their music can be heard on the
double CD Count Ossie and the Mystic Revelation of Rastafari, Grounation, The
Roots of Reggae (European Union: Proper/Retro, 1998).
25. Cited in Beverley Hall-Alleyne, "The Evolution of African Languages in Jamaica,"
ACIJ Research Review (Insitute of Jamaica) no. 1 (1984): 21–46. For an excellent
description of the role of Count Ossie in the development of Jamaican music, see
Verena Reckford, "From Burru Drums to Reggae Riddims: the Evolution of Rasta
Music," in N. S. Murrell, W. Spencer, and A. McFarlane, eds., *Chanting Down
Babylon* (Kingston, Jamaica: Ian Randle, 1998), chap. 14.
26. Bob Marley, "Trench Town," on CD *Confrontation*.
27. Ibid.
28. See Lawrence Kramer, *Music as Cultural Practice* (Berkeley: University of California Press, 1993), chap. 1, for an impressive discussion of Kant on this point.
29. Ernst Bloch, *The Spirit of Utopia* (Stanford, Calif.: Stanford University Press,
2000), 47.
30. Samuel A. Floyd, Jr., *The Power of Black Music* (Oxford: Oxford University Press,
1995), 8.
31. For a good description of this process in America, see Mark Anthony Neal, *What
the Music Said: Black Popular Music and Black Public Culture* (New York: Routledge, 1999), introduction.
32. Steven Seidman, ed., *Jürgen Habermas on Society and Politics: A Reader* (Boston:
Beacon Press, 1989).
33. For a fuller discussion of this, see James Scott, *Domination and the Arts of Resistance* (New Haven, Conn.: Yale University Press, 1990).
34. Erna Brodber and Edward Greene, *Reggae and Cultural Identity in Jamaica*,
Working paper no. 35. (Kingston, Jamaica: ISER, 1988), 7.
35. Kenneth Bilby, "Jamaica," in Peter Manuel, ed., *Caribbean Currents: Caribbean
Music from Rumba to Reggae* (Philadelphia: Temple University Press, 1995),
151–152.
36. Brodber and Greene, *Reggae and Cultural Identity*, 3.
37. See, for a very good discussion of this point, Anita M. Waters, *Race, Class and Political Symbols: Rastafari and Reggae in Jamaican Politics* (New Brunswick, N.J.:
Transaction, 1989).
38. Garth White, "The Evolution of Jamaican Music," in *Social and Economic Studies*
47, no. 1 (March 1998): 5–19.
39. Ibid.
40. Bilby, "Jamaica," 152.
41. Ibid., 159–160.
42. Ibid., 153.
43. Today *mento* as musical form is danced at staged festivals that celebrate Jamaican
heritage. They are many *mento* bands that play in the tourist areas of the island.
Their musical repertoire includes some calypso numbers. For a fairly wide selection of this music, listen to the CD *Mento Music in Jamaica, Vol. 1* (Jamaica Cultural Development Commission, Kingston, Jamaica, 2000).
44. Carolyn Cooper, *Noises in the Blood* (London: Macmillan Caribbean, 1993),
chap. 7.
45. Ibid., 118.
46. Bob Marley, "Coming in from the Cold," from *Uprising* (Tuff Gong: Island
Records, 1980).

47. Swami Anand Prahlad, *Reggae Wisdom: Proverbs in Jamaican Music* (Jackson: University Press of Mississippi, 2001), 4.

48. Kwame Dawes, *Natural Mysticism: Towards a New Reggae Aesthetic* (London: Peepal Tree, 1999), 14.

49. Bob Marley, interview on . . . *So Much Things to Say* (Tuff Gong: Ras Records, 1996).

50. Greg Tate, "Preface to One-hundred-and Eighty Volume Patricide," in Gina Dent, ed., *Black Popular Culture* (Seattle, Wash.: Bay Press, 2002), 244–245.

51. Marley, interview on *So Much Things to Say.*

52. V. Y. Mudimbe, *Parables and Fables: Exegesis, Textuality, and Politics in Central Africa* (Madison: University of Wisconsin Press, 1991), 89.

53. Ibid., 89–90.

54. The last album, *Confrontation,* was released posthumously in 1983, and therefore all the tracks cannot properly be said to be the ones Marley would have recorded if he had lived, though Marley had approved the album cover.

55. Bob Marley, "Buffalo Soldier," on the CD *Confrontation* (Tuff Gong: Island Records, 1983).

56. Marley interview, on . . . *So Much Things to Say.*

57. Marley, "Buffalo Soldier."

58. Sylvia Wynter, " 'We Know Where We Are From': The Politics of Black Culture from Myal to Marley," unpublished paper (November 1977) in OWTU library, San Fernado, Trinidad.

59. Ibid., 38.

60. Ibid., 44–45.

61. Pierre Bourdieu, *Language and Symbolic Power* (Cambridge, Mass.: Harvard University Press, 1995), 48.

62. Ibid., 166.

63. Michael Walzer, *Interpretation and Social Criticism* (Cambridge, Mass.: Harvard University Press, 1985), 81.

64. Here I follow the first-class discussion of prophecy in Africa in David M. Anderson and Douglas H. Johnson, *Revealing Prophets,* (London: James Curry, 1995).

65. For a discussion of this, see B. Babcock, *The Reversible World: Symbolic Inversion in Art and Society* (Ithaca, N.Y.: Cornell University Press, 1978).

66. Liner notes on *Survival* (Tuff Gong: Island Records, 1979).

67. Neville Garrick was the visual artist for all three concept albums. One can see other aspects of his work in Neville Garrick, *A Rasta Pilgrimage* (Calif.: Pomegranate, 1998).

68. Horace Campbell, *Rasta and Resistance: From Marcus Garvey to Walter Rodney* (Trenton, N.J.: Africa World Press, 1987), 146.

69. For a discussion of Jamaican "nation-language," see Edward Kamau Brathwaite, *History of the Voice* (London: New Beacon Books, 1984).

70. For a dictionary of Jamaican language that explains many of these things, see F. G. Cassidy and R. B. Le Page, eds., *Dictionary of Jamaican English* (Cambridge: Cambridge University Press, 1967).

71. Mario Vargas Llosa, "Trench Town Rock," *American Scholar* 71, no. 3 (Summer 2002): 53–56.

Select Bibliography

Newspapers, Leaflets, and State Archives

Newspapers

Daily Gleaner (Kingston, Jamaica), December 16, 1933.
Daily Gleaner, March 14, 1934.
Daily Gleaner, March 15, 1934.
Daily Gleaner, March 16, 1934.
Daily Gleaner, October 11, 1960.
Daily Gleaner, October 13, 1960.
Daily Gleaner, October 25, 1960.
Jamaica Times (Kingston, Jamaica), July 19, 1941.
New York Times, July 27, 1960.
Trinidad Express (Port of Spain, Trinidad and Tobago), August 21, 1979.

Leaflets

Henry, Claudius. *Standing in the Gap with Unquestionable Truth Repairing the Breach to Fall the Nations.* Kingston. January 15, 1960.
Negus, Ras. *Abeng* leaflet no. 1. Kingston, Jamaica, n.d.

Archives

Classified General Records, 1956–1962. Records of the Foreign Service Posts of Department of State. Record Group 84. Washington, D.C.: National Archives.

Music

Bounty Killer. *Ghetto Dictionary: The Mystery.* New York VP Records, 2002.
Count Ossie and The Mystic Revelation of Rastafari. *Grounation, the Roots of Reggae.* European Union: Proper/Retro, 1998.
Marley, Bob, and The Wailers. *Survival.* Tuff Gong: Island Records, 1979.
Marley, Bob, and The Wailers. *Uprising.* Tuff Gong: Island Records, 1980.
Marley, Bob, and The Wailers. *Confrontation.* Tuff Gong: Island Records, 1983.
Marley, Bob. Interviews. *So Much Things to Say.* Tuff Gong: Ras, Records, 1995.

Books and Articles

Allahar, Anton, ed. *Caribbean Charisma: Reflections on Leadership, Legitimacy and Populist Politics.* Kingston, Jamaica: Ian Randle, 2001.

Allen, James. *Reconstruction: The Battle for Democracy.* New York: International Publishers, 1937.

Allen, James, ed. *Without Sanctuary: Lynching Photography in America.* Santa Fe, N.M.: Twin Palms, 2000.

Anderson, David M., and Douglas H. Johnson. *Revealing Prophets.* London: James Currey, 1995.

Ankersmit, F. R. *Historical Representation.* Stanford, Calif.: Stanford University Press, 2001.

Aptheker, Herbert, ed. *A Documentary History of the Negro People in the United States.* Vol. 2. New York: Citadel Press, 1992.

Arendt, Hannah. *Origins of Totalitarianism.* New York: Harcourt Brace Jovanovich, 1968.

Arendt, Hannah. *Between Past and Future.* New York: Penguin, 1977.

Ascherson, Neal. *The King Incorporated: Leopold the Second and the Congo.* London: Granta, 1999.

Austin, J. L. *How to Do Things with Words.* Cambridge, Mass.: Harvard University Press, 1975.

Babcock, B. *The Reversible World: Symbolic Inversion in Art and Society.* Ithaca, N.Y.: Cornell University Press, 1978.

Balibar, Etienne. *Masses, Ideas and Politics.* London: Verso, 1994.

Baker, Lee D. *From Savage to Negro: Anthropology and the Construction of Race, 1896–1954.* Berkeley: University of California Press, 1998.

Bartolovich, Crystal, and Neil Lazarus, ed., *Marxism, Modernity and Post Colonial Studies.* Cambridge: Cambridge University Press, 2002.

Bauman, Z. *Legislators and Interpreters.* Stanford, Calif.: Stanford University Press, 1987.

Bederman, Gail. *Manliness and Civilization: A Cultural History of Gender and Race in the United States, 1880–1917.* Chicago: University of Chicago Press, 1995.

Benda, Julien. *The Treason of Intellectuals.* New York: Norton, 1963.

Benjamin, Walter. *Illuminations: Essays and Reflections.* New York: Schocken Books, 1968.

Benn, Denis. *The Growth and Development of Political Ideas in the Caribbean, 1772–1983.* Kingston, Jamaica: Institute of Social and Economic Studies, 1987.

Berlin, Isaiah. *The Power of Ideas.* Princeton, N.J.: Princeton University Press, 2000.

Berlin, Isaiah. *Four Essays on Liberty.* Oxford: Oxford University Press, 1969.

Berlin, Isaiah. "Does Political Theory Still Exist?" In his *The Proper Study of Mankind.* New York: Farrar, Straus and Giroux, 1998.

Berlin, Isaiah. "Political Judgment." In Isaiah Berlin, *Studies in Ideas ands Their History: The Sense of Reality.* New York: Farrar, Straus and Giroux, 1998.

Bernstein, Richard J. *Radical Evil: A Philosophical Interrogation.* Cambridge: Polity Press, 2002.

Bernstein, Richard J. *Praxis and Action: Contemporary Philosophies of Human Activity.* Philadelphia: University of Pennsylvania Press, 1971.

Bhabha, Homi K. *The Location of Culture.* New York: Routledge, 1994.

Bilby, Kenneth. "Jamaica." In Peter Manuel, ed., *Caribbean Currents: Caribbean Music from Rumba to Reggae.* Philadelphia: Temple University Press, 1995.

Blight, David W. *Race and Reunion.* Amherst: University of Massachusetts Press, 2001.

Blight, David W. *Beyond the Battlefield: Race, Memory, and the American Civil War.* Amherst: University of Massachusetts Press, 2002.

Bloch, Ernst. *The Spirit of Utopia.* Stanford, Calif.: Stanford University Press, 2000.

Bloch, Ernst. *The Principle of Hope.* Cambridge, Mass.: MIT Press, 1986.

Bogues, Anthony. "Nationalism and Jamaican Political Thought." In Glen Richards and Kathleen E. A. Monteith, eds., *Jamaica in Slavery and Freedom: History, Heritage and Culture.* Kingston, Jamaica: University of the West Indies Press, 2002.

Bogues, Anthony. *Caliban's Freedom: The Early Political Thought of C. L. R. James.* London: Pluto, 1997.

Bogues, Anthony. "Politics, Nation and Post Colony." *Small Axe* no. 11 (March 2002): 1–30.

Bontemps, Arna, ed. *Great Slave Narratives.* Boston: Beacon Press, 1969.

Boors, Diane. "History and Symbols in Ideology: A Jamaican Example." *Man* 14, no 3 (September 1979):

Bourdieu, Pierre. *Language and Symbolic Power.* Cambridge, Mass.: Harvard University Press, 1995.

Bourdieu, Pierre. *Outline of a Theory of Practice.* Cambridge: Cambridge University Press, 1977.

Bradley, Lloyd. *Bass Culture.* London: Viking, 2000.

Bradley, Patricia. *Slavery, Propaganda and the American Revolution.* Jackson: University Press of Mississippi, 1998.

Brathwaite, Edward Kamau. *History of the Voice: The development of Nation-Language in Anglophone Caribbean Poetry.* London: New Beacon Books. 1984.

Brathwaite, Edward Kamau. "Dialect and Dialectic." *African Studies Association of the West Indies Bulletin* no. 6. (December 1973) 89–99.

Brathwaite, Kamau. "Caribbean Man in Space and Time." *Savacou* 11/12 (1975), 1–11.

Bremer, Thomas, and Ulrich Fleishmann, eds. *History and Histories in the Caribbean* Madrid: Iberoamericana, 2001.

Brodber, Erna, and Edward Greene. *Reggae and Cultural Identity in Jamaica.* Working paper no. 35. Kingston, Jamaica: ISER, 1988.

Buhle, Paul, ed. *C. L. R. James: His Life and Work.* London: Allison & Busby, 1986.

Butchart, Alexander. *The Anatomy of Power: European Constructions of the African Body.* London: Zed Press, 1998.

Cabral, Amilcar. "The Weapon of Theory." In his *Revolution in Guinea: An African People's Struggle..* London: Stage One, 1971.

Cabral, Amilcar. *Return to the Source.* Conakry, Guinea: PAIGC, 1973.

Campbell, Horace. "The Impact of Walter Rodney and Progressive Scholars on the Dar es Salaam School." *Social and Economic Studies* (Institute of Social and Economic Research, University of the West Indies) 40, no. 2 (June 1991): 99–135.

Campbell, Horace. *Rasta and Resistance: From Marcus Garvey to Walter Rodney.* Trenton, N.J.: Africa World Press, 1987.

Carby, Hazel. "On the Threshold of Woman's Era": Lynching, Empire, and Sexuality in Black Feminist Theory." In Henry Louis Gates, Jr., ed., *"Race," Writing and Difference.* Chicago: University of Chicago Press, 1986.

Carby, Hazel V. *Reconstructing Womanhood: The Emergence of the African-American Novelist.* Oxford: Oxford University Press, 1987.

Carrithers, Michael, Steven Collins, and Steven Lukes. *The Category of the Person: Anthropology, Philosophy, History.* Cambridge: Cambridge University Press, 1999.

Cassidy, F. G., and R. B. Le Page, eds. *Dictionary of Jamaican English.* Cambridge: Cambridge University Press, 1967.

Cavarero, Adriana. "Politicizing Theory." *Political Theory* 30, no. 4 (August 2002): 506–532.

Césaire, Aimé. *A Tempest.* Translated by Richard Miller. New York: Ubu Repertory Theater Publications, 1993.

Césaire, Aimé. *Discourse on Colonialism.* New York: Monthly Review Press, 2000.

Césaire, Aimé. *Letter to Maurice Thorez.* Paris: Presence Africaine, 1957.

Césaire, Suzanne. "Leo Frobenius and the Problem of Civilization." In Michael Richardson, ed., *Refusal of the Shadow: Surrealism and the Caribbean.* London: Verso, 1996.

Chartier, Roger. *On the Edge of the Cliff: History, Language and Practices.* Baltimore: Johns Hopkins University Press, 1997.

Chevannes, Barry. *Rastafari: Roots and Ideology* Kingston: The Press, University of the West Indies, 1995.

Chevannes, Barry. "Repairer of the Breach: Reverend Claudius Henry and Jamaican Society." In Frances Henry, ed., *Ethnicity in the Americas.* The Hague: Mouton, 1976.

Clapham, Christopher. "The Context of African Political Thought." *Journal of Modern African Studies.* 8, no. 1 1970.

Collingwood, R. G. *The Idea of History.* Oxford: Oxford University Press, 1994.

Collins, Patricia Hill. "Introduction." In Ida B. Wells-Barnett, *On Lynchings.* New York: Humanity Books, 2002.

Comaroff, John, and Jean Comaroff. *Of Revelation and Revolution: The Dialectics of Modernity on a South African Frontier.* 2 vols. Chicago: University of Chicago Press, 1997.

Cooper, Carolyn. *Noises in the Blood.* London: Macmillan Caribbean, 1993.

Cosentino, Donald, ed. *Sacred Arts of Haitian Vodou.* Los Angeles: University of California Press, 1995.

Costanzo, Angelo, ed. *The Interesting Narrative of the Life of Olaudah Equiano.* Peterbourgh, Ontario: Broadview Press, 2001.

Cugoano, Quobna Ottobah. *Thoughts and Sentiments on the Evil of Slavery.* Edited by Vincent Carretta. London: Penguin, 1999.

Davidson, A. B. "African Resistance and Rebellion Against the Imposition of Colonial Rule." In T. O. Ranger, ed., *Emerging Themes of African History.* Dar es Salaam: East Africa Publishing House, 1965.

Davis, Angela Y. *Women, Race and Class.* New York: Random House, 1981.

Davis, David Brion. *The Problem of Slavery in Western Culture.* Oxford: Oxford University Press, 1966.

Davis, David Brion. *The Problem of Slavery in the Age of Revolution 1770–1823.* Ithaca, N.Y.: Cornell University Press, 1975.

Dawes, Kwame. *Natural Mysticism: Towards a New Reggae Aesthetic.* London: Peepal Tree, 1999.

Dayan, Joan. *Haiti, History and the Gods.* Berkeley: University of California Press, 1998.

De Certeau, Michel. *The Writing of History.* New York: Columbia University Press, 1988.

De La Rue, Andre. "Ujamaa on the March." In Lionel Cliffe and John S. Saul, eds., *Socialism in Tanzania: An Interdisciplinary Reader* Vol. 2, *Policies.* Dar es Salaam: East African Publishing House, 1973.

Dewey, John. *Liberalism and Social Action.* New York: Prometheus Books, 2000.

Diderot, Denis. *Political Writings.* Cambridge: Cambridge University Press, 1992.

Drake, St. Clair. *The Redemption of Africa and Black Religion.* Chicago: Third World Press, 1977.

Dray, Philip. *At the Hands of Persons Unknown: The Lynching of Black America.* New York: Random House, 2002.

Du Bois, W. E. B. *The Souls of Black Folks.* New York: Dodd, Mead, 1979.

Du Bois, W. E. B. *Black Reconstruction in America 1860–1880.* New York: Atheneum, 1969.

Du Bois, W. E. B. *Darkwater Voices from Within the Veil.* New York: Schocken Books, 1969.

Du Bois, W. E. B. *Dusk of Dawn.* New York: Schocken Books, 1968.

Du Bois, W. E. B. *The Souls of Black Folks.* Edited by Henry Louis Gates, Jr., and Terri Hume Oliver. New York: W. W. Norton, 1999.

Dunayevskaya, Raya. *Marxism and Freedom.* New York: Columbia University Press, 1988.

Dunn, John. *The History of Political Theory and Other Essays.* Cambridge: Cambridge University Press, 1996.

Dunn, John. *Western Political Theory in the Face of the Future*. Cambridge: Cambridge University Press, 1993.

Duster, Alfreda M., ed. *Crusade for Justice: The Autobiography of Ida B. Wells*. Chicago: University of Chicago Press, 1970.

Eco, Umberto. *Kant and the Platypus: Essays on Language and Cognition*. Translated by Alastair McEwen. New York: Harcourt, 1999.

Edgar, Robert, and Hilary Sapire. *African Apocalypse*. Athens: Ohio University Press, 2000.

Elkins, W. F. *Street Preachers, Faith Healers and Herb Doctors in Jamaica, 1890–1925*. New York: Revisionist Press, 1977.

Eudell, Demetrius. *Political Languages of Emancipation in the British Caribbean and the U.S. South*. Chapel Hill: University of North Carolina Press, 2002.

Fanon, Frantz. *Towards the African Revolution*. New York: Grove Press, 1967.

Fanon, Frantz. *Black Skin, White Masks*. New York: Grove Press, 1967.

Fanon, Frantz. *The Wretched of the Earth*. New York: Grove Press, 1963.

Feierman, Steven. *Peasant Intellectuals: Anthropology and History in Tanzania*. Madison: University of Wisconsin Press, 1990.

Femia, Joseph V. *Gramsci's Political Thought*. Oxford: Clarendon Press, 1987.

Ferguson, Moira. *Colonialism and Gender Relations: From Mary Wollstonecraft to Jamaica Kincaid*. New York: Columbia University Press, 1993.

Fetter, Bruce, ed. *Colonial Rule in Africa: Readings from Primary Sources*. Madison: University of Wisconsin Press, 1979.

Fick, Carolyn. *The Making of Haiti: The Saint Domingue Revolution from Below*. Knoxville: University of Tennessee Press, 1990.

Fink, Leon, Stephen T. Leonard, and Donald M. Reid. *Intellectuals and Public Life*. Ithaca, N.Y.: Cornell University Press, 1996.

Floyd, Samuel A., Jr. *The Power of Black Music*. Oxford: Oxford University Press, 1995.

Foner, Philip S., ed. *Frederick Douglass: Selected Speeches and Writings*. Abridged and Adapted by Yuval Taylor. Chicago: Lawrence Hill Books, 1999.

Foucault, Michel. *Madness and Civilization*. New York: Vintage, 1988.

Foucault, Michel. *The Archaeology of Knowledge*. London: Routledge, 1992.

Foucault, Michel. *The Order of Things*. New York: Vintage, 1973.

Fredrickson, George M. *Black Liberation: A Comparative History of Black Ideologies in the United States and South Africa*. Oxford: Oxford University Press, 1995.

Freeden, Michael. *Ideologies and Political Theory*. New York: Oxford University Press, 1986.

Freyhold, Michaela von. *Ujamaa Villages in Tanzania*. New York: Monthly Review Press, 1979.

Gaines, Kevin K. *Uplifting the Race*. Chapel Hill: University of North Carolina Press, 1996.

Gates, Henry Louis, Jr., *The Signifying Monkey*. Oxford: Oxford University Press, 1988.

Gates, Henry Louis, Jr., and William L. Andrews. *Pioneers of the Black Atlantic*. Washington, D.C.: Civitas Counterpoint, 1998.

Geertz, Clifford. *The Interpretation of Cultures*. New York: Basic Books, 1973.

Geggus, David. *Slave Resistance Studies and Saint Domingue Slave Revolt: Some Preliminary Considerations*. Occasional Paper, 4. Latin American and Caribbean Center, Miami, Winter 1993.

Genovese, Eugene D. *From Rebellion to Revolution: Afro-American Slave Revolts in the Making of the Modern World*. Baton Rouge: Louisiana State University Press, 1979.

Giddings, Paula. *When and Where I Enter: The Impact of Black Women on Race and Sex in America*. New York: Bantam Books, 1984.

Glaude, Eddie S., Jr. *Exodus! Religion, Race and Nation in early Nineteenth-Century Black America*. Chicago: University of Chicago Press, 2000.

Goldberg, David Theo. *The Racial State*. Oxford: Blackwell, 2002.

Goodman, Dena. *Criticism in Action*. Ithaca, N.Y.: Cornell University Press, 1989.

Goodwyn, Lawrence. "Populist Dreams and Negro Rights: East Texas as a Case Study." *American Historical Review* (December 1971): 1435–1456.

Gordon, Lewis. "The Unacknowledged Fourth Tradition: An Essay on Nihilism, Decadence, and the Black Intellectual Tradition in the Existential Pragmatic Thought of Cornel West." In George Yancy, ed., *Cornell West: A Critical Reader*. Oxford: Blackwell, 2001.

Gordon, Lewis. "Fanon's Tragic Revolutionary Violence." In Lewis R. Gordon, T. Denean Sharpley-Whiting, and Renee T. White, eds., *Fanon: A Critical Reader*. Oxford: Blackwell, 1996.

Gordon, Lewis R. *Bad Faith and Anti-Black Racism*. Atlantic Highlands, N.J.: Humanities Press, 1995.

Gordon, Lewis R. *Existentia Africana*. New York: Routledge, 2000.

Gorman, William. "W. E. B. Du Bois and His Work." *Fourth International* 11, no. 3 (May–June 1950).

Goveia, Elsa. *Historiography of the British West Indies*. Washington, D.C.: Howard University Press, 1980. Originally published Mexico City: Instituto Panamericano de Geografiá historia, 1956.

Graham, Shirley. *Julius K. Nyerere, Teacher of Africa*. New York: Julian Messner, 1975.

Gramsci, Antonio. *Selections from Prison Notebooks*. New York: International Publishers, 1987.

Gregoire, Henri. *An Enquiry Concerning the Intellectual and Moral Faculties and Literature of Negroes*. Translated by D. B. Warren. College Park, Md.: McGrath, 1967.

Guha, Ranajit. *Dominance Without Hegemony*. Cambridge, Mass.: Harvard University Press, 1997.

Guha, Ranajit, and Gayatri Spivak. *Selected Subaltern Studies*. Oxford: Oxford University Press, 1982.

Gutman, Patrick Hutton, ed. *Technologies of the Self*. Amherst: University of Massachusetts Press, 1998.

Gyekye, Kwame. *Tradition and Modernity: Philosophical Reflections on the African Experience*. Oxford: Oxford University Press, 1997.

Habermas, Jürgen. *The New Conservatism: Cultural Criticism and the Historians' Debate*. Cambridge, Mass.: Harvard University Press, 1989.

Hailey, Lord William. *An African Survey: A Study of Problems Arising in Africa South of the Sahara*. London: Oxford University Press, 1938.

Hall, Catherine. *Civilising Subjects*. Chicago: University of Chicago Press, 2002.

Hall, Stuart. "What Is this 'Black' in Black Popular Culture." In Gina Dent, ed., *Black Popular Culture*. A project by Michele Wallace. Seattle, Wash.: Bay Press, 1992.

Hall-Alleyne, Beverley. "The Evolution of African Languages in Jamaica." *ACIJ Research Review* (Institute of Jamaica) no. 1 (1984) 21–46.

Hallen, Barry. *A Short History of African Philosophy*. Bloomington: Indiana University Press, 2002.

Hardt, Michael, and Antonio Negri. *Empire*. Cambridge, Mass.: Harvard University Press, 2000.

Harris, Wilson. *History, Fable and Myth in the Caribbean and Guianas*. Wellesley, Mass.: Calaloux Publications, 1995.

Harrison, Lawrence E., and Samuel P. Huntington. *Culture Matters: How Values Shape Human Progress*. New York: Basic Books, 2000.

Hart, Richard. *Slaves Who Abolished Slavery*. 2 vols. Kingston, Jamaica: ISER, 1982–1985.

Hatch, John. *Two African Statesmen*. Chicago: Henry Regnery, 1976.

Hawkins, Mike. *Social Darwinism in European and American Thought, 1860–1945.* Cambridge: Cambridge University Press, 1997.

Hedlund, Stefan, and Mats Lundahl. *Ideology as a Determinant of Economic Systems: Nyerere and Ujamaa in Tanzania.* Research Report no. 84. Uppsala: Scandinavian Institute of African Studies, 1999.

Henry, Paget. *Caliban's Reason: Introducing Afro-Caribbean Philosophy.* New York: Routledge, 2000.

Hill, Christopher. *The World Turned Upside Down.* London: Penguin, 1991.

Hill, Christopher. *The English Bible and the Seventeenth-Century Revolution.* London: Penguin, 1994.

Hill, Robert A. *Dread History: Leonard P. Howell and the Millenarian Visions in the Early Rastafarian Religion.* Kingston, Jamaica, Chicago: Research Associates/School Times Publications and Miguel Lorne, 2001.

Hobsbawm, Eric. *Primitive Rebels.* Manchester, U.K.: Manchester University Press, 1978.

Hochschild, Adam. *King Leopold's Ghost.* New York: Houghton Mifflin, 1999.

Holt, Thomas. *The Problem of Freedom: Race, Labour, and Politics in Jamaica, 1832–1938.* Kingston, Jamaica: Ian Randle, 1992.

Hoogvelt, Ankie M. M. *The Third World in Global Development.* London: Macmillan, 1982.

Hooker, James. *Black Revolutionary: George Padmore's Path from Communism to Pan-Africanism.* London: Pall Mall Press. 1967.

Hopkins, Elizabeth. "The Nyabingi Cult of Southwestern Uganda." In Robert Rotberg and Ali Mazrui, eds., *Protest and Power in Black Africa.* New York: Oxford University Press, 1970.

Isichei, Elizabeth. *A History of African Societies to 1870.* Cambridge: Cambridge University Press, 1997.

Jacoby, Russell. *The Last Intellectuals: American Culture in the Age of Academe.* New York: Basic Books, 1987.

James, C. L. R. *The Black Jacobins.* New York: Vintage, 1989.

James, C. L. R. "The Old World and the New." In his *At the Rendezvous of Victory.* London: Allison & Busby, 1984.

James, C. L. R. "The West Indian Intellectual." In J. J. Thomas, *Froudacity.* London: New Beacon, 1969.

James, C. L. R. "Rodney and the Question of Power." In Edward A. Alpers and Pierre-Michel Fontaine, eds., *Walter Rodney, Revolutionary and Scholar: A Tribute.* Los Angeles: Center for Afro-American Studies and African Studies Center, University of California, 1982.

James, C. L. R. "Revolution and the Negro." In Scott McLemee and Paul Le Blanc, eds., *C. L. R. James and Revolutionary Marxism: Selected Writings of C. L. R. James 1939–1949.* Atlantic Highlands, N.J.: Humanities Press, 1994.

James, C. L. R. *Notes on Dialectics.* London: Allison & Busby, 1980.

James, C. L. R. Transcript of talk at Tougaloo College, May 9, 1972. C. L. R. James Institute.

James, C. L. R. "Lectures on *The Black Jacobins.*" *Small Axe* no. 8 (September 2000): 65–112.

James, C. L. R. *A History of Negro Revolt.* 3rd ed. London: Race Today Publications, 1985.

James, C. L. R. *Beyond a Boundary.* London: Serpent's Tail, 1994.

James, C. L. R. *Beyond a Boundary.* London: Hutchinson, 1963.

James, Joy. "The Profeminist Politics of W. E. B. Du Bois with Respects to Anna Julia Cooper and Ida B. Wells Barnett." In Bernard W. Bell, Emily R. Grosholz, and

James B. Stewart, eds., *W. E. B. Du Bois on Race and Culture*. New York: Routledge, 1996.

James, Joy. *Shadowboxing: Representations of Black Feminist Politics*. New York: Palgrave, 2002.

James, Joy. *Transcending the Talented Tenth*. New York: Routledge, 1997.

Jennings, Jeremy, and Anthony Kemp-Welch, eds. *Intellectuals in Politics*. London: Routledge, 1997.

Jordan, Winthrop D. *White over Black: American Attitudes Toward The Negro, 1550–1812*. Chapel Hill: University of North Carolina Press, 1969.

Judy, Ronald A. T., ed. "Sociology Hesitant: Thinking with W. E. B. Du Bois." *boundary 2* 27, no. 3 (Fall 2000). (Special issue.)

July, Robert. *An African Voice: The Role of Humanities in African Independence*. Durham, N.C.: Duke University Press, 1987.

Kaunda, Kenneth D. *A Humanist in Africa*. London: Longmans, 1966.

Kiros, Teodros, ed. *Explorations in African Political Thought*. New York: Routledge, 2001.

Kohler, Lotte, and Hans Saner, eds. *Hannah Arendt/Karl Jaspers: Correspondence 1926–1969*. New York: Harcourt Brace Jovanovich, 1992.

Koselleck, Reinhart. *The Practice of Conceptual History: Timing History, Spacing Concepts*. Stanford, Calif.: Stanford University Press, 2002.

Kramer, Lawrence. *Music as Cultural Practice*. Berkeley: University of California Press, 1993.

Kymlicka, William. *Contemporary Political Philosophy*. Oxford: Oxford University Press, 1990.

Kymlicka, William. *Multicultural Citizens: A Liberal Theory of Minority Rights*. Oxford: Clarendon Press, 1995.

La Capra, Dominick. *Writing History, Writing Trauma*. Baltimore: Johns Hopkins University Press, 2001.

Lake, Obiagele. *Rastafari Women: Subordination in the Midst of Liberation Theology*. Durham, N.C.: Carolina Academic Press, 1998.

Lamming, George. "Foreword." In Walter Rodney, *A History of the Guyanese Working People, 1881–1905*. Baltimore: Johns Hopkins University Press, 1981.

Lamming, George. *Pleasures of Exiles*. London: Allison & Busby, 1984.

Langley, J. Ayo. *Ideologies of Liberation in Black Africa, 1856–1970*. London: Rex Collings, 1979.

Laslett, Peter, ed. *Philosophy, Politics and Society*. 1st ser. Oxford: Blackwell, 1956.

Lemert, Charles, and Esme Bhan, eds., *The Voice of Anna Julia Cooper*. New York Lanham: Rowman and Littlefield, 1998.

Levitas, Ruth. "Educated Hope: Ernst Bloch and Abstract and Concrete Utopia." In Jamie Owen Daniel and Tom Moylan, eds., *Not Yet: Reconsidering Ernst Bloch*. London: Verso, 1997.

Lewis, David Levering. *W. E. B. Du Bois: The Fight for Equality and the American Century, 1919–1963*. New York: Henry Holt, 2000.

Lewis, Gordon. *Main Currents in Caribbean Thought*. Kingston, Jamaica: Heinemann Educational Books Caribbean, 1983.

Lewis, Rupert. "Learning to Blow the Abeng: A Critical Look at Anti-establishment Movements of the 1960's and 1970's." *Small Axe* (Kingston, Jamaica) no. 1 (1997): 5–17.

Lewis, Rupert. "Marcus Garvey and the Early Rastafarians." In N. S. Murrell, W. D. Spencer, and A. A. McFarlane, eds., *Chanting Down Babylon*. Kingston, Jamaica: Ian Randle, 1998.

Lewis, Rupert. *Walter Rodney's Intellectual and Political Thought*. Kingston, Jamaica: University of the West Indies Press, 1998.

Lindsay, Louis. *The Myth of Independence.* Working Paper no. 6. Kingston, Jamaica: ISER, 1975.

Linebaugh, Peter, and Marcus Rediker. *The Many Headed Hydra.* Boston: Beacon Press, 2000.

Locke, John. *Two Treatises of Government.* Edited by Peter Laslett. Cambridge: Cambridge University Press, 1988.

Lukes, Steven. "Equality and Liberty, Must They Conflict." In David Held, ed., *Political Theory Today.* Stanford, Calif.: Stanford University Press, 1991.

Mamdani, Mahmood. *Citizen and Subject: Contemporary Africa and the Legacy of Late Colonialism.* Princeton, N.J.: Princeton University Press, 1996.

Mannheim, Karl. *Ideology and Utopia.* London: Routledge, 1966.

Marqusee, Mike. *Redemption Song.* London: Verso, 2000.

Marshall, P. J., and Glyndwr Williams. *The Great Map of Mankind.* Cambridge: Cambridge University Press, 1982.

Martin, William G., and Michael O. West. *Out of One, Many Africas: Reconstructing the Study and Meaning of Africa.* Urbana: University of Illinois Press, 1999.

Marx, Karl. *Capital.* Vol. 1. London: Penguin, 1976.

Masolo, D. A. *African Philosophy in Search of Identity.* Bloomington: Indiana University Press, 1995.

Mbembe, Achille. *On the Postcolony.* Berkeley: University of California Press, 2001.

McDonald, David A., and Eunice Njeri Sahle, eds. *The Legacies of Julius Nyerere: Influences on Development Discourse and Practice in Africa.* Trenton, N.J.: Africa World Press, 2002.

McMurray, Linda O. *To Keep the Waters Troubled: The Life of Ida B. Wells.* New York: Oxford University Press, 1998.

Meeks, Brian. *Narratives of Resistance.* Kingston, Jamaica: University of the West Indies Press, 2000.

Michael, John. *Anxious Intellects.* Durham, N.C.: Duke University Press, 2000.

Mill, John Stuart. *On Liberty.* London: Penguin, 1974.

Mills, Charles. *Racial Contract.* Ithaca, N.Y.: Cornell University Press, 1997.

Mittelman, James H. *The Globalization Syndrome: Transformation and Resistance.* Princeton, N.J.: Princeton University Press, 2000.

Mlimuka, A. K. L. J., and P. J. A. M. Kabudi. "The State and the Party." In Issa G. Shivji, ed., *The State and the Working People in Tanzania.* Dakar: CODESRIA, 1986.

Montesquieu, C. L. *The Spirit of the Laws.* Edited by Anne Cohler, Basia Miller, and Harold Stone. Cambridge: Cambridge University Press, 1989.

Moore-Gilbert, Bart. *PostColonial Theory: Contexts, Practices, Politics.* London: Verso, 2000.

Mudimbe, V. Y. *The Invention of Africa: Gnosis, Philosophy, and the Order of Knowledge.* Bloomington: Indiana University Press, 1988.

Mudimbe, V. Y. *Parables and Fables: Exegesis, Textuality, and Politics in Central Africa.* Madison: University of Wisconsin Press, 1991.

Munro, Ian, and Reinhard Sander. *Kas-Kas Interviews with Three Caribbean Writers in Texas.* Austin: African and Afro-American Institute, University of Texas, 1972.

Murrell, Nathaniel Samuel, William David Spencer, and Adrian Anthony McFarlane, eds. *Chanting Down Babylon.* Kingston, Jamaica: Ian Randle, 1998.

Nagel Thomas. *Equality and Partiality.* Oxford: Oxford University Press, 1991.

Neal, Mark Anthony. *What the Music Said: Black Popular Music and Black Public Culture.* New York: Routledge, 1999.

Nettleford, Rex. *Identity, Race and Protest in Jamaica.* New York: William Morrow, 1972.

Nkrumah, Kwame. *Class Struggle in Africa.* London: Panaf Books, 1970.

Nyerere, Julius. "Freedom and Development." In Andrew Coulson, ed., *African Socialism in Practice: The Tanzanian Experience,* Nottingham, U.K.: Spokesman, 1982.

Nyerere, Julius. *The Rational Choice—Capitalism or Socialism*. Tunapuna, Trinidad: New Beginning Movement, 1974.

Nyerere, Julius. *Freedom and Development, Uhuru na Maendele: A Selection from Writings and Speeches, 1968–1973*. Dar es Salaam: Oxford University Press, 1974.

Nyerere, Julius. *Freedom and Unity*. Dar es Salaam: Oxford University Press, 1966.

Nyerere, Julius. *Uhuru na Ujamaa: Freedom and Socialism. A Selection from Writings and Speeches, 1965–1967*. Dar es Salaam: Oxford University Press, 1968.

O'Neill, Onora. "Transnational Justice." In David Held, ed., *Political Theory Today*. Stanford, Calif.: Stanford University Press, 1991.

Ojo, Adebayo. *Bob Marley: Songs of African Redemption*. Lagos: Malthouse Press, 2000.

Oosthuizen, Gerhardus C. *The Healer-Prophet in Afro-Christian Churches*. Leiden, N.Y.: E. J. Brill, 1992.

Oyewumi, Oyeronke. *The Invention of Women: Making an African Sense of Western Gender Discourses*. Minneapolis: University of Minnesota Press, 1997.

Padmore, George. *Pan-Africanism and Communism*. New York: Anchor Books, 1972.

Pagden, Anthony. *Peoples and Empires*. New York: Modern Library, 2001.

Paine, Thomas. "African Slavery in America." In Michael Foot and Isaac Kramnick, eds., *The Thomas Paine Reader*. London: Penguin, 1987.

Paine, Thomas. *The Rights of Man*. In Michael Foot and Isaac Kramnick, eds., *The Thomas Paine Reader*. London: Penguin, 1987.

Painter, Nell Irvin. *Sojourner Truth: A Life, a Symbol*. New York: W. W. Norton, 1996.

Patterson, Orlando. *Slavery and Social Death: A Comparative Study*. Cambridge, Mass.: Harvard University Press, 1982.

Planno, Mortimer. *The Earth Most Strangest Man: The Rastafarian*. (www.rism.org/planno/.)

Pocock, J. G. A. *The Machiavellian Moment: Florentine Political Thought and the Atlantic Republican Tradition*. Princeton, N.J.: Princeton University Press, 1975.

Pollard, Velma. *Dread Talk: The Language of Rastafari*. Kingston, Jamaica: Canoe Press, 1994.

Post, Ken. *Arise Ye Starvelings*. The Hague: Martinus Nijhoff, 1978.

Post, Ken. "The Bible as Ideology: Ethiopianism in Jamaica, 1930–38." In Christopher Allen and R. W. Johnson, eds., *African Perspectives*. Cambridge: Cambridge University Press, 1970.

Prahlad, Swami Anand. *Reggae Wisdom: Proverbs in Jamaican Music*. Jackson: University Press of Mississippi, 2001.

Prescod, Colin. "Guyana's Socialism: An Interview with Walter Rodney." *Race and Class* 18 (Autumn 1976): 2: 111–128.

Rampersad, Arnold. *The Art and Imagination of W. E. B. Du Bois*. New York: Schocken Books, 1990.

Ranger, Terence. "The Invention of Tradition in Colonial Africa." In Terence Ranger and Eric Hobsbawm, *The Invention of Tradition*. Cambridge: Cambridge University Press, 1983.

Reckford, Verena. "From Burru Drums to Reggae Riddims: The Evolution of Rasta Music." In N.S. Murrell, W. Spencer, and A. McFarlane, eds., *Chanting Down Babylon*. Kingston, Jamaica: Ian Randle, 1998.

Retamar, Roberto. *Caliban and Other Essays*. Minneapolis: University of Minnesota Press, 1997.

Richardson, Heather Cox. *The Death of Reconstruction: Race, Labor and Politics in the Post Civil-War North, 1865–1901*. Cambridge, Mass.: Harvard University Press, 2001.

Ricoeur, Paul. "Heidegger and the Question of the Subject." In his *The Conflict of Interpretations*. Evanston, Ill.: Northwestern University Press, 1974.

Ricoeur, Paul. *Time and Narrative*. Chicago: University of Chicago Press, 1983.

Ricoeur, Paul. *History and Truth.* Evanston, Ill.: Northwestern University Press, 1965.

Ripley, C. Peter, ed. *The Black Abolitionist Papers.* Vols. 1–4. Chapel Hill: University of North Carolina Press, 1985–1991.

Robinson, Cedric. *Black Marxism.* Chapel Hill: University of North Carolina Press, 2000.

Rodney, Walter. "Some Aspects of the Political Economy of the Caribbean." Unpublished text of a speech in author's possession.

Rodney, Walter. "Marxism in Africa." Undated and unpaginated pamphlet in author's possession.

Rodney, Walter. "Problems of Third World Development." *Ufahamu* 3, no. 2 (Fall 1972): 27–47.

Rodney, Walter. "Tanzanian Ujamaa and Scientific Socialism." *Africa Review* 1, no. 4, (1971): 61–76.

Rodney, Walter. "Contemporary Political Trends in the English-Speaking Caribbean." *Black Scholar* vol. 7, no. 1. (September 1975): 15–21.

Rodney, Walter. *How Europe Underdeveloped Africa.* Washington, D.C.: Howard University Press, 1982.

Rodney, Walter. *Sign of the Times.* London: WPA Support Group, n.d.

Rodney, Walter. "Pan-Africanism and Neo-Colonialism in Africa." *Black Liberator* 2, no. 3 (June 1974/January 1975): 256–66.

Rodney, Walter. *Groundings with My Brothers.* London: Bogle L'Overture, 1971.

Rodney, Walter. *Walter Rodney Speaks: The Making of an African Intellectual.* Introduction by Robert Hill and Foreword by Howard Dodson. Trenton, N.J.: Africa World Press, 1990.

Rogers, Robert Athlyi. *The Holy Piby: The Blackman's Bible.* Chicago and Kingston, Jamaica: Research Associates/School Times Publications and Headstart Printing and Publishing, 2000.

Root, Deborah. "Speaking Christian: Orthodoxy and Difference in Sixteenth Century Spain." *Representations* 23 (Summer 1998): 18–134.

Rorty, Amelie Oksenberg. *The Many Faces of Evil: Historical Perspectives.* New York: Routledge, 2001.

Said, Edward. *Representations of the Intellectual.* New York: Vintage, 1996.

Sandel, Michael. *Democracy's Discontent,* Cambridge, Mass.: Harvard University Press, 1996.

Sander, Reinhard. *West Indian Literature of the 1930's.* Westport, Conn.: Greenwood Press, 1988.

Sandiford, Keith A. *Measuring the Moment: Strategies of Protest in Eighteenth-Century Afro-English Writing.* London: Associated University Presses, 1988.

Schechter, Patricia A. *Ida B. Wells Barnett and American Reform, 1880–1930.* Chapel Hill: University of North Carolina Press, 2001.

Scott, David. *Refashioning Futures: Criticism After Postcoloniality.* Princeton, N.J.: Princeton University Press, 1999.

Scott, David. "The Archaeology of Black Memory: An Interview with Robert A. Hill." *Small Axe* no. 5 (March 1999): 80–150.

Scott, David. Interview with Sylvia Wynter. *Small Axe.* no. 8 (September 2000) 119–207.

Scott, James C. *Domination and the Arts of Resistance.* New Haven, Conn.: Yale University Press, 1990.

Scott, James C. *Seeing like a State.* New Haven, Conn.: Yale University Press, 1998.

Seidman, Steven, ed. *Jürgen Habermas on Society and Politics: A Reader.* Boston: Beacon Press, 1989.

Senghor, Léopold. "Nationhood: Report on the Doctrine and Program of the Party of African Federation." In Okwui Enwezored, ed., *The Short Century: Independence and Liberation Movements in Africa, 1945–1994.* New York: Prestel, 2002.

Shapiro, Herbert. *White Violence and Black Response.* Amherst: University of Massachusetts Press, 1988.

Shepperson, G. "Ethiopianism: Past and Present." In C. G. Baeta, ed., *Christianity in Tropical Africa.* Oxford: Oxford University Press, 1968.

Shivji, Issa. *The Silent Class Struggle.* Dar es Salaam: Tanzanian Publishing House, 1974.

Shivji, Issa G. *Class Struggles in Tanzania.* London: Heinemann, 1976.

Silverman, Bertram, ed. *Man and Socialism in Cuba: The Great Debate.* New York: Atheneum, 1973.

Singham, A. W., and Shirley Hune. *Non-Alignment in the Age of Alignments.* London: Zed Press, 1986.

Skinner, Quentin. *Liberty Before Liberalism.* Cambridge: Cambridge University Press, 1998.

Skinner, Quentin. "Meaning and Understanding." In James Tully, ed., *Meaning and Context: Quentin Skinner and His Critics.* Princeton, N.J.: Princeton University Press, 1988.

Skocpol, Theda. *Social Revolutions in the Modern World.* Cambridge: Cambridge University Press, 1994. 5.

Small, Helen, ed. *The Public Intellectual.* Oxford: Blackwell, 2002.

Smith, Daniel R. *The Influence of the Fabian Colonial Bureau on the Independence Movement in Tanganyika.* Africa series, no. 44. Athens: Ohio University Press, 1985.

Smith Frances Foster. "Frances Ellen Watkins Harper (1825–1911)." In Darlene Clark Hine, ed., *Black Women in America: An Historical Encyclopedia.* New York: Carlson, 1993.

Smith, Rogers. *Civic Ideals.* New Haven, Conn.: Yale University Press, 1997.

Spivak, Gayatri. *A Critique of PostColonial Reason.* Cambridge, Mass.: Harvard University Press, 1999.

Spivak, Gayatri. "Can the Subaltern Speak?" In Cary Nelson and Lawrence Grossbergeds, ed., *Marxism and the Interpretation of Culture.* Chicago: University of Illinois Press, 1988.

Stanton, Elizabeth Cady. "Address to the New York State Legislature." In Miriam Schneir, ed., *Feminism: The Essential Historical Writings.* New York: Vintage Books, 1992.

Stephens, Gregory. *On Racial Frontiers.* Cambridge: Cambridge University Press, 1999.

Stoger-Eising, Viktoria. "European Influences in Nyerere's Social and Political Thought." *Africa.* 70, no. 1 (2000): 118–34.

Stone, Carl. *Class, Race and Political Behaviour in Urban Jamaica.* Kingston, Jamaica: ISER, 1973.

Strauss, Leo. *What is Political Philosophy?* Chicago: University of Chicago Press, 1988.

Sundkler, Bengt. *Bantu Prophets in South Africa.* Oxford: Oxford University Press, 1961.

Tate, Greg. "Preface to One-hundred-and Eighty Volume Patricide." In Gina Dent, ed., *Black Popular Culture.* Seattle, Wash.: Bay Press, 2002.

Taylor, Ula Y. " 'Negro Women Are Great Thinkers as Well as Doers': Amy Jacques-Garvey and Community Feminism in the United States, 1924–1927." *Journal of Women's History* 12, no. 2 (Summer 2000): 104–126.

Thiong'o, Ngugi wa. *The First Walter Rodney Memorial Lecture.* London: Bogle L'Overture, n.d.

Thiong'o, Ngugi wa. *Decolonising the Mind: The Politics of Language in African Literature.* London: Heinemann, 1986.

Thiong'o, Ngugi wa. "The Politics of Self-Reliance." In David A. McDonald and Eunice Njeri Sahle, eds., *The Legacies of Julius Nyerere: Influences on Development Discourse and Practice in Africa.* Trenton, N.J.: Africa World Press, 2002.

Thompson, E. P. *The Poverty of Theory and Other Essays.* London: Merlin Press, 1978.

Thompson, E. P. *Making of the English Working Class*. New York: Vintage, 1966.

Thorton, John K. "African Soldiers in the Haitian Revolution." *Journal of Caribbean History* 25, nos. 1 and 2 (1991): 58–80.

Trouillot, Michel-Rolph. *Silencing the Past: Power and the Production of History*. Boston: Beacon Press, 1995.

Tully, James, ed. *Meaning and Context: Quentin Skinner and His Critics*, Princeton, N.J.: Princeton University Press, 1988.

Tully, James. *An approach to political philosophy: Locke in Contexts*. Cambridge: Cambridge University Press, 1993.

Ulyanovsky, R. *Socialism and the Newly Independent Nations*. Moscow: Progress Publishers, 1975.

Vaughan, Megan. *Curing Their Ills: Colonial Power and African Illness*. Stanford, Calif.: Stanford University Press, 1991.

Villa, Dana R. *Politics, Philosophy, Terror: Essays on the Thought of Hannah Arendt*. Princeton, N.J.: Princeton University Press, 1999.

Walcott, Derek. "The Muse of History." In his *What the Twilight Says*. New York: Farrar, Straus and Giroux, 1998.

Wallerstein, Immanuel. "A Left Politics for the 21st Century? Or, Theory and Praxis Once Again." *New Political Science* 22, no. 2 (June 2000): 143–159.

Wallerstein, Immanuel. *The End of the World as We Know It*. Minneapolis: University of Minnesota Press, 1999.

Walvin, James. *An African Life: The Life and Times of Olaudah Equiano, 1745–1797*. London: Continuum, 1998.

Walzer, Michael. *The Company of Critics*. New York: Basic Books, 2002.

Walzer, Michael. *Interpretation and Social Criticism*. Cambridge, Mass.: Harvard University Press, 1987.

Ward, June. "The Master's Tools: Abolitionist Arguments of Equiano and Cugoano." In Tommy Lott, ed., *Subjection and Bondage*. New York: Rowman and Littlefield, 1998.

Waters, Anita M. *Race, Class and Political Symbols: Rastafari and Reggae in Jamaican Politics*. New Brunswick, N.J.: Transaction, 1989.

Webking, Robert H. *The American Revolution and the Politics of Liberty*. Baton Rouge: Louisiana State University Press, 1989.

Wedderburn, Robert. *The Horrors of Slavery and Other Writings*. Edited by Ian McCalman. Kingston, Jamaica: Ian Randle, 1997.

Wells, Ida B. *A Red Record: Lynchings in the United States*. In Jacqueline Jones Royster ed., *Southern Horrors and Other Writings: The Anti-Lynching Campaign of Ida B. Wells, 1892–1900*. Boston: Bedford Books, 1997.

West, Cornel. *Keeping Faith*. New York: Routledge, 1993.

White, Garth. "The Evolution of Jamaican Music." *Social and Economic Studies* 47, no. 1 (March 1998): 5–19.

White, Garth. "Rudie, Oh Rudie!" *Caribbean Quarterly* 13 (September 1967): 39–44.

White, Hayden. *The Content of the Form: Narrative Discourse and Historical Representation*. Baltimore: Johns Hopkins University Press, 1987.

White, Deborah Gray. *Too Heavy a Load: Black Women in Defense of Themselves, 1894–1994*. New York: W. W. Norton, 1999.

White, Walter. *Rope and Faggot*. Notre Dame, Ind.: University of Notre Dame Press, 2001.

Williams, Raymond. *Keywords: A Vocabulary of Culture and Society*. New York: Oxford University Press, 1983.

Williams, Raymond. *Problems in Materialism and Culture*. London: Verso, 1980.

Worcester, Kent. *C. L. R. James: A Political Biography*. Albany: State University of New York Press, 1996.

Wynter, Sylvia. " 'We Know Where We Are From': The Politics of Black Culture from Myal to Marley." November 1977. Unpublished paper.

Young, Robert. *White Mythologies: Writing History and the West.* London: Routledge, 1990.

Young, Robert. *Postcolonialism: An Historical Introduction.* Oxford: Blackwell, 2001.

Zamir, Shamoon. *Dark Voices.* Chicago: University of Chicago Press, 1995.

Zartman, I. William. *Collapsed States: The Disintegration and Restoration of Legitimate Authority.* London: Lynne Rienner, 1995.

Ph.D. Dissertations

Augusto, Geri. "Knowing Differently, Innovating Together? A Study of Transepistemic Relations in a South Africa Biotechnology Project." George Washington University, 2003.

Van Dijk, Frank Jan. "Jahmaica: Rastafari and Jamaican Society, 1930–1990." University of Utrecht, 1993.

Index